Qualitative Inquiry in Everyday Life

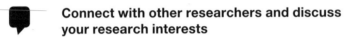
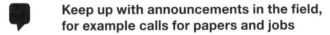

Qualitative Inquiry in Everyday Life

Svend Brinkmann

Los Angeles | London | New Delhi
Singapore | Washington DC

Los Angeles | London | New Delhi
Singapore | Washington DC

SAGE Publications Ltd
1 Oliver's Yard
55 City Road
London EC1Y 1SP

SAGE Publications Inc.
2455 Teller Road
Thousand Oaks, California 91320

SAGE Publications India Pvt Ltd
B 1/I 1 Mohan Cooperative Industrial Area
Mathura Road
New Delhi 110 044

SAGE Publications Asia-Pacific Pte Ltd
3 Church Street
#10-04 Samsung Hub
Singapore 049483

Editor: Katie Metzler
Assistant editor: Anna Horvai
Production editor: Ian Antcliff
Copyeditor: Sarah Bury
Proofreader: Kate Harrison
Marketing manager: Ben Griffin-Sherwood
Cover design: Francis Kenney
Typeset by: C&M Digitals (P) Ltd
Printed and bound by CPI Group (UK) Ltd,
Croydon, CR0 4YY

Library of Congress Control Number: 2011944977

British Library Cataloguing in Publication data

A catalogue record for this book is available from
the British Library

MIX
Paper from
responsible sources
FSC
www.fsc.org   FSC® C013604

ISBN 978-0-85702-475-6
ISBN 978-0-85702-476-3 (pbk)

To know
That which before us lies in daily life
Is the prime wisdom

John Milton, Paradise Lost

Table of contents

About the author

Svend Brinkmann is Professor of Psychology in the Department of Communication and Psychology at the University of Aalborg, Denmark, where he serves as director of the Center for Qualitative Studies (with Lene Tanggaard). His research is particularly concerned with philosophical, moral, and methodological issues in psychology and other human and social sciences. He is the editor of *Qualitative Studies* and author and co-author of numerous articles and books, including *InterViews: Learning the Craft of Qualitative Research Interviewing* (in its second edition).

Acknowledgements

This book began as a coincidence. I was reviewing a book proposal for Sage, and at the bottom of the review form was a section in which to put down any ideas of my own for possible book projects. I thought about this for a few minutes, and then it occurred to me that I would like to write a book on how to do small-scale research based on the researcher's own life and experiences. I don't know why this struck me at that particular moment, but, as I developed the idea further, it became clear to me that this is how I do much of my own work. Although I have been working like this for some years, I have yet to find a book that tells me that this is a legitimate way of working or one that instructs me in how to do it well. As a consequence, I decided to write the book myself, and the result can be found on the following pages.

I work like this for two reasons, I believe, one practical and the other more factual, one might say. Firstly, and practically, I work like this because it represents a possible (and rather enjoyable) way to do research in an otherwise hectic academic life, and, secondly, because I believe that interpretative qualitative research should build on questions and problems that are of genuine interest to the researcher herself. If our human and social science research projects are not existentially important to ourselves, there is a real risk that they will not be important to anyone. On the other hand, if they are urgent and important from our own everyday life perspective, there is at least a chance that they will be so from the perspectives of others too.

I wish to thank the people at Sage for getting back to me about this project and for supporting me as I went on to write the book. I thank in particular Katie Metzler for her encouragement and proficient editorship, and also Anna Horvai and Ian Antcliff for facilitating a smooth process. I am grateful to my colleague Lene Tanggaard for having read and commented on large parts of the manuscript and to Jacob Klitmøller for reading the whole thing at a late stage in the process and for providing me with very helpful comments. Portions of the book have been published previously in articles and book chapters, and I thank the various editors and reviewers for their comments. I am particularly grateful for comments and criticism from Jaan Valsiner, Joshua Clegg and Norman Denzin. I owe a particular debt of gratitude to Ole Jacob Madsen, who is the first author of the text on which the empirical example of Chapter 7 is based.

This book contains materials from the following manuscripts that have previously been published:

Brinkmann, S. (2007). Could interviews be epistemic? An alternative to qualitative opinion-polling. *Qualitative Inquiry*, 13(8): 1116–1138.

Brinkmann, S. (2009). Literature as qualitative inquiry: The novelist as researcher. *Qualitative Inquiry*, 15(8): 1376–1394.

Brinkmann, S. (2010). Guilt in a fluid culture: A view from positioning theory. *Culture & Psychology*, 16(2): 253–266.

Brinkmann, S. (in press). The practice of self observation in the phenomenological traditions. In J.W. Clegg (Ed.), *Self Observation in the Social Sciences*. New Brunswick, NJ: Transaction Publishers.

Brinkmann, S. & Kvale, S. (2008). Ethics in qualitative psychological research. In C. Willig & W. Stainton-Rogers (Eds), *The SAGE Handbook of Qualitative Research in Psychology* (pp. 263–279). London: Sage.

Madsen, O.J. & Brinkmann, S. (in press). Lost in paradise: *Paradise Hotel* and the showcase of shamelessness. *Cultural Studies ⇔ Critical Methodologies*.

Introduction: Making less more

In the last few decades, there has been a boom in qualitative inquiry. In many fields and disciplines, from the human and social sciences to health and education, qualitative research methods are now considered legitimate and necessary for a number of research purposes. Although hostility towards qualitative inquiry still exists here and there, not least in my own field of psychology, qualitative methods are now broadly accepted. This is a good thing, but it sometimes leads to what may be called 'methodolatry', or a worship of method, at the cost of careful theoretical and conceptual reflection. We see this, for example, in some of the current method books that aim to 'sell' some research method, wholly disconnected from theoretical considerations about the nature of the subject matter. I am often led to wonder how methods are supposed to make sense in abstraction from an understanding of the subject matter to which they are applied. The popularity of qualitative research methods has also led to a certain inflation of qualitative research projects that grow in scope with more and more participants. This book counters both these tendencies from the perspective that *less can be more* in qualitative inquiry.

Qualitative methods are often taught and practised as something that requires numerous hours of interviewing, observation or fieldwork. This is the result, perhaps, of a reasonable desire to gain scientific legitimacy, or perhaps of an ambition simply to do thorough and rigorous work. Researchers and also students frequently aspire to carry out very large qualitative research projects, possibly in order to impress the relevant funding agencies and examiners. But such large-scale projects too often result in the researcher 'drowning in data', and it is quite common that researchers and students have insufficient time to analyse their huge amounts of data given all the other tasks that they must carry out in their academic lives (teaching, administration, examinations, etc.). It is not unusual that the many hours of 'data collection' could have been used in ways that would have been better and more conducive to high-quality research. In general, too much time is spent on accumulating material; too little time is spent on theoretically reflecting upon, and writing about, the concrete details of what one has observed.

Why read this book?

This book aims to make qualitative inquiry possible in a busy life of research and learning. It is meant as a 'survival guide' for students and researchers who would like to conduct a qualitative study with limited resources (time and money). The book suggests that a way forward is to use everyday life materials, such as books, television, the internet, the media and everyday conversations, situations and interactions, as topics for qualitative analyses. As living human beings in cultural worlds, we are constantly surrounded by 'data' that call for analysis, and, as we cope with the different situations and episodes of our lives, we are in fact engaged in understanding and interpreting the world in ways that are always already qualitative forms of inquiry. We tend to forget that there are extremely rich sources of data in our everyday lives and that a disciplined awareness of these sources can lead to insightful analyses of our social and personal life processes.

What I argue in this book is that qualitative research into everyday life materials is not just possible, but that it can be enjoyable, a personal learning experience and of high scientific quality, potentially equal to the quality of much larger research projects. The book is thus written for novices and experienced researchers alike, who would like to look carefully at materials from their own life in order to be able to understand the larger social world. I should make clear that I am not the first to consider this approach. Here is sociologist Clinton Sanders, telling us about moving from Chicago to Philadelphia as a young researcher, without knowing a lot of people there, and watching a lot of television to make time pass:

> One sunny Saturday afternoon I was mindlessly viewing my second or third horror film of the day and feeling guilty about wasting my life. Suddenly, the realization struck me that I wouldn't have to feel guilty about watching crummy horror films if I simply began to take notes on them. I could turn a waste of time into work and, once again, begin to feel that I was moving in a potentially productive direction. Although this project eventually resulted in only minimal professional returns […], it did help to get me out of my doldrums and brought home to me the fact that doing qualitative sociology offers the unique opportunity of turning casual interests to account. (Sanders, 1999, p. 43)

Sanders articulates one kind of motive that may exist for reading this book: turning casual interest into research interests. Using parts of your everyday life in a qualitative research project can make idle activities professionally useful, and this book will provide you with arguments in favour of doing so and tools for how to do it. I believe that this is one legitimate motive for reading this book, but I will point to two other, and perhaps more expected, occasions that will give you a reason to read the book:

- As you live your life, you stumble upon a problem or a situation that surprises you or makes you worry. This book argues that such situations are often very useful as occasions for qualitative inquiry that may not just enable you personally to get a clearer view of what surprised or worried you, but which may also throw light on larger social issues as these are reflected through your life. Qualitative researchers can read this book with this in mind.
- If you are a student, you are more likely to read this book because you are taking a course in qualitative research. If your teacher is using this book, she will likely encourage you to think of research somewhat along the lines of what I just said: use your own feelings of surprise and worry to guide your choice of a situation of inquiry. If you are told instead to do research on a particular topic (e.g. anger or embarrassment) or field (e.g. television or material culture), you may use this book to orient yourself in how the relevant phenomenon emerges in your own life as self-observed (Chapter 4), in conversations and interactions that you participate in (Chapter 5), or in the media (Chapter 6), movies and television (Chapter 7) and in books (Chapter 8). You can choose to focus on just one source of material (this will often be sufficient in order to do a decent empirical analysis), or you may choose to combine representations and enactments of your phenomenon from different everyday life sources.

Whichever motive you might have, you should bear in mind that a central message of the book is that high-quality research is not antithetical to small-scale inquiries. The argument does significantly *not* entail that larger, and more traditional, qualitative research projects are ill-founded, but I hope to demonstrate that it is legitimate to add small-scale analyses of everyday life materials to the canon of qualitative research methods. Most people will recognise that anecdotes from our everyday lives can be enlightening when we teach or explain what we mean to others, but this book argues that 'anecdotes' (e.g. from everyday observations and conversations), when properly conceived, can be much more than 'merely anecdotal'!

Unlike method books that simply tell the reader what to do, this book tries to *show* it by ending most of its chapters (5, 6, 7 and 8) with rather thorough empirical analyses of everyday life phenomena or objects that exemplify the way of working that the chapter has brought forth. This is in line with the crafts philosophy that informs the book, according to which one cannot learn a way of working without being presented with exemplars of possible end results of one's efforts. It would be absurd to suppose that a cabinetmaker could learn his or her craft excellently without acquiring an understanding of the products that are to be produced. Something similar is the case with research. Practice and an acquaintance with research products are sorely needed. The examples should also serve as reminders that techniques, procedures and methods should never be thought of as goals in themselves – the goal of qualitative analyses of everyday life is always to *understand the world better*. Thus, through its analyses of empirical examples, the book can also be read as a portrait of the contemporary culture in Western consumer society; of how people in this culture deal with existential and spiritual questions (Chapter 5), how they construct their 'emotionology' and negotiate feelings of guilt and morality (Chapter 6), how they navigate issues of shame and sex in a televised world (Chapter 7), and how they produce books of fiction that articulate existential concerns of meaninglessness and loneliness (Chapter 8).

Theories as tools in qualitative inquiry

The book is based on the premise that observing and analysing our everyday lives for research purposes is something most people can learn to do quite well. What brings rigour and scientific quality to small-scale projects is a disciplined and analytic awareness informed by theory. Consequently, the book's approach to qualitative inquiry in everyday life is far from being anti-theoretical, but rather builds on the insight from pragmatism (e.g. Dewey, 1929) that theories in the human and social sciences are tools that enable us to understand and cope with the world. Theoretical concepts are sensitising instruments, to borrow a term from Herbert Blumer, that we use to help us look in fruitful directions and helpful ways (see Clarke, 2005, p. 28). We use theoretical tools in coping with the situations and processes of the world, and such coping occurs all the time, in research and in our personal lives, and a fundamental assumption of this book is that there is no clear difference between 'doing a research project' and 'living a life'. Not because a life is – or should be – a dry, mechanical and methodological affair, but because qualitative research can be lively, engaging and existentially important.

Recently, anthropologist Tim Ingold (2011) has advocated C. Wright Mills' plea for intellectual craftsmanship, destroying traditional divisions between 'theory' and 'method'. We do not (or should not) begin social research with a theoretical agenda that is then operationalised into testable hypotheses through methods. Rather, we should acknowledge, Ingold says, 'that there is no division, in practice, between work and life. [An intellectual craft] is a practice that involves the whole person, continually drawing on past experience as it is projected into the future' (p. 240). We do research for purposes of living, and theories of social and psychological life are just some of the tools we employ in the process (others are art and education).

Although I have referred to the book as a survival guide, it is not uniquely so. It is more importantly an argument to the effect that our everyday lives are a unique context for discovering who we are and what is at stake in human living in the twenty-first century. Writers of fiction are often adept at depicting the small details of the everyday lives of their characters in ways that are informative about larger social issues. In my view, writers such as Bret Easton Ellis, Douglas Coupland and Michel Houellebecq, for example, share a style of writing that closely observes the everyday doings and sufferings of people, which provides the reader with an understanding of our post-traditional consumer society and its challenges to human living (I analyse Houellebecq's works in Chapter 8). Today, following Lyotard's now classic analysis of the postmodern condition (1984), it has become a commonplace that the grand modernist narratives have become problematic, and instead we must look to our local, everyday modes of crafting small narratives to find the meanings that organise our lives – and the ruptures that disorganise them (Frosh, 2007). Qualitative researchers can learn much from fiction in this regard, and this book is based on the assumption that the twin skills of *observing* and *writing* about the intersection between one's everyday life and the larger social world are best cultivated together. Thus, the book advocates Laurel Richardson's idea that writing about our lives should be conceived as a key method of social inquiry in itself (Richardson & St. Pierre, 2005).

I often hear from both experienced researchers and novices that they experience a lack of time to do research. One solution to this problem can be to work with the materials that already surround us in our lives. There is a risk, however, that this leads to overly confessional and personalised reports that are not always interesting or enlightening for readers (see the critical discussion in Hammersley, 2008). This book advocates keeping a clear focus on what everyday life materials can tell us about our *social worlds*. Not that the book is against the personal, the confessional or the biographical – quite the contrary – but it argues that the personal dimensions in research should be seen as instrumental for understanding more general issues about culture and society. Mills (1959) famously pointed towards the use of the sociological imagination for researchers 'to grasp what is going on in the world, and to understand what is happening in themselves as minute points of the intersections of biography and history within society' (p. 7). Biography and social history intersect within society, and if good qualitative inquiry lives in this intersection, we should focus on both lines of the intersection, not least in order for our analyses to be interesting as research. I continuously develop the argument that theory in a broad sense is what enables researchers to go from personalised analyses to social analyses with broader validity and generality (and I return to Mills' position at the end of Chapter 2).

Qualitative inquiry as empirical philosophy

There are other books that have used the concept of 'everyday life' in relation to the practice of qualitative inquiry (e.g. Glassner & Hertz, 1999), but the present book differs from these in not simply using social science to understand different everyday life issues at work or at home, but to argue that human life as such is a research process, a hermeneutic process of inquiry that makes it impossible to draw a line between 'doing research' and 'being alive'. In that way, the present book is not built upon methodological rules as such, but rather upon a philosophical anthropology, i.e., a philosophically informed perspective on human beings as fundamentally interpreting, inquiring creatures for whom 'social science' is simply a condensed or crystallised form of the everyday activity of understanding one's life in a social world. Theories – from philosophy, sociology, psychology, anthropology and related fields – can be useful in understanding one's life and can be used to help us act together in fruitful ways, but they are ultimately to be thought of and assessed as tools rather than objective mirrors of the world.

As a consequence of this approach, and its emphasis on theoretical reflection, the book could also be said to advocate an approach to qualitative inquiry as 'empirical philosophy', a term used by Annemarie Mol, whom we encounter in the next chapter. Empirical philosophy breaks down the boundaries between traditional philosophical work that deals with purely theoretical and conceptual analyses on the one hand, and the empirical sciences that study concrete objects and phenomena on the other. Philosophy needs the empirical in order not to be empty, and qualitative inquiry needs theoretical and philosophical reflections in order not to be blind.

Elizabeth St. Pierre (2011) has recently argued that if we do not read the philosophical literature as qualitative researchers, 'we have nothing much to think with during analysis except normalized discourses that seldom explain the way things are' (p. 614). This, for her, means that the study of philosophy should precede the study of research methodology. And Peter Winch, in his classic *The Idea of a Social Science and Its Relation to Philosophy*, made a similar point in his own way by arguing that 'any worthwhile study of society must be philosophical in character and any worthwhile philosophy must be concerned with the nature of human society' (Winch, 1963, p. 3). There is a complex interpenetration of philosophy, social science and qualitative research, which this book aims to make the best of instead of trying to purify them into distinct domains. Winch's book is furthermore an early and thorough defence of a thesis that is central to the present book as well: that a so-called 'scientific' understanding of human life and human action is not, as long as it qualifies as 'understanding', different in nature from the mundane forms of understanding that humans make use of in living their everyday lives.

The book chapters

The book is divided into two parts: The first part describes the background and the epistemological and ethical issues involved in this approach. A whole philosophical theory of inquiry supports the book's approach. This is an approach that argues that being alive as a human being is necessarily to be engaged in interpretative processes of inquiry. This means that what we call qualitative research rests on a focused cultivation of the human skills of conversation, observation, interaction and communication. A main point of the ethics chapter is that ethics cannot be something external to the process of inquiry, but must be seen as an inherent part of research in all its stages. In principle, there are no issues in life or in research that are free from ethical considerations, just as there are no questions that are uniquely ethical. The ethical stance is one among others that are necessary in our lives, but there are at the same time no aspects of our lives that are beyond the ethical.

The second part looks at five different sources of everyday life materials. The chapters have a craft approach to the production of knowledge in line with Kvale & Brinkmann (2008). Qualitative researchers should think of themselves as craftspersons who engage creatively with the materials and should not be rigid methodologists who mechanically follow pre-defined steps. The theories and analytical approaches that are presented are therefore seen as tools for the craftsperson.

The five sources that structure the chapters are self observations (Chapter 4), everyday conversations (Chapter 5), media materials, including social media (Chapter 6), movies, television and other images (Chapter 7) and finally books of fiction (Chapter 8). Each chapter introduces theoretical and analytical tools with which to work and then (apart from Chapter 4, which is more theoretical) demonstrates concretely how to apply them to a particular piece of everyday life material encountered by myself (several of the concrete analyses build on my own published research). Chapters 4 and 5 mainly deal with materials that are constructed or 'collected' intentionally by the researcher for a specific research purpose: Chapter 4 introduces a phenomenological perspective on self observation and shows how self observation data can be used in everyday life research, whereas Chapter 5 gives a broad introduction to conversations as relevant for quality inquiry before developing a more specific use of conversations with inspiration from Socrates.

The particular examples that are included at the end of the chapters are chosen to demonstrate the wide variety of issues that analyses of everyday life materials can inform us about, ranging from the tiniest micro processes of human interactions and emotions (e.g. Chapters 4 and 5) to the largest macro issues resulting in cultural diagnoses of social imaginaries as reflected in books and television (Chapters 6, 7 and 8). Chapters 6, 7 and 8 primarily include materials that are not constructed for a research purpose, but which are there anyway as a part of the researcher's life (media materials, audiovisual materials and books). Chapter 5 recounts the story of how I lost contact with a friend who joined a religious sect.

Chapter 6 interprets the cultural significance of guilt as an emotion through an analysis of a medialised confession of a famous cyclist who admitted having used performance-enhancing drugs. Chapter 7 looks at the television series *Paradise Hotel* to understand issues of shame and sexuality in the postmodern world, and Chapter 8 includes a reading of a number of novels to ask what we may learn about our lives from fiction. Can fiction be considered qualitative inquiry? In the concluding chapter I return to more general issues about quality in everyday life analyses: How can we assess the quality of the research that may stem from this book's approach?

Each chapter closes with one or more practical exercises that the reader can do in order to get started doing everyday life research herself. This supports the craft-oriented approach of the book and hopefully underlines the idea that rigorous, high-quality research into everyday life materials demands training and discipline. The craft approach is also seen in the book's practical perspectives on how to focus one's attention on particular issues and salient features of the social world; how to remember important details; how to write them down and handle note books, mind-maps and matrixes; how to include theoretical perspectives as ways of ordering one's observations and ideas; how to read one's material, looking for patterns and contradictions; how to use writing as a way of analysing the material; how to relate one's analyses to the extant literature and how ultimately to publish interesting research reports.

PART I

ONE

Qualitative research and everyday life

Not long ago, my oldest child, a boy, started school. The school is located very close to where we live, and the sunny morning I walked him there, both of us were quite excited. We talked about the classmates he was soon going to meet. Some of them he knew in advance from the Kindergarten he had attended, but most of them would be new to him. Almost all his friends – at least the ones that had been invited to play in our house in the past – were boys, and my wife and I hoped that he would have a chance to expand his circle of friends to include some girls. We find it important to try to avoid the common segregation of children into groups of boys and girls, and, in our own childhood from the late 1970s and into the early 1980s, both of us had had as our best friend a child of the opposite sex.

Our ideals were quickly challenged, however, for already at the first school meeting, when all the parents had a chance to meet each other and exchange contact information, two lists circulated among the parents on which they were supposed to write down their telephone numbers. One list for the parents of boys and another for the parents of girls. It was tacitly assumed that boys would only play with other boys and girls with other girls. Not just this list, but also much of the micro architecture of the school worked for, rather than against, a segregation of the two sexes. In the rooms where the children play after school until they are picked up by their parents, there is one section where boys can put their clothes and another one for the girls. 'The boys rummage much more than the girls', as one of the pedagogues explained, 'and we don't want the boys to bother the girls'. Even the refrigerators contain separate shelves for boys and girls to put their lunch boxes. Obviously, when attending after school activities such as sports, the children are also divided according to gender, although there are no physical differences at this young age that warrant it.

As a result, my son plays almost exclusively with other boys. Although his interests are not just stereotypically boyish (soccer, violent video games), but also more gender neutral (he loves things like theatre, nature and music), he becomes quite embarrassed when we suggest that we invite one of the girls home to play with him. There are clearly numerous social factors that support a segregation of boys and girls and position them in stereotypical ways at this quite early age, even if the official school policy is meant to counter such tendencies. When he has occasionally (very rarely) played with a girl after school, it is important for him that this is kept as a secret from his class mates. Otherwise, there is a risk of teasing or even bullying.

These few remarks are meant to illustrate what I mean in this book when I address qualitative inquiry in everyday life. We have an everyday life occurrence – a child beginning school life – and we have a situation that causes the researcher (in this case myself) to stop and wonder. Something seems strange, confusing and maybe even worrying. An ideology of gender equality and positive relationships is seemingly contradicted by the social practices of school life. The short description given above draws upon two main sources:

- The researcher's experience of something strange, but interesting, from his everyday life. This would not be strange and interesting to everyone, but it was to me, given my personal background and childhood experiences, and also my theoretical readings of some feminist literature that have sensitised me to certain phenomena rather than others. The biographical and theoretical here meets the concrete social reality, and this is where qualitative inquiry often happens.
- I use my own memory of the encounter with the school. I remember a specific conversation with a professional pedagogue there, and I refer to observations of the school architecture and a few episodes of after school activities. There are thus both symbolic and material factors present that inform this micro analysis, based on my own experience.

This situation from everyday life could form the beginning of what I mean by a qualitative research project into everyday life. In order for me to turn this into a more focused study, I would have to supplement the initial observations and recollections with further ones. I would have to consider the ethical implications of writing about people I know and who know me. I would have to read about research that has already been done on the topic and think about how this could inform the way I see the situation now. I would have to consult theories about sex, gender and school life. And I would have to reflect upon my own role in the process of inquiry: Why have I not confronted the school with my observations and criticisms? Why is it so important to me that children have friends of the opposite sex?

If I were to do these things, and write about them in the process, I would likely end up with a piece of everyday life research that could perhaps even be published and be of interest to others. Hopefully, I would become able to comprehend the situation better. I could possibly even use my analysis to try to change the situation if I still felt a need to do so. Or perhaps I would be forced to conclude that there are legitimate reasons why the local social world operates like this that will have to be respected. These questions are not rhetorical, for I honestly do not know the answers, but that is exactly the point, since I have not yet done the study – I have only taken the most preliminary steps towards an understanding of the phenomenon as laid out above.

Steps in the research process

An outline of the steps that are needed to carry out an everyday life research project (such as the one just described) would give us something like this:

1 *Choose a topic.* Normally this will be based on something that genuinely interests you, bothers you or confuses you. It is preferably based on something you do not yet understand and which you would like to understand, perhaps in order to be able to act more appropriately towards it. The first step can often be conceptualised as a breakdown in understanding. Good social science frequently springs from a breakdown ('I don't understand this'), coupled with a mystery (e.g. the framing of the breakdown as a riddle) and then a possible resolution of the riddle, e.g. based on a novel perspective on the matter that confused you (Alvesson & Kärreman, 2011). If you are in the process of learning how to do research, you may be 'forced' by the teacher or the curriculum to choose a topic that might not constitute a breakdown. In this case, you can favourably practise breaking down your own understanding of the phenomenon you are going to study. Later in this chapter (and also in the next one), I present some techniques that can help you to defamiliarise yourself with the phenomena that you take for granted, thus creating a sense of curiosity that is conducive to good qualitative research.
2 *Collect materials.* When you choose a topic, you are simultaneously collecting materials. These steps are deeply related – as are all of them. Recollections that you write down, newspaper articles that you read, commercials that annoy you or conversations that seem to stick in your memory can all be examples of materials that may enter into defining the topic that interests you. From the point of view of the present book, 'data collection' is not a separate process that starts only after the research project is designed, but something we all constantly do as living human beings with memories.
3 *Consult the literature.* We should never underestimate the insights that other researchers have provided us with, so it is important to read about empirical analyses in the topical area, and it is also important to develop one's imagination and powers of observation by reading theoretical literature. Who knows, maybe Hegel's dialectics of recognition can inform my understanding of the issue of gender segregation? Or maybe I need Judith Butler or Erving Goffman?
4 *Continue collecting materials.* Try to think broadly about what may be needed and include visual as well as textual materials whenever possible. Don't try to purify data

(e.g. by conducting only standardised research interviews), but use everything that helps you clarify the situation. Have you read novels about your phenomenon? Or media stories or television programmes? Where and how is your phenomenon represented in the social world? As Bruno Latour (2005) argues in a recent book on *Reassembling the Social*, from now on, when you think of what you are doing as a research project, *everything is data*! That everything is data in everyday life research is both a burden and a blessing. It is a blessing since it makes it easy to get started on an often enjoyable research quest, but it is also a burden since the researcher risks losing focus. The researcher must therefore frame the research project very carefully in order not to end up with a deeply fragmented analysis. My argument is that *theory* is the most important tool to help in this regard, which means that you must constantly go back to step number three.

5   *Do analytic writing.* I have already quoted Laurel Richardson that writing is a method of inquiry. I call the writing that you need to do 'analytic' to stress the idea that good qualitative writing often uses theoretical concepts to analytically unpack the social situations, events and processes that are scrutinised. I am not saying that you should avoid using the concepts of everyday language to write about everyday life – indeed you often must use the vernacular – but I am saying that the concepts of everyday language are theoretically loaded in the first place, and you can do a much better analysis if you understand both *how* they are so loaded, and can *evaluate* whether this works for or against what you want to say (e.g. my way of talking about boys and girls above used everyday language, but in a way that possibly reinforces some of the distinctions that I would like to deconstruct).

6   *Publish your text.* Your writing is done when things have cleared up for you, when the breakdown in understanding is somehow mended, and you are able to explain to others how you now understand things (differently) and possibly even to convince them that your understanding is helpful. Sometimes you must adjust your text to fit certain standard ways of reporting if you aim to publish it. Sometimes you may even have to downplay the fact that you have done a piece of everyday life research and reconstruct the steps that you have taken to make them fit into more standardised formats. You should never lie, of course, but some disciplines and journals will not be open to what I recommend in this book. You can sometimes work your way around this by writing that the empirical examples of your analysis 'illustrate' some general point instead of saying that your materials made you discover something new in the social world. Other journals – often those that use the word 'qualitative' in their names – are completely open to the kind of research that this book is about.

Some will no doubt find these six steps overly loose and unmethodical. But my point is that good research very often rests on a cultivation of common human capabilities of understanding and communicating with others rather than on mechanical methodological procedures. This is not a licence to do sloppy work – quite the contrary. It demands a lot from the researcher: she must learn to focus her attention, spend hours reading and writing and be a master of linking theoretical concepts with the empirical world. One can only learn to do this by trying it again and again and by reading examples of research that have employed this procedure. This explains why I have devoted a considerable number of pages in this book to examples of concrete everyday life analyses. It is not enough to say what one should do – it needs to be shown.

If this way of working appeals to you, I encourage you to try it out for yourself. One way would be to just do it – following the loosely outlined steps above – and then return to the rest of this book afterwards as a kind of after-thought that may enhance the quality of the analysis. Another way would be to read the book first and experiment with some of the practical exercises along the way. In any case, I believe that it is very important to work concretely with some everyday life materials while reading this book. In the final sections of this chapter, I will present three examples of everyday life research that may serve as sources of inspiration.

On everyday life

It seems reasonable to begin a book entitled *Qualitative Inquiry in Everyday Life* by explaining its main concepts: qualitative inquiry and everyday life. In the rest of this chapter, I will first briefly address the notion of everyday life before moving on to qualitative inquiry, both of which are harder to define than one would think. I recommend approaching qualitative inquiry as a vital human activity that all living human beings are engaged in. In the next chapter, I draw upon varieties of pragmatic and hermeneutic paradigms (that emphasise the idea that being alive as a human being should be conceived as an interpretative process of inquiry) to develop a philosophical anthropology of the human knower.

The term 'everyday life' has entered many corners of the social sciences today. Classical works have investigated 'the presentation of self in everyday life' (Goffman, 1959), 'everyday life in the modern world' (Lefebvre, 1968) and 'the practice of everyday life' (de Certeau, 1984). More specific approaches, such as ethnomethodology (Garfinkel, 1967) and symbolic interactionism (Blumer, 1969), have also advocated a focus on the mundane details of human interaction as the key to understanding social processes. A focus on our everyday lives becomes particularly central in a postmodern era, when society 'has been broken apart and reconstituted as everyday life' (Ferguson, 2009, p. 160). In a postmodern world in fragments, where larger social structures and processes are experienced as disjointed, everyday life has become the essential 'theatre of fragmentation' that must be studied if we want to understand our lives (p. 157).

Social science began with the emergence of modern, industrial society, when individuals and society were conceived as separate entities, and when this separation was seen as problematic, resulting in disintegration, anomie and the modern malaises (such as excessive individualism, loneliness and neuroses). More specifically, we can say that the particular social science focus on everyday life began at the University of Chicago in the late nineteenth century, when there was a need to understand the experiences of people living in the new big cities (Jacobsen, 2009). The urban experience has since intensified in the postmodern epoch, which, among other things, is characterised by the fact that Society (conceived as a stable, hierarchical social order) seems to be breaking apart and is reconfigured as heterogeneous networks and practices that have a more precarious and fluid character. Some refer to these emerging social forms as network sociality (Wittel, 2001) and others argue that they result in deeply fragmented forms of human experience that demand a fragmented rendition in writing (Baudrillard, 2007).

In any event, what seems to be the case is that 'the social' in broad terms is recast as everyday life in the social sciences. The social is no longer primarily conceived as a hierarchical and rigidly structured sphere (like the Marxian base-superstructure or the Habermasian system-lifeworld), but as something that is much more mundane, fluid and heterogeneous. This does not mean that inequalities have disappeared and that everyone shares the same perspective on culture and society – far from it – but it does mean that it has become more difficult for people to know their own society, for the social no longer has an obvious centre. Our 'social imaginary' (Taylor, 2004) no longer revolves around one central deity, state or nation. Rather, the flow and flux of our everyday lives is what now constitutes the social. We simply tend to imagine the social in terms of everyday life.

Can we approach a more specific definition of everyday life? One suggestion is that the everyday in a literal sense refers to 'a host of routine activities, private and public, carried out on a regular, if not actually daily, basis; such as eating, sleeping, working, commuting, shopping and so on' (Ferguson, 2009, p. 164). These activities, although trivial at first sight, turn out to be rich sources of information about who we are in a postmodern era. I will soon illustrate this by referring to some seemingly trivial events and objects (such as a tube of toothpaste) that turn out to be richly informative about our lives. Furthermore, as Ferguson adds, the everyday is 'the inclusive arena in which occasional, incidental, and unusual events *also* take place' (p. 164). So not only the commonplace, the daily, but also the exceptional can be a significant object for everyday life analyses. It is not the prevalence of something that makes it ordinary; rather, something is ordinary because it appears in our everyday lives. A divorce, for example, must be considered an everyday life event, even if the person is only divorced once in her life.

As these initial analyses testify, it is notoriously difficult to define everyday life. There are numerous ways of characterising the term and it seems to be 'overloaded with meaning' (Jacobsen, 2009, p. 9). Still, the term directs our attention in an important direction. Everyday life can be described as a place (e.g. the home), a temporal dimension (e.g. what happens daily), an attitude (the unreflective, practical stance), as specific artefacts (everyday objects), a theoretical approach (focusing on lived experience), an academic abstraction, and as a set of experiences (p. 14). Elias has attempted a characterisation of everyday life by contrasting it with what it is *not*: holidays, the bourgeois sphere, the life of the privileged, exceptional events, public life, the artificial and the unspontaneous (Elias, 1998). Others have argued more specifically that the everyday is confined to four types of quotidian space: workspaces, urban/mobile spaces, living spaces and non-places (between contexts) (Scott, 2009, p. 1). Although it can be helpful to keep these distinctions in mind, I doubt that they exhaustively define or delineate our everyday lives. The difficulties of pinpointing everyday life are probably related to the fact that everyday life is our paramount reality, the life world (to speak with the phenomenologists), the ubiquitous interaction order (to speak with Goffman), or the immortal ordinary society (to speak with Garfinkel). Everyday life is everywhere, and we live through it like fish proverbially live in the water.

In this book, I take a pragmatic attitude to everyday life and define it relative to the everyday life of the *researcher* and what mediates her activities and experiences. Everyday life *objects* are thus those that the researcher in question appropriates and uses in her daily living (e.g. consumer products, technologies, pieces of art), and everyday *situations* and *events* are those that the researcher experiences in her life (e.g. conversations, parties, work, rituals). Throughout the book, I try to focus equally on objects and events. These are not unrelated: something appears as an object for human beings in the course of events as these are unfolding, and there is hardly any event in the social process that does not include objects (Latour, 1996). Qualitative researchers, however, often tend to forget about objects and materialities and concentrate on studying 'social interaction' as if this could exist in some kind of material vacuum.

Needless to say, the discussion about where and how 'the social' shows itself is unresolved. How does one capture human experience, sociocultural life or the *Zeitgeist*? Rather than postulating macrosocial entities like social structures or systems that should be studied by social and human scientists, this book follows the microsocial turn to the everyday that has become increasingly important during the last fifty years or so. Everyday life, in this perspective, is not 'the rest', i.e., what is left over when we have looked at important institutions such as work, education and health care, but everyday life is rather the zone where acting persons *conduct* or *lead* their lives (Dreier, 2008). Phenomenologists often refer to this zone as the *life world* (*Lebenswelt*), an intersubjective world where objects and events appear as meaningful prior to those theorisations we may engage in about them. For example, before my condition is a clinical depression, perhaps caused by a dysfunctional serotonin level in the brain, it is a disheartened way in which the world appears to me as uninviting (I return to phenomenology several times, but most thoroughly in Chapter 4).

On qualitative inquiry and the everyday

There is no simple relationship between qualitative inquiry and social science theories that look at our everyday lives, but in the box below, I mention some paradigms that more or less explicitly take an interest in everyday life research from a qualitative perspective.

BOX 1.1

On qualitative everyday life theories

In books on everyday life sociology, a number of well-known theories and disciplines are usually rehearsed as specifically concerned with everyday life. Scott lists psychoanalysis, social psychology, structural functionalism, interpretivist sociology, phenomenology, ethnomethodology, symbolic interactionism, dramaturgy, structuration theory, cultural studies, post-structuralism and the so-called new sociologies of everyday life, which includes the theories of de Certeau and Lefebvre (Scott, 2009, pp. 11–31). Although Scott has helpful discussions of each of these, it is hard to see what warrants recruiting all of them as qualitative everyday life sociologies. In fact, they more or less seem to encompass the entire field of sociology, and the inclusion of all of them under the heading of everyday life risks emptying the concept of meaning. Since the present book is not confined to sociological analyses, I will not go through these theories here, but I do try to flesh out some more general theoretical points below.

Jacobsen's introduction to the sociologies of everyday life – or of the 'unnoticed', as he prefers – has a more focused selection of theories that includes the Chicago School, pragmatism, phenomenology, symbolic interactionism, existential sociology, critical everyday life sociologies, Marxism, Goffman, ethnomethodology, conversation analysis and the sociology of the absurd (Jacobsen, 2009). What such diverse theoretical orientations share can perhaps be explained with reference to Maffesoli's account of the three (cross-theoretical) defining features of everyday life studies (Maffesoli, 1989):

- *First*, the researcher is seen as involved in the object of inquiry, which means that the researcher is first and foremost understood as a *participant* rather than a spectator in social life. As an everyday life researcher, she writes from her own participating stance in the social world.
- *Second*, everyday life research is focused on human *experience* in a broad sense, and the theories mentioned above differ to a considerable extent concerning their views on whether human experience is an authentic, experiential realm

(posited by some schools of phenomenology) or whether it is constructed linguistically and discursively (as argued by some conversation analysts, for example).

- *Third*, the theme of everyday life demands *conceptual audacity* so that descriptions and analyses of mundane life can be intellectually interesting and challenging. A conceptual audacity can 'break the closure of the political-economic logic which still underlies many analyses' (p. v). We use (audacious) concepts not to neutrally mirror the world, but as tools that enable us to see new and perhaps surprising aspects of the everyday lives that we lead. This may in turn generate new forms of human action.

In Box 1.1 I have attempted to say something general, i.e. across theories, about everyday life research and how it pertains to qualitative inquiry. Concerning Maffesoli's third point, conceptual audacity, this book argues that a focused use of theoretical concepts can help researchers become defamiliarised from their lives and distance themselves adequately from their subject matters in ways that facilitate research with a critical edge. Without theories and philosophies, everyday life research would become nothing but a trivial recounting of our quotidian activities (Jacobsen, 2009, p. 17). Unlike other contemporary texts on qualitative inquiry that follow more or less anti-theoretical currents, the present book advocates using theoretical concepts as tools with which to see the unnoticed in everyday life. Theories are in this sense epistemologically important in the production of knowledge, just as hammers and nails are important in the carpenter's activities of producing objects.

When we take an interest in how people obtain knowledge about their everyday lives (e.g. about the *Lebenswelt*), we are beginning to address what is usually called qualitative inquiry. Human inquiry is qualitative when it concerns the *how* of our lives: How do we experience the world? How do we collectively construct social worlds that subsequently seem to be independent of our constructive efforts? How do we accomplish everyday acts such as producing or consuming objects, or educating the young? These are questions that can be answered only by using what is now conventionally called qualitative methods. Qualitative methods throw light on the qualities of experience, actions and emotions, whereas quantitative methods are used to chart the causal effects of independent variables on dependent ones.

For an initial, generic definition of qualitative research that is close to the spirit of this book, I will refer to Denzin and Lincoln:

> *Qualitative research* is a situated activity that locates the observer in the world. Qualitative research consists of a set of interpretive, material practices that make the world visible. These practices transform the world. They turn the world into a series of representations, including fieldnotes, interviews, conversations, photographs, recordings, and memos to the self. At this level, qualitative research

involves an interpretive, naturalistic approach to the world. This means that qualitative researchers study things in their natural settings, attempting to make sense of or interpret phenomena in terms of the meanings people bring to them. (Denzin & Lincoln, 2011, p. 3)

The keywords are *situated* (the researcher is placed in a historical and social situation that informs her analyses), *interpretative* (qualitative analyses concern meanings that must be interpreted), *material* (all research takes place in a material situation, which includes economical and institutional factors that shape the activity) and *transform* (qualitative inquiry never leaves the world as it was).

This book is written from the more specific premise that the social world inhabited by acting persons is one that cannot be understood as controlled by causal laws (Harré, 2004). There are no social structures, institutions or powers that *cause* us to do, think or feel in certain ways. Instead, persons are the only efficacious agents in the social world (Slocum-Bradley, 2009). The social is that which is continually *done* by persons. Only persons act, but they could obviously not do so without discursive practices that render certain acts intelligible and thereby meaningful. And they could not do so without a range of enabling conditions that are material, such as brains, bodies and artefacts, and this whole network of discourses and materialities is, in principle, relevant when one engages in qualitative analyses of social processes (Brinkmann, 2011b). If it is true that the social world in which we conduct our everyday lives is one where persons are agents, then we can only understand the lives and experiences of these agents by engaging in qualitative inquiry. We should not, first and foremost, explain what *happens* (as in quantitative research traditions), but rather understand how people *conduct their lives*, i.e., understand what they *do*. Table 1.1 summarises some simplified (and rather caricatured) differences between these two modes of thought.

In qualitative inquiry, we study things that are done, conducted or performed. This means that we approach human beings as agents. Humans are not just

Table 1.1 Two forms of inquiry

	Qualitative inquiry	*Quantitative inquiry*
Subject matter	Relations of meaning	Causally related entities
Purpose	Understanding actions and events	Uncovering causal relations
Ontology	Performances that are done	Things that happen
Methods	Interpreting human actions, practices and cultural productions	Establishing correlations between variables
Materials	Texts	Numbers

causally reacting entities, but acting persons that can often give accounts of what they do and may try to justify their actions. Unlike the causal processes in non-human nature, human actions are based on reasons and motives that are important to describe when we seek to understand the things that are done. Often this will involve interpretation, for actions, and the reasons on which they are based, are not always transparent to onlookers, and may not even be clear to the persons who are performing them. Typically, an action makes sense *as* an action, when it is part of a broader social practice that has a social history and involves other people who participate in the practice. It is impossible to understand the concrete actions at school described in the example above, for example, if one does not take the history of education and practices of boys and girls into account. Human beings perform the social here-and-now, but they always do so on the background of social practices that have a history. When we study how actions are related to other actions, and how an individual action is part of a historical practice of carrying out that action, we are seeking to understand relations of meaning. In qualitative inquiry, we are not trying to pinpoint a specific causal factor that may have brought about a certain action (such as the school division between boys and girls), but we are rather trying to understand how a certain action makes sense to the people involved, what constitutes the conditions for it being performed, and how the action may be related to other ensuing actions and events. In short, we are interested not in causal relations, but in meanings.

Qualitative research methods, such as interviews, fieldwork and paradigmatic approaches like phenomenology or discourse analysis, have been developed in order to throw light upon human experience and social life. Statistical averages are not in focus, but researchers are rather concerned with understanding concrete human beings and how they think, feel, act, learn or develop as persons. Few qualitative researchers are, as such, against generalising their results, but they believe that generalisation must proceed by means other than statistical tests (see the next chapter). Qualitative researchers are committed to a study of the human world of meaning and value and take an interest in how actors themselves experience the world. In that sense, researchers strive to understand human life 'from the inside', i.e., from inside the local practices where life is led, rather than 'from the outside' at a distance through objectifying methods.

The main challenge when doing research 'from the inside' is that so much is taken for granted in our everyday life. It can be very difficult to understand the obvious. This has been articulated well by Hall, Lashua and Coffey:

> How are we to know that which we begin by taking for granted? This is precisely no problem at all when it comes to 'doing' daily life, in everyday ways – fluency here follows from our very unconscious familiarity with the mundane – though much harder when it comes to knowing the everyday and making it the explicit object of attention and understanding. Here the everyday resists, or rather

eludes, scrutiny. Attending to the everyday can require an estranging sensitivity, one that is more often found in the arts than the sciences. (Hall, Lashua, & Coffey, 2008, pp. 1021–1022)

When I refer to examples from the arts in this book, it is not just because of the aesthetic qualities of novels, poems and films, but also because of what the authors above refer to as the required 'estranging sensitivity', in relation to which art is often helpful. Art can defamiliarise us with our lives in a way that can be conducive to understanding it better.

Three stances and examples of qualitative inquiry in everyday life

Before moving on, it might be useful to see some concrete examples of what I mean by qualitative analyses of everyday life, i.e., of research that has given us significant insight into human lives by using very few and everyday pieces of 'data'. I will describe three examples of research below that deal with quite mundane materials in ways that are both theoretically rich and insightful in relation to broader human and social issues. These examples of everyday life research are published as short and highly readable articles, and they make clear that less can be more. Each deal with a single everyday life phenomenon that all of us have access to. I have chosen these three specific examples because they illustrate three different but related analytic stances or strategies that are helpful to bear in mind when one conducts everyday life research, and which I will return to throughout this book. Although these stances point in different directions, they can all help us in knowing the obvious, or that which we take for granted, as we shall see. Inspired by Noblit and Hare (1988), these strategies are:

1 Making the obvious obvious
2 Making the hidden obvious
3 Making the obvious dubious

These are quite general strategies across different paradigms in the social sciences and humanities, and the distinction between them comes from Noblit and Hare's book on meta-ethnography, which is the art of synthesising results and analyses from different qualitative studies (Noblit and Hare emphasise that this art is an interpretative affair and not a simple aggregative or cumulative exercise). I generalise the strategies here and present them as three wide-ranging stances in qualitative inquiry that are all important today, and particularly so in relation to our everyday lives. After presenting the stances, I provide an example of each of them.

Phenomenological stance: Making the obvious obvious

The first can be called a phenomenological stance that seeks to describe human experience by making the obvious obvious. I present phenomenology more thoroughly in Chapter 4, but, in colloquial terms, it is meant to help us see the trees as a forest and the forest as an array of trees. In everyday life research, this can be much harder than it seems, as the example below will indicate. In this context, we may quote Pelias, who argues that what I call a phenomenological stance is really the stance of poetry: 'Science is the act of looking at a tree and seeing lumber. Poetry is the act of looking at a tree and seeing a tree' (Pelias, 2004, p. 9). The poet, argues Pelias, is really the one who can see the world clearly as it is; at least those aspects of the world that are 'poetic' and 'aesthetic' rather than instrumental (the term 'aesthetic' originates from the Greek word for experience).

Critical stance: Making the hidden obvious

The second stance is a critical stance that is shared among Foucauldian discourse analysts and Marxists critics of capitalism. To criticise is here to uncover the hidden power structures that regulate human behaviours and influence human experience. Marxists talk about ideologies and Foucauldians about discourses, but the point is to see through the surface and demonstrate the working mechanisms behind the phenomena. Marx famously argued that 'all science would be superfluous if the outward appearance and the essence of things directly coincided'.[1] Science is needed to go beyond appearance or the surface to critically uncover a truer reality. Some of the authors who approach the world from the critical angle are at odds with the assumption in this book that persons are the only efficacious agents in the social world. Some critical scholars invoke hidden social structures or systems as causal agents, whereas I advocate seeing social and cultural artefacts as mediators that acting persons may use in living their lives, but nevertheless it may still be relevant to take a critical stance and ask what hidden roles such mediators may play in our everyday lives.

Deconstructive stance: Making the obvious dubious

The final stance is the deconstructive. This stance implies an attempt to question what we take for granted, not necessarily to uncover hidden mechanisms, but rather to show that meanings and understandings are unstable and

---

[1]Cited from the internet edition: www.marxists.org/archive/marx/works/1894-c3/ch48.htm

endlessly ambiguous. The relations of meaning, referred to in Table 1.1, could always appear in different ways, and deconstruction is the art of bringing these differences to light. The concept of deconstruction was introduced by Derrida as a combination of 'destruction' and 'construction'. It involves destructing one understanding of a text and opening for construction of other understandings (Norris, 1987). The focus is not on 'what really happens' or 'the real meaning of what was done', but on presenting alternative versions of the real. It is affiliated with the 'hermeneutics of suspicion' of the critical stance, but it does not search for any underlying genuine or stable meanings hidden beneath a text or an event. Meanings of words are conceived in relation to an infinite network of other words in a language. What we take for granted in our everyday lives – e.g. that we must work, love and consume according to the logics of late modern capitalism – can be deconstructed, thereby opening up for other images of human existence.

The phenomenological, critical and deconstructive stances are not confined to their own traditions (phenomenology, critical theory and deconstruction), although these schools of thought tend to cultivate such specific perspectives. Obviously, a phenomenologist can be critical and even deconstructive, and vice versa, so here I use the terms more generally to point to analytic strategies that may be useful to bear in mind when one does qualitative inquiry in everyday life. The logic of one's study, and the way one presents and analyses the material, may differ relative to one's interest in either making the obvious obvious, making the hidden obvious or making the obvious dubious.

In Box 1.2 we shall look at an example of the first strategy of making the obvious obvious in everyday life.

BOX 1.2

Throwing like a girl: Making the obvious obvious

In a classic article entitled 'Throwing like a girl: A phenomenology of feminine body comportment, motility and spatiality', political scholar and feminist Iris Marion Young addressed the extremely mundane activity of throwing objects (Young, 1980). Young began by quoting the phenomenologist Erwin Straus, who, in an earlier essay from 1966, had observed what he called a 'remarkable difference in the manner of throwing of the two sexes' (p. 137). Girls at the age of five, Straus had noted, do not make any use of lateral space when throwing an object such as a ball. A boy of the same age, on the other hand, uses his entire body when throwing, which results in a much faster acceleration of the ball. Straus ascribed this observed difference to an innate biological difference, a specific 'feminine attitude' that girls have in relation to the world and to space that is not as such anatomical, but biological at some deeper level. This difference between boys and girls results

---

in the derogatory expression 'he throws like a girl', which is used, for example, as an insulting comment in American baseball.

Young finds Straus's descriptions compelling, but she disagrees with his essentialist explanation, which invokes 'a mysterious feminine essence' (p. 138) in order to account for the difference between boys and girls. So Young significantly expands on Straus's description through an extremely close portrayal of the motions of gendered bodies. Let me quote some of Young's words here:

> [G]irls do not bring their whole bodies into the motion as much as the boys. They do not reach back, twist, move backward, step, and lean forward. Rather, the girls tend to remain relatively immobile except for their arms, and even the arm is not extended as far as it could be. (p. 142)

Young goes on to describe further differences in body style between boys and girls, and men and women, concerning how they sit, stand and walk:

> Women generally are not as open with their bodies as men in their gait and stride. Typically, the masculine stride is longer proportional to a man's body than is the feminine stride to a woman's. The man typically swings his arms in a more open and loose fashion than does a woman and typically has more up and down rhythm in his step. (p. 142)

And there are many other rich descriptions in Young's essay, for example concerning how women tend to lift heavy objects:

> [W]omen more often than men fail to plant themselves firmly and make their thighs bear the greatest proportion of the weight. Instead, we tend to concentrate our effort on those parts of the body most immediately connected to the task – the arms and shoulders – rarely bringing the power of the legs to the task at all. (p. 143)

Young's prose is precise, descriptive and quite dry, but she manages to take the mundane movements of girls and women and present them as a very relevant and interesting topic for analysis. As a reader, one is convinced by her accurate descriptions; there is an immediate feeling of recognition. In a sense, we know already what Young is saying, but we don't know that we know it, and in that way, she is making the obvious obvious for us, something that is extremely difficult to do in such an insightful way.

In the essay, Young wants to say that women are holding themselves back, not just concerning their bodily movements, but also more generally in society. Unlike boys, who learn to be assertive, aggressive and proactive, and grow up to act in this way as adult men, girls are not taught to use their full bodily capacities 'in free and open engagement with the world' (p. 152). Consequently, they often become insecure, restricted and self-enclosed as adult women. This, for Young, is not to be explained with reference to anatomy, physiology or by invoking a mysterious feminine essence, but is rather a result of the particular situation of women in a patriarchal and thus oppressive society. If this analysis is valid, it ought to have significant consequences for how to conceive of gender inequality, which turns out not just to be a matter of discourses and the symbolic, e.g. concerning unequal rights and treatments. Gender inequality may be rooted in the very bodily habits that persons acquire from a very early age, which may be quite difficult to change. A first step towards improvement, however, can be taken when these inequalities are made obvious for us.

Young does not stay with the merely descriptive. She also invokes theoretical concepts to present an explanation of the phenomenon that she has observed. And we can even say that her initial descriptive stance is theoretically informed, namely through the phenomenology of the body, as developed by Merleau-Ponty (1945). Phenomenology builds on an ambition to describe the world as it is experienced pre-reflectively by human subjects, and, for Merleau-Ponty, by *embodied* subjects specifically. We know the world through our bodily engagement in the world, and we develop as subjects as our bodily habits are formed. To be a subject is to have the capacity for *transcendence*, i.e., for projecting oneself into the future, and this is a capacity Merleau-Ponty ascribes to the body. However, Young points out that enacting the existence of women in patriarchal society implies a contradiction: as a human subject, a woman participates in transcendence, but the societal conditions that shape her habits simultaneously deny her that very transcendence (p. 141).

Box 1.2 summarises some of the points of Young's analysis of 'throwing like a girl'. There are several other points worth mentioning, but I will refer the reader to Young's essay for further details. The analysis exemplifies many virtues of everyday life research when well carried out: it deals with an aspect of human existence that is pervasive in everyday life – gendered ways of moving our bodies – that is at the same time sufficiently specific to be analysed in a rather short essay. It is primarily based on the researcher's own observations, which are described very closely and directly. But although based on ordinary observations, the analysis is far from a-theoretical. Young helps us understand the phenomenon better by invoking phenomenological theory and by introducing theoretical concepts that crystallise the everyday phenomenon of feminine movement and its contradictory modalities: ambiguous transcendence (a transcendence of the body that is simultaneously laden with immanence), inhibited intentionality (when the feminine body under-uses its real capacities) and a discontinuous unity (meaning that the part of the body that is transcending towards an aim is discontinuous with the rest of the body) (Young, 1980, pp. 145–147). These contradictions, for Young, are rooted in the cultural tendency to make the feminine body both subject and object for itself at the same time, and, in this way, her mundane observations are related to much larger social issues about gender inequalities. By making the obvious obvious, these analyses can potentially assist in changing the oppressive character of the patriarchy. Given the significance of

Young's contribution, it seems reasonable to conclude that her essay has indeed contributed to greater social justice and gender equality.

The next example tries to go beyond the obvious to critically uncover hidden discourses at work in a mundane object.

BOX 1.3

Toothpaste and discourse: Making the hidden obvious

In a short paper called 'Discursive complexes in material culture', critical psychologist Ian Parker presents an analysis of a text found on the back of a toothpaste tube. The text reads:

Directions for use

Choose a children's brush that has a small head and add a pea-sized amount of Punch & Judy toothpaste. To teach your child to clean teeth, stand behind and place your hand under the child's chin to tilt head back and see mouth. Brush both sides of teeth as well as tops. Brush after breakfast and last thing at night. Supervise the brushing of your child's teeth until the age of eight. If your child is taking fluoride treatment, seek professional advice concerning daily intake.

Contains 0.8 per cent Sodium Monofluorophosphate. (Parker, 1996, p. 189)

It is difficult to think of a more mundane piece of prose, and it may initially strike one as completely uninteresting to invest time and energy in analysing it. However, from an everyday life perspective, even the most dull objects and routine activities have the potential to teach us important things about our cultural worlds. In Parker's case, it is a discourse analytic reading that enables him to open up the object and reveal the hidden discursive complexes within it. As he says: 'What seems trivial can be seen as symptomatic of patterns of regulation, and the toothpaste text in question can now no longer be read with an innocent eye' (p. 185).

Parker is particularly interested in uncovering the culturally prescribed understandings about the nature of subjectivity that circulate in society and influence even such things as toothpaste texts. Any text, according to Parker, 'interpellates' the reader. Interpellation is a term from the French structuralist Althusser, and it refers to readers being 'hailed' by the text, whether they choose to agree with its message or try to resist it. In this case, the reader is interpellated through four discourses that Parker identifies in the text: a rationalist discourse that hails the reader as someone who can follow 'directions for use' and who accepts health authorities; a familial discourse in which one has ownership (cf. 'your child') of family members and a duty to care for them; a developmental-educational discourse, which concerns the education and training of children's skills and abilities; and, finally, a medical discourse, according to which the use of toothpaste is linked to hygiene within a complex of knowledge about health and disease.

Parker recognises not just the discourses that are visible in the text, but also those that are invisible. He finds it interesting that gender as a category is repressed,

---

illustrated by the absence of gendered pronouns ('to clean teeth', 'sides of teeth') (p. 191). And he introduces psychoanalytic notions of the Oedipal triangle and the reality principle to analyse the activity of brushing the interior (indeed a Freudian cue word) of the mouth after restraining the head. An activity is presented 'in which the child is physically restrained while a cleaning implement is inserted in the mouth. There is powerful affect running alongside meaning, and it is helpful to attend to our "emotional response" to the text, to images in the text here as varieties of affect produced in discourse' (p. 190). We come to witness 'a scene in which an adult with power gazes upon and acts upon the child' (p. 193). Parker asks us to use our own emotional response as a way of reading the text.

Parker's relationship with psychoanalysis in this paper and elsewhere is ambiguous. On the one hand, he employs psychoanalytic concepts as theoretical tools in concert with discourse analysis to study social and psychological processes in everyday life. On the other hand, he argues that psychoanalysis has shaped the culture and the subjectivities that inhabit it, so, in a sense, he says that we need psychoanalytic concepts to understand our lives, because psychoanalysis has constructed the way that we interpret ourselves. In any case, his reading is deeply informed by theoretical concepts that enable him to make the hidden obvious.

In Box 1.3, I have summarised some of the main points of Parker's discursive and psychoanalytic reading of an object that nearly all of us possess: a tube of toothpaste. His research interests concern the discourses that shape subjectivities, and these discourses are doing their work in the most unlikely places in our everyday lives, even on toothpaste tubes. By using his psychoanalytic and discourse analytic theoretical tools, Parker manages to reveal how certain discourses, which are normally hidden to our eyes, function to interpellate us and invite us to act as subjects within specific discursive complexes.

The most important part of taking the critical stance exemplified by Parker concerns what he calls taking a 'step back' (Parker, 1996, p. 190). This is described as an essential part of discourse analysis, and I would add that it is nearly always a crucial part of any study of everyday life. It consists of producing a critical distance between the reader (or researcher) and the text (object or event) so that one becomes able to pose the question: 'what collections of relationships and theories of self must obtain for this material to make sense?' (p. 190). This is a question we can pose in relation to literally any everyday life object or event: what are its conditions of possibility as a meaningful phenomenon? An answer to this question will nearly always include references to numerous discourses, symbolic systems and material structures. I will suggest that this question ought to accompany any qualitative study of everyday life from the outset, since it has the potential of stimulating our (sociological) imagination. What collections of relationships and theories of self must obtain, for example, for you to be able to read this book?

The final example of everyday life research involves a deconstructive reading of a seemingly trivial activity, leading to a destabilisation of our commonsense understanding of ourselves as subjects.

BOX 1.4

I eat an apple: Making the obvious dubious

In just a little more than six printed pages of text, the ethnographer and philosopher Annemarie Mol uses the mundane process of eating an apple as a basis for theorising subjectivity (Mol, 2008). And she doesn't just theorise subjectivity – the *I* who eats an apple – she also suggests explicitly in her conclusion that if we draw upon exemplary situations to do with eating as we engage in philosophy, many things, including subjectivity, may change (p. 34). Without using the term herself, I propose that she is using her analysis of apple eating to deconstruct our traditional notion of the subject as a discrete, bounded self with agency. 'The eating self', as she says, 'does not control "its" body at all' (p. 30). And it is worth continuing the quote:

> Take: *I eat an apple*. Is the agency in the *I* or in the *apple*? I eat, for sure, but without apples before long there would be no 'I' left. And it is even more complicated. For how to separate us out to begin with, the apple and me? One moment this may be possible: here is the apple, there I am. But a little later (bite, chew, swallow) I have become (made out of) apple; while the apple is (a part of) me. *Transsubstantiation*. What about that for a model to think with? (p. 30)

By describing the everyday occurrence of eating an apple, Mol wants to make us think about how to remodel the subject. The subject emerges in her text as much more embedded in the world, or saturated with the world, so to speak, than on traditional accounts. The subject emerges in her analysis as something with semipermeable boundaries (p. 30). Mol takes the 'thin' situation of apple eating as her starting point, but she goes on to provide much more 'thick' history around it. Thus, she tells us the cultural history of apples, how the apple has biblical connotations, how apples came to the Netherlands (her home country), and how there is a politics of apples (Mol dislikes Granny Smiths, because they used to be imported from Chile during the Pinochet dictatorship). Eating apples is an everyday phenomenon that is radically situated, and which is made possible because of complex webs of relationships (agricultural, religious, geographical, political, etc.) that it is possible and interesting to study.

Instead of confining action, activity, uniquely to human subjects, Mol deconstructs the whole subject–object split and posits an image of *inter-activity* – 'shared activity all round' (p. 31). And her deconstructive tools are deeply poetical. Consider the following statement:

In the orchard, the apples. The trees carefully grafted. The colours and textures and tastes and cellar life attended to and the best fruit selected. And again. Without the work of ever so many generations of cultivators my apple would not have been. The cultivators, meanwhile, owed their lives to their apples. When and where in all these flows does subjectivity emerge? Where to stop the flow and point at it? (p. 31)

Should we consider this as poetry, philosophy or as an ethnography of apple eating in everyday life? In my view, it qualifies as all three things, and the result is a beautiful account of subjectivity as always already in transaction with its surroundings.

Mol's elegant text is written almost without specific theoretical concepts, and yet it can be argued that it is her theoretical stance (feminist science studies) that enables her to see the mundane practice of eating an apple in a new, deconstructed light. As a reader one immediately recognises what she describes, but then one suddenly loses one's hold on the world, when subjectivity slips away in the deconstructive movement. But then subjectivity reappears in the text; only now in a mutualist form that is deeply integrated with apples – and the world more generally. There are references and a few theoretical discussions in the paper, but these are confined to the footnotes.

Mol's text illustrates that it is possible to do provocative and interesting deconstructive work simply by taking an everyday occurrence as a starting point. She makes our 'obvious' preconceptions of subjectivity dubious by showing us other possible ways of thinking that are immanent in eating practices. In the process, the world itself appears as re-enchanted; the world is no longer a collection of lifeless objects in Newtonian space, but an active process of change and becoming. This re-enchantment is achieved by a movement similar to Richard Rorty's Deweyan advice that 'the way to re-enchant the world, to bring back what religion gave our forefathers, is to stick to the concrete' (Rorty, 1991, p. 175). Perhaps we can say that this, exactly, is the virtue of qualitative inquiry in everyday life – it enables us to re-enchant the world without fleeing into abstraction or mysticism, but precisely by sticking to the concrete.

We can see that Maffesoli's three defining features of everyday life research (researcher as participant, a focus on experience and conceptual audacity) are richly present in all three examples of everyday life research, albeit in different ways. All examples can be seen as pieces of 'empirical philosophy', grounded in phenomenology, discursive psychoanalysis, and a form of feminist materialism, respectively. Thus, the three researchers use philosophical positions and theoretical ideas to open up everyday objects and practices in audacious ways that enable us to understand more.

Concluding comments

In this chapter I have provided three examples to indicate what I mean by qualitative everyday life research. It is research that deals with particular objects or events that are found in the researcher's everyday life, and which can inform us about more general issues in human life. These objects and events do not suddenly fall from the sky, but are chosen because they disturb, annoy or simply interest the researcher. They are usually chosen because of some kind of breakdown in the researcher's understanding.

I have also argued that in order for the researcher to engage in fruitful analyses of such everyday life materials, it is often indispensable to master theoretical concepts. These should not be thought of as eternally true reflections of the social world, but as sensitising instruments that can assist us in understanding and eventually coping with the different situations and materials (I further unfold this pragmatist epistemology in the next chapter). I have also discussed different characterisations of qualitative inquiry in everyday life and I have introduced a number of stances to one's material that are worth considering (phenomenological, critical, deconstructive).

EXERCISE

Choose a particular event that you have experienced and which made you stop and reflect. It may be something that confused you or simply something that made you wonder.

Describe the event in less than 1,000 words. Provide an answer to the questions: What made this event possible? What common rules and regularities were involved (and possibly broken)? What was taken for granted by the participants – and why?

Take your analysis and consider whether it primarily made the obvious obvious, the hidden obvious or the obvious dubious. Discuss your analysis and your reading of it with others.

If you find it worthwhile to do further work on your analysis, try to rewrite it by explicitly taking one or more of the analytic stances (phenomenological, critical, deconstructive).

TWO

The epistemology of working with everyday life materials

In the previous chapter, I introduced the idea of qualitative everyday life research, which was defined as research that takes some situation (event, episode, object) encountered by the researcher in her life as the point of departure for analyses of social life. I presented three pieces of research as exemplary texts that have taught researchers something new about human life. But what makes these exemplars good? What makes their analyses valid? Is it possible to say anything general on the background of such particular examples? These questions concern *epistemology*. Epistemology is the theory of knowledge, and modern philosophy (roughly from the Renaissance until the late twentieth century) became preoccupied with the question about knowledge and its validity and thus inaugurated a long epistemological tradition (Taylor, 1995). Usually, the epistemological questions were posed from an assumption that the human being is an isolated knower, who stands outside the world and aims to represent it correctly. True knowledge, on this account, means correct representation. This is still the dominant picture in positivist philosophies and methodologies.

This chapter presents a different take on epistemology. It is based on the idea that knowing is not something that simply happens – as if we were able to magically represent the world 'as it is' – but rather that knowing is an activity. Knowing is something people *do*, as part of their lives. Although humans 'do knowing' in their everyday lives, they have also invented certain practices that help them know in specific ways (we usually refer to these as sciences), but these practices are *human* activities and can never give us a God's-eye view of the universe. Unlike the illusory 'view from nowhere' that is posited by positivist epistemologies (see Nagel, 1986, for a classic discussion), we need to desacralise knowledge and admit that if knowing is a human activity, it is always already situated somewhere – in some cultural, historical and social situation. This has been stressed for a couple of decades now by people who subscribe to postmodern epistemologies, arguing that knowledge isn't unitary or even necessarily methodical, but local, situated, embodied, relative, intersubjective, relational, discursive, gendered and many other things.

Before the postmodern turn, the philosophies of pragmatism (primarily in the United States) and hermeneutics (primarily in Europe) developed sophisticated accounts of knowing that in many ways prefigured the postmodern analyses, but without the extreme relativism that is sometimes advocated by postmodernists. In my view, what distinguishes these earlier philosophies is the fact that for them, epistemological questions are always intimately connected to anthropological and ontological ones. For if knowing is an activity, something acting human beings *do*, then we must surely characterise these human beings in order for us to understand what knowing is. There is no knowledge in abstraction from people who know and their activities of knowing. And the name for the philosophical subfield that sets itself the task of characterising human knowers is 'philosophical anthropology'.

This chapter therefore presents an epistemological analysis of knowing through a philosophical anthropology that is relevant when working with everyday life materials. I shall first present an analysis of the social world in which everyday life research is carried out, and after that I address the philosophies of pragmatism and hermeneutics. I end the chapter with a discussion of some of the standard issues in the philosophy of science, such as validity, generalisation and objectivity, and return to the relevance of these philosophical discussions for qualitative inquiry in everyday life.

An ontology of the social world

Epistemology is the discipline that asks what knowledge is and how it is obtained, but this is always related to the question of ontology: How is what we call the (social) world constructed? What are its constituents? Different theoretical perspectives on qualitative inquiry obviously answer this question in quite different ways. Phenomenologists argue that the human world is made of intentional acts of consciousness (Husserl, 1954), symbolic interactionists (unsurprisingly) believe that the social is made up of symbolic interactions (Blumer, 1969), discourse analysts find that the social world is discursively constituted (Potter & Wetherell, 1987) and Actor-Network-Theorists work with an ontology of actants that affect each other in material-semiotic chains of networks (Latour, 2005). And the list could go on. The pragmatism that informs this book has the advantage that it does not force us to choose just one of these. Pragmatists want us to think of ontologies as practical tools to think with, and it would be just as

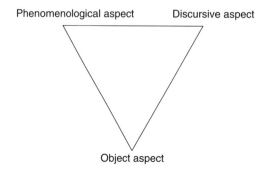

Figure 2.1 The ontological triangle

foolish to demand that we stick to a single bounded ontology of the social, as it would be to demand of the carpenter that she should use only a saw in her work. Those ontologies that prove to be fruitful in the collective efforts of humans to build social worlds are valid and justified, and those that prove to be unfruitful are deemed invalid by pragmatists. Working with an ontology of social atomism, for example, which posits human beings as essentially asocial, discrete entities that are only capable of pursuing private interests, would quite possibly lead to impoverished experiences of the world and to malfunctioning forms of human life (Taylor, 1985a). Thus, pragmatists would reject such an ontology.

I thus want to advocate *pragmatic pluralism* in thinking ontologically about the social world. This gives us the possibility of creatively synthesising a number of different positions in qualitative inquiry, relying on the assumption that different traditions each have something interesting and valid to say about the 'stuff' of the social. In Figure 2.1, I present an 'ontological triangle', which depicts three aspects of the social world that have been highlighted by three quite different traditions.

The legs of the triangle can be related to the three analytic stances that were introduced in the previous chapter:

- The phenomenological leg was described as a stance or strategy of making the obvious obvious. Phenomenologists study human *experience*, i.e., how the world appears to human beings, and the 'how' of experience is often so implicit in our life processes that we fail to recognise it. This was made evident in Iris Marion Young's analysis of throwing like a girl (1980). In the phenomenological camp we find not just phenomenologists proper, but also researchers working with interpretative approaches in the tradition of hermeneutics.
- The discursive leg of the triangle has been emphasised by those who believe that the social world and its practices are primarily constituted by conversations in a broad sense, i.e., by the human capacities for account-giving, drawing upon discourses and interpretative repertoires. In this camp we find discourse analysts, ethnomethodologists

(who also have a foot in the phenomenological camp) and conversation analysts. Ian Parker's analysis of the tube of toothpaste (1996) recounted in the previous chapter exemplifies how to work from this perspective, making the hidden discursive mechanisms obvious.

- Finally, we have the object leg of the triangle, which has received less attention in the social sciences. Recently, however, the social sciences seem to have taken a 'material turn', looking at the role of objects and materialities in constructing the social world. Annemarie Mol's (2008) materialist deconstruction of subjects and objects through the activity of eating represented an analytic stance that engaged with the object leg of the ontological triangle (with the apple as salient object), thereby attempting to make the obvious dubious.

Actor-Network-Theory (Latour, 2005) probably represents the best example of a well worked-out perspective so far that begins from the object leg, but pragmatists have also long taken an interest in how the social world is mediated and held together by material objects, and some analysts even talk about the need for a materialist social constructionism today (Clarke, 2005, p. 7). This is a social constructionism which acknowledges that the social world is not just made up of texts and symbolic interaction, but equally so of bodies, buildings, roads, tools, foods and numerous other material entities. If we go back to the example from my son's school that opened the previous chapter, we saw that an awareness of many things that are 'material' (e.g. the way things were arranged spatially) contributed to the construction of specific relationships between the children. The challenge in everyday life inquiry is to find analytic ways of moving between the different legs of the triangle and include so many different things – some symbolic, some experiential and some material – in our analyses. Social scientists have become used to treating these separately, typically thinking that they deal with social interaction only and thereby forgetting that almost all social interaction is mediated by material objects.

The main point of introducing the triangle above, depicting the ontology of the social world, is to stress that *the social is made of all these things*: experience, discourse and objects. We can begin from any of the legs when we analyse social happenings and episodes, but we should be careful not to exclude the other legs, and some of the best social analyses take all three into account. Notably, we should not ignore the fact that almost all forms of human interaction involve technologies and artefacts (Latour, 1996). We can 'uphold' relations between us, so to speak, without close interactions, because we have buildings, institutions, infrastructure, databases, parliaments and numerous other things. In many ways, these 'things' enable what we call human *culture*. Traffic, to take an obvious example, is only possible because of the existence of roads, cars, trains, etc., and Latour's point is that these things are not just *means* that we use to realise our intentions to move around, but they are *mediators*, and as such actively shape the intentions we have. I can only have the intention of writing this book because of the existence of such technological and material mediators as computers, alphabets, scholarly networks of publication channels and readers and many other things. When studying relations of meaning and how things are done, experienced and understood, which is the goal of qualitative inquiry (cf. Table 1.1), we often need to be aware of such material mediators, objects or cultural resources that enable us to act and continually uphold social life and shared practices.

What about the other legs, then, those of experience (phenomenology) and conversation (discursivity)? These have been much more discussed in the literature on qualitative inquiry, and there has been a significant debate going on whether qualitative researchers should study 'lived experience' (phenomenology) or 'lived textuality' (discourse analysis) (Denzin, 1995, p. 197). Again, from a pragmatic perspective, we do not have to choose, for they are like poles in the social world rather than mutually exclusive, although I do believe that there is reason to voice scepticism concerning an ambition ever to reach something like pure, unmediated experience. For pragmatists and hermeneuticists, experience is always mediated (by relationships, discourse, culture, symbolic resources, etc.), and qualitative inquiry should study these mediators, but this does not preclude a focus on how we actually experience the world.

Qualitative inquiry in everyday life may take as its starting point any of the three legs in the triangle. We can begin with an *experience* of something that troubles us (like my experience at my son's school), we can begin with the conversational and *discursive practices* within which we live our lives (see Chapter 5) or we can begin with *cultural objects* that for some reason become salient (like Parker's tube of toothpaste). As Martin Packer has argued in a recent book on the science of qualitative research, what we study in qualitative inquiry is *constitution*, i.e., the mutual relationship between people and their form of life (Packer, 2011) – and this constitution, I will add, can be approached from any of the angles in the ontological triangle. For both experience, discourse and objects enter into the constitution of a form of life, and are simultaneously constituted by a form of life in a dialectical process.

Connecting the triangle's legs

Some of the most interesting methodological developments in qualitative inquiry are those that try to approach a topic from several or all of the legs in the triangle. One example is the broad tradition of Cultural Studies, the study of culture 'as a set of contested interpretive, representational practices' (Denzin, 2003, p. 999). Another example is Adele Clarke's development of situational analysis (Clarke, 2003, 2005), which is a regenerated version of grounded theory that seeks to go beyond those postmodern approaches that simply focus on 'voice' and its representation (e.g. interpretive phenomenologies, narrative analyses, etc.). The goal is to include what Clarke calls 'the full situation of inquiry' in social analyses. The analytic means are 'cartographic', e.g. in the form of situational maps that include the main human, non-human, discursive and material elements that influence situations, and the analyst is encouraged to try to understand the relations between them.

The construction of situational maps is intended 'to capture and discuss the messy complexities of the situation in their dense relations and permutations' (Clarke, 2003, p. 559). A situational map of my son's school, for example, would include everything from conversations with children, teachers and pedagogues, discourses that are mobilised, descriptions of buildings and rooms, and institutional self-understandings as found in the school's official documents on the internet etc. Working with situational maps is intentionally messy, because the world is a messy place. Like the everyday life analyses favoured in the present book, Clarke wants situational analysis to make 'the usually invisible and inchoate social features of a situation more visible' (p. 572), as she puts it, but a significant difference is that Clarke (perhaps because of her background in grounded theory and its sometimes empiricist leanings) does not rely on theory – and theoretical concepts as research tools – to the same extent as the present book.

Nevertheless, Cultural Studies and situational analysis share much with the present outlook, not least an eye for research taking place in 'situations', i.e., episodes of breakdown, a conception taken from pragmatist philosophy. For Dewey, a situation is the name we give to instabilities in our dealings with the world that make it difficult for us to proceed as usual (Dewey, 1938). When situations in this sense arise, there is a need to do inquiry, i.e., to develop and test different understandings to see if one of these can help us. This is something we do in our everyday lives, and it is what we do under the banner of science. Life and method, for Dewey, are therefore inextricably intertwined. This means that one 'learns about methods by thinking about how one makes sense of one's own life' (Denzin, 2004, p. 449). This is essential to qualitative inquiry in everyday life, and it takes us directly to pragmatism, especially in Dewey's version, as one of the main philosophical pillars of this book's approach.

Pragmatism and hermeneutics

Based on pragmatism and hermeneutics, I shall now attempt to develop a comprehensive epistemology of everyday life inquiry. Without doubting the value of the specialised qualitative methodologies that we find in conversation analysis or grounded theory, for example, this book builds upon a much more generic approach to working with qualitative materials. Rather than being a specific method or even paradigm, the approach can more adequately be characterised as a qualitative *stance* towards the social and personal worlds in which we live. Although I intend to develop this stance in the following pages, where it is exemplified in relation to concrete materials, I also believe that it is important to acknowledge those philosophical and theoretical schools that serve as the main sources of inspiration for how to work with everyday life materials in qualitative research. The traditions of pragmatism and hermeneutics are particularly important in this regard.

Pragmatism

Louis Menand has aptly characterised pragmatism as a single idea that was shared among its founders: Charles Sanders Peirce, William James, John Dewey, and also the (philosophically less known) supreme judge Oliver Wendell Holmes. This is an idea about ideas: 'ideas are not "out there" waiting to be discovered, but are tools – like forks and knives and microchips – that people devise to cope with the world in which they find themselves' (Menand, 2002, p. xi). In many ways, this pragmatist idea about ideas was, and is, a revolutionary proposal that turns Western thought on its head. Ideas are not representations or copies of how the world is, but are tools, with which we transform, engage, and cope with the world as we go about living our lives (Brinkmann & Tanggaard, 2010).

Dewey's pragmatic theory of inquiry is particularly interesting for everyday life researchers because it blurs any hard-and-fast distinctions between scientific knowing and human knowing in general. In other words, science is just a condensed form of human knowing, or a focused form of the activity of coping with the world that we are constantly engaged in as living human beings. In this sense, Dewey's pragmatism is a philosophical anthropology of the human knower. Dewey tried from the beginning of his career to overcome the view of the knower as a passive spectator that we have inherited from the Greeks. He argued that stimuli do not passively impinge on the human senses, but instead arise when active knowers are engaged in various activities. This is clear in the following early quote, where Dewey discusses the stimulus of a noise:

> If one is reading a book, if one is hunting, if one is watching in a dark place on a lonely night, if one is performing a chemical experiment, in each case, the noise has a very different psychical value; it is a different experience. (Dewey, 1896, p. 361)

This simple example should alert us to the idea that stimuli are constituted only on the background of activities and practices (see also Brinkmann, 2004). Experiences are not passive happenings, but aspects of human beings' everyday doings and engagements with the world and each other. Contrary to the epistemological tradition from Descartes and the British empiricists, according to which knowledge is a passive representation of the world, it means that there are no experiential elements that are simply *given* in the mind of a spectator. Dewey wants to replace the image of something being *given* with the image of something being *taken*:

> The history of the theory of knowledge or epistemology would have been very different if instead of the word 'data' or 'givens', it had happened to start with calling the qualities in question 'takens' [...] *as* data they are *selected* from this total original subject-matter which gives the impetus to knowing; they are discriminated for a purpose: – that, namely, of affording signs or evidence to define and locate a problem, and thus give a clew to its resolution. (Dewey, 1929, p. 178)

We *take* bits and pieces of the world – such as qualitative materials – when we need to do so in order for us to go on living in fruitful ways. We discriminate for a purpose, as Dewey says, when we are in a situation and find a need to solve a problem. Dewey treated thinking as what we do in such situations when we reflect intelligently (Dewey, 1910). He defined thinking as: '*Active, persistent, and careful consideration of any belief or supposed form of knowledge in the light of the grounds that support it, and the further conclusions to which it tends*' (p. 6). Thinking is thus partly about testing the grounds for belief and partly about developing one's beliefs in light of further beliefs that one entertains. In line with fellow pragmatists Peirce and James, Dewey thought that such processes are necessitated in and by a problematic situation, or what he called 'a *forked-road* situation' (p. 11), where one's activity is stuck. All thinking, all forms of reflective understanding of the world, emerge from such situations. As an existential affair in this sense, thinking is not something that can be formalised methodologically, but is a whole, active and situational life process. Being alive means doing inquiry.

Dewey insisted that all thinking occurs in relation to a background understanding that can break down. If this happens, the situation appears to be lacking in meaning. We never encounter a problem with a virginal mind, but always with 'certain acquired habitual modes of understanding, with a certain store of previously evolved meanings' (Dewey, 1910, p. 106). When we think, it is quite rare that an end is clear to us and that we only need to find the most efficient means of reaching the end. It is more often the case that we are confronted with an unclear and problematic situation, which stimulates the development of hypotheses that can be tested in practice. Unlike most psychological studies of thinking that begin with presenting preconceived problems to subjects, Dewey's view is much closer to our everyday lives, where a large part of solving a problem usually consists of getting clear about the nature of the problem in the first place. It may also involve getting clear about the 'habitual modes of understanding' with which we meet a problematic situation.

In summary, we can say that pragmatism, and Dewey's pragmatism in particular, contributes with the following lessons:

- Knowing is a human activity of coping with the world. Knowing is related to *action* – participation in social practices – as the relationship between what we do and what subsequently happens (knowledge is not a representation of the world, as in the representationalist or spectator theories of knowledge).
- Knowing is something we do in our everyday lives as much as it is something that takes place in universities and laboratories. In fact, we should only count something as knowledge if it makes a difference to how we experience the world or act in social practices.
- Theories are therefore tools that demonstrate their validity in practice, as aids in problem-solving.
- The process of inquiry is a general life process that succeeds when an indeterminate situation is transformed into a more determinate situation that can lead us to further forms of human experience. Qualitative research is simply a condensed and reflective form of such inquiry.

Pragmatism, including Dewey's, has had quite an effect on later social thought and qualitative inquiry, and here we may think of the Chicago School in sociology, symbolic interactionism, and also the more postmodern versions that arose later in the twentieth century, not least that influenced by the work of Richard Rorty (e.g. Rorty, 1982). Denzin's (2001a) interpretive interactionism stands as a bridge between the action-oriented stance of pragmatism and the interpretative stance of hermeneutics. The interpretive process, Denzin says, seeks to connect personal troubles with public issues, and the emphasis on interpretation takes us to hermeneutics, for 'in the world of human experience, there is only interpretation' (p. xii). But what is interpretation? And who interprets?

Hermeneutics

Hermeneutics is the other main tradition that inspires the philosophical anthropology of the present book. Originally, with Friedrich Schleiermacher, hermeneutics was developed as a methodology for interpreting texts, notably biblical texts (see Brinkmann, 2005). With Wilhelm Dilthey in the late nineteenth century, hermeneutics was extended to human life itself, conceived as an ongoing process of interpretation. And Heidegger's *Being and Time* from the early twentieth century is often cited as the work that inaugurated the shift to ontological hermeneutics proper (Heidegger, 1927). The question of methodological hermeneutics (e.g. Schleiermacher) had been: How can we correctly understand the meaning of texts? Epistemological hermeneutics (e.g. Dilthey) had asked: How can we understand our lives and other people? But ontological hermeneutics – or 'fundamental ontology' as Heidegger also called it (p. 34) – prioritises the question: 'What is the mode of being of the entity who understands?' (Richardson, Fowers, & Guignon, 1999, p. 207). *Being and Time* aims to answer this question and can thus be said to be an interpretation of interpreting, or a philosophical anthropology.

Heidegger's name for the entity that understands is *Dasein*, and the being of *Dasein* is unlike the being of other entities in the universe. Physical entities such as molecules, tables and chairs are things that have categorical ontological characteristics, whereas human beings, or *Dasein*, are *histories* or *events* and have existentials as their ontological characteristics (Polkinghorne, 2004, pp. 73–74). The difference between *Dasein* and physical entities corresponds quite closely to the two columns of Table 1.1 that was discussed in the previous chapter – with *Dasein*, obviously, on the qualitative side. The existentials that make up the basic structure of *Dasein* are *affectedness (Befindtlichkeit)* (we always find ourselves 'thrown' into situations where things already matter and affect us), *understanding (Verstehen)* (we can use the things we encounter in understanding the world), and *articulation* or *telling (Rede)* (we can to some extent articulate the meanings things have) (Dreyfus, 1991). In short, humans are creatures that are affected by what happens, can understand their worlds, and communicate with others. Of course, humans also have living physical bodies with categorical characteristics, we are *alive*, but in addition we have *lives* that unfold in time, and evolve around what is deemed meaningful and valuable. Understanding lives, on this account, means to understand their unique, qualitative features.

Dasein primarily exists as involved in a world of meanings, relations and purposes, and only derivatively in a world of objectified properties. In our everyday lives we live absorbed in pre-established structures of significance, or what Heidegger called *equipment*, which serve as a background that enables specific things to show up as immediately meaningful and value-laden, given our participation in different social practices. This is close to the concept of lifeworld found in the work of other phenomenologists. We do not experience meanings and values as something we subjectively project onto the world, for the qualitative world in which we live meets us as always already imbued with meaning and value. Only when our everyday, unreflective being-in-the-world breaks down, when our practices of coping with the equipment somehow become disturbed, do entities appear with 'objective' characteristics distinguishable from human subjects. This is similar to what pragmatists describe as a need for inquiry when our unreflective, habitual coping becomes disturbed.

For Heidegger and later hermeneuticists such as Gadamer and Taylor, understanding is not something we occasionally do, e.g. by following certain procedures or rules. Rather, understanding is the very condition of being human

(Schwandt, 2000, p. 194). We always see things *as* something, human behaviour *as* meaningful acts, letters in a book *as* conveying some meaningful narrative. In a sense, this is something we do, and hermeneutic writers argue that all such understanding is to be thought of as interpretation. This, however, should not be understood as implying that we normally make some sort of mental act in interpreting the world. 'Interpretation' here is not like the mental act of interpreting a poem, for example. It is not an explicit, reflective process, but rather something based on skilled, everyday modes of comportment (Polkinghorne, 2000).

Interpretation depends on certain *pre-judices*, as Gadamer famously argued, without which no understanding would be possible (Gadamer, 1960). Knowledge of what others are doing, and also of what my own activities mean, 'always depend upon some background or context of other meanings, beliefs, values, practices, and so forth' (Schwandt, 2000, p. 201). There are no fundamental 'givens', for all understanding depends on a larger horizon of non-thematised meanings. This horizon is what gives meaning to everyday life activities, and it is what we must engage with as we do qualitative inquiry; both as something that can break down and necessitate a process of inquiry, and as something that we can try to make explicit in an attempt to attain a level of objectivity. The latter is often referred to, by qualitative methodologists, as making one's preunderstanding explicit.

According to hermeneutics, we are self-interpreting animals (Taylor, 1985b), who make sense of the world through storylines that generate meanings. The writer of fiction Douglas Coupland puts it well through one of his characters in the novel *Generation A*: 'How can we be alive and not wonder about the stories we use to knit together this place we call the world? Without stories, our universe is merely rocks and clouds and lava and blackness' (Coupland, 2009, p. 1). We can understand the world in which we live only by attending to the relations of things, including our relations to things and to ourselves, and this we do most importantly, 'by telling their stories', as Ingold says, and he continues: 'For the things of this world *are* their stories, identified not by fixed attributes but by the paths of movement in an unfolding field of relations' (Ingold, 2011, p. 160). Our human lives – actions, thoughts, and emotions – are nothing but physiology if considered as isolated elements outside narrative and interpretative contexts. A life, as Paul Ricœur has said, 'is no more than a biological phenomenon as long as it has not been interpreted' (Ricœur, 1991, p. 28).

That we are self-interpreting creatures that use stories to constitute our identities (Brinkmann, 2008b) and as means of self-understanding does not imply that any individual person can make himself Napoleon by trying to interpret himself that way, i.e., by telling the story that he is Napoleon, but it means that human communities of interpreters and their historical and narrative traditions constitute the meanings of our self-interpretations. Gadamer has said:

> In fact history does not belong to us; we belong to it. Long before we understand ourselves through the process of self-examination, we understand ourselves in a self-evident way in the family, society, and state in which we live. The focus of subjectivity is a distorting mirror. The self-awareness of the individual life is only a flickering in the closed circuits of historical life. *That is why the prejudices of the individual, far more than his judgments, constitute the historical reality of his being.* (Gadamer, 1960, pp. 276–277)

Gadamer argues that this makes the condition of human and social science quite different from the one we find in the natural sciences 'where research penetrates more and more deeply into nature' (Gadamer, 1960, p. 284). In the human and social sciences, there can be no 'object in itself' to be known (p. 285), for interpretation is an ongoing and open-ended process that continuously reconstitutes its object. The interpretations of social life offered by researchers in the human and social sciences are an important addition to the repertoire of human self-interpretation, and influential fields of description offered by human science, such as psychoanalysis, can even affect the way whole cultures interpret themselves. As Richardson and colleagues spell out Gadamer's view, this means that 'social theories do not simply mirror a reality independent of them; they define and form that reality and therefore can transform it by leading agents to articulate their practices in different ways' (Richardson, Fowers, & Guignon, 1999, p. 227). Like the pragmatists would say, social theories are tools that may affect and transform those agents and practices that are theorised.

If the prejudices of the individual is what constitutes her being, as Gadamer puts it in the quote above, it also implies that any understanding of social processes runs in two directions at the same time: towards the social, on the one hand, with an eye to the historical and cultural processes that form our habits and prejudices, but also towards the one who lives in the social and cultural world – the person of the researcher – who must take her own biography (and prejudices) into account and do her analytic work in the intersection between the personal and the social, as C. Wright Mills also advocated. This, exactly, is the springboard for qualitative inquiry in everyday life.

In summary, we should learn the following lessons from hermeneutics:

- Knowing is conceived as understanding. Understanding is an interpretative affair that constantly takes place on a background of human activity.
- As knowers, we are thrown into a world that is already imbued with meaning. This is a world that is historically and socially constituted.
- Only when our everyday practical understandings 'break down' is inquiry necessitated, and in these cases the world appears as an 'objective reality', seemingly detached from human activities.

- Like the pragmatists, hermeneuticists reject the idea of something being 'given' in human experience, and they would much prefer to talk about aspects of the world being 'taken' relative to our life projects and social practices. Explicating how we 'take' the world is a form of hermeneutic objectivity.

Breakdown and abduction

Following from pragmatism and hermeneutics, a key assumption becomes that qualitative inquiry, and the construction of an understanding, primarily occurs in situations of breakdown. Agar has even described ethnography as 'a process of coherently resolving breakdowns' (Agar, 1986, p. 39), and Alvesson and Kärreman have recently made this idea the backbone to a qualitative approach, which they refer to as breakdown-oriented research (Alvesson & Kärreman, 2011). The main idea in breakdown-oriented research is that researchers should frame situations of breakdown as a mystery, which is a first step towards resolving the breakdown. When one has understood what the problem is, one has often already come a long way towards a resolution. Classically, this method is used by writers of crime fiction, who take the reader through the mystery before resolving it.

When breakdowns occur naturalistically, i.e., without the researcher intentionally trying to create them, there is an authentic chance to do qualitative inquiry with wider cultural significance. This is often where private troubles meet public concerns (Denzin, 2001a), or where the biographical meets the social world (Mills, 1959). But when breakdowns do not simply happen, qualitative researchers may try to bring them about. The three stances described in the previous chapter represent very general ways of doing this (making the obvious obvious, making the hidden obvious and making the obvious dubious), but Scott has pointed to somewhat more concrete techniques in qualitative analyses of everyday life, with the first and third ones being directly breakdown-inducing (Scott, 2009, pp. 4–5). These techniques are:

1 *Make the familiar strange.* Everything from bedtime rituals to shopping lists (and also habits of throwing objects, toothpaste tubes and apples!) can become interesting topics if we defamiliarise ourselves from them and acknowledge their contingent natures (i.e., acknowledge that they could have been different, provided that there had been other social practices and meaning horizons to construct them). Such mundane sources of data are also capable of yielding significant insights into larger and more general social and psychological processes.
2 *Search for underlying rules, routines and regularities.* The episodes and events of our lives are not usually chaotic and anomic, but display an order that everyday life studies can uncover. This order is not causal, but normative. It concerns the *oughtness* of human life. As I argued in the previous chapter, when doing qualitative inquiry we are studying

how things are done, and not simply what happens, and when things are done, we can always raise the normative question whether they were done *well*. In fact, it is this very normativity that constitutes actions as actions rather than as mechanical behaviours (Brinkmann, 2011a).

3 *Challenge the taken-for-granted assumptions.* Social order is often revealed when the norms and rules (the webs of 'oughtness') are broken, as Garfinkel (1967) demonstrated. Breaking the rules in order to disclose them can be used as a deliberate everyday life research strategy (more on this in Chapter 4). And even without deliberately breaking the rules in practice, the everyday life researcher may challenge the taken for granted in other ways, e.g. by analysing the power relations that are at work in the ongoing production of the social world.

Such techniques and approaches are useful when confronted with, or intentionally trying to bring about, breakdowns. However, a breakdown must subsequently be resolved or used to understand something – otherwise it would simply be a form of anarchy or anomie – and since breakdowns are always concrete, there is a need to think of the knowledge-producing activity following a breakdown in a particular way, namely as *abduction*, which is something different from more traditional models of reasoning in research processes such as induction and deduction.

- *Induction* is the process of observing a number of instances in order to say something general about the given class of instances. According to traditional formal logic (which is deductive), inductive inference is not strictly valid, for even if the first 99 girls we have observed do in fact 'throw like a girl', it may be the case that the 100th does not. Nevertheless, qualitative research is frequently characterised as inductive, since researchers will often enter the field without too many preconceived ideas to test, but will rather let the empirical world decide which questions are worth seeking an answer to. Grounded theory is an example of an approach that seeks to optimise the inductive process in qualitative inquiry.

- *Deduction* is a phase in the knowledge-producing process of deducing testable hypotheses from general theories, and then seeking to falsify these. In philosophy of science, this theory was famously developed by Karl Popper and was known as *falsificationism*. The idea was that only those theories that result in hypotheses that are in principle falsifiable deserve to be called scientific. This, according to Popper, excluded Marx and Freud from the rank of scientists. The deductive model may serve the natural sciences well, but is less helpful as a general model in the human and social sciences. The main problem with the deductive approach and falsificationism is that scientists will often not know whether to reject their hypothesis (in light of seemingly contrary evidence) or ignore their observations (because they are methodologically weak, for example) in cases where empirical observations apparently contradict one's hypothesis and general theory. That said, qualitative inquiry can work deductively and, for example, use single cases as a testbed for general theories, following a deduction like 'If this is (not) valid for this case, then it applies to all (no) cases'. (Flyvbjerg, 2006, p. 230)

Both induction and deduction as models of reasoning take for granted that we already know what we are talking about in the research process; that we have some stable entity that we can study repeatedly in a number of cases to build general knowledge (induction) or that we already have general ideas from which we can deduce particular consequences (deduction). But when we talk about everyday life, with all its practices and breakdowns, this is often not the case. Thus we need a different kind of reasoning, and fortunately we have what is known as abduction.

- *Abduction* as a form of reasoning is associated with the pragmatist Charles S. Peirce. Peirce is often credited with being *the* original pragmatist because of his formulation of what has since been known as the 'pragmatic maxim': 'Consider what effects, which might conceivably have practical bearings, we conceive the objects of our conception to have. Then our conception of these effects is the whole of our conception of the object' (quoted from Bernstein, 2010, p. 3). According to Peirce, things *are* their effects. Abduction is a form of reasoning that we employ in situations of uncertainty; when we need an understanding or explanation of some effect. It can be formalised as follows: (1) We observe X, (2) X is unexpected and breaks with our normal understanding, (3) but if Y is the case, then X makes sense, (4) therefore we are allowed to claim Y, at least provisionally. As an example, let us say (1) that we observe a person, who waves her arms wildly. And let us say (2) that this is unexpected in the context (the situation is not, for example, an aerobics class). We can then conjecture (3) that an aggressive wasp is attacking the person. This would make the person's behaviour understandable, even expected, and therefore (4) we infer that this is the case (at least until we arrive at a better interpretation).

As the example testifies, abduction is a very pervasive form of reasoning in everyday life. And it is likewise widespread, although more implicitly, in qualitative analyses. In most forms of qualitative inquiry, there is an abductive aspect, especially connected to (3), which we may refer to as the creative moment in the interpretative process. This is when researchers employ their sociological imagination (Mills, 1959), which may be aided by a number of *heuristics*. Heuristics are interpretative tools – or thinking tools – that can be used to create new ideas (Abbott, 2004), among them ideas about what would count as a warranted interpretation (the 'Y' in the abductive process), enabling a possible understanding of something (the 'X').

In Andrew Abbott's book on heuristics, he introduces a number of fruitful distinctions between different kinds of heuristics (Abbott, 2004). Two major kinds are *search heuristics*, which borrow creatively from other fields to create a viable interpretation of something, and *argument heuristics*, which include what I have called 'making the obvious dubious' and also 'reversal', the strategy of turning common understandings upside down. An example of search heuristics could be to study romantic relations between people as if they were economical or business relations – or the opposite: studying modern capitalism and work life as a romantic life arena (see Illouz, 2007, for an example of the latter). An example of argument heuristics could be to study not how a child acquires a learning disability, but how a learning disability, through complex social processes, acquires a child (see McDermott, 1993). A third kind of heuristics is reconceptualisation, where something is reconceptualised as something else (can we understand something about crime, for example, by thinking of it not as socially disruptive, but rather as confirming social norms by highlighting them?). Social science in general is full of such heuristics, but, apart from Abbott's work, these have rarely been addressed, although they are crucial to the ways that ideas and interpretations are generated, not least at step three in the abductive process, when we articulate interpretations that resolve breakdowns in understanding.

Concluding comments: Knowing after methodology

In this chapter, I have presented a way of thinking about human knowers based on pragmatism and hermeneutics. A fundamental assumption is that humans are participants in social practices. Social practices are the fabric of our social lives that have (at least) three aspects: experience, discourse and objects. Sometimes social life presents us with difficulties or even breakdown. In such cases, we are forced to step back and engage in inquiry about the social world in order to understand it and become able to act. We can also intentionally try to defamiliarise ourselves with our everyday lives, thus creating disturbances and breakdowns that are helpful in making processes of inquiry take off. We can ask 'How is this possible?' and force ourselves to think about what we take for granted in our lives.

A note on validity

I would like to stress that conceiving the human knower in this way is not antithetical to traditional scientific virtues like validity, objectivity and generalisability. These are exactly that: intellectual virtues that enable knowers to know and act responsibly (Zagzebski, 1996). A core idea that follows from the philosophies of pragmatism and hermeneutics is that our everyday life analyses are valid when they enable us to understand and act. This means that we have reason to leave the representational idiom behind and stop thinking of validity and truth as correspondence and representation. We should think of validity in much more active terms: our analyses are valid when they enable us to *do* certain things. When we experience breakdowns, good analyses are those that enable us to regain an understanding and cope with the situation. And objectivity can still find a place, only reconceived in pragmatic terms as 'allowing the object to object' (Latour, 2000). Dewey defined an object as 'that which objects, that to which frustration is due' (Dewey, 1925, p. 239). Objectivity is attained when objects reveal themselves through acts that frustrate the researcher's preconceived ideas – or what I have referred to as breakdowns.

A note on generality

Generality can be attained in everyday life analyses, even if it does not have to be a goal in all cases. It is true that we cannot work with statistical averages, but we can find what Denzin (following Psathas) calls 'instances'. We should take 'each instance of a phenomenon as an occurrence that evidences the operation of a set of cultural understandings currently available for use by cultural members' (Denzin, 2001a, p. 63). An instance is an occurrence that is evidence that 'the machinery for its production is culturally available' (Psathas, quoted by Denzin, p. 63). When faced with an instance in this sense, we should ask 'How is it possible?' This corresponds to Parker's question that we met in the previous chapter: What relationships and theories of self must obtain for this material, this instance, to make sense? These are questions that invite us into *abductive* reasoning, as I have argued. And if these questions are answered thoroughly and faithfully, we can obtain knowledge about the general features of cultural life that bring a certain instance into existence. If done well, readers will not even feel a need to ask 'But how do you know that this can be generalised?' (think, for example, of Iris Marion Young on 'throwing like a girl' from the previous chapter). When no one wants to raise this question, we have a good pragmatic indication that a certain analysis has given us an insight into social life with some generality.

The question of method

The approach to qualitative inquiry that is advocated here is one that tries to avoid the dangers of 'methodolatry', the worship of method (Curt, 1994). To mechanically follow certain specified methodological steps does not guarantee scientific truth, let alone interesting research. Instead of distrusting our ordinary human capacities for observing and communicating about our lives, and allocating understanding to specific methods instead, a number of significant social scientists have argued that the person of the researcher is the actual research instrument that human and social researchers can and must work with. This is expressed, for example, by anthropologist Jean Lave in the following interview sequence, where Steinar Kvale (SK) acts as interviewer:

SK: Is there an anthropological method? If yes, what is an anthropological method?

JL: I think it is complete nonsense to say that we have a method. First of all I don't think that anyone should have *a* method. But in the sense that there are 'instruments' that characterise the 'methods' of different disciplines – socio-logical surveys, questionnaire methods, in psychology various kinds of tests and also experiments – there are some very specific technical ways of inquir-ing into the world. Anthropologists refuse to take those as proper ways to study human being. I think the most general view is that the only instrument that is sufficiently complex to comprehend and learn about human existence is another human. And so what you use is your own life and your own experi-ence in the world. (Lave & Kvale, 1995, p. 220)

Mills (1959) also depicted social research in general as 'intellectual craftsman-ship'. A mastery of the relevant methods and theories is here important for the craft of social research, but should not become autonomous idols of scientific inquiry. 'They [methods] are like the language of the country you live in; it is nothing to brag about that you can speak it, but it is a disgrace and an incon-venience if you cannot' (p. 121). Instead of using methods mechanically, Mills believed in the power of the researcher-craftsperson herself to generate insight-ful research:

Be a good craftsman: Avoid any rigid set of procedures. Above all, seek to develop and to use the sociological imagination. Avoid the fetishism of method and technique. Urge the rehabilitation of the unpretentious intellectual crafts-man, and try to become such a craftsman yourself. Let every man be his own methodologist; let every man be his own theorist; let theory and method again become part of the practice of a craft. (p. 224)

All in all, I believe that good social and human science research goes beyond formal rules and encompasses more than technical methods. What the prag-matists called inquiry depends upon human *judgement*, something that was also emphasised by the hermeneuticists. The proficient craftsperson does not focus on the techniques, but on the task and on the material with which he or she works. Fortunately, we are all – knowingly or not – experts on the eve-ryday lives that we lead, and we can all learn to deal with the exciting mate-rials of our lives in more focused and creative ways in order to throw light on them. I believe that the concepts and vocabularies of significant theories can assist us in doing just that. Such theories are tools in the toolbox of the researcher-craftsperson.

Look through standard textbooks in your field and analyse the conception of knowledge that prevails – implicitly or explicitly.

Compare that conception to the pragmatic-hermeneutic conception advocated in this chapter. What are the strengths and weaknesses of the respective positions?

THREE

The ethics of working with everyday life materials

As we have seen in the previous chapters, qualitative research in everyday life entails the power to explore human existence in great detail. It gives access to human experience and allows researchers to describe intimate aspects of people's life worlds. The human interaction in qualitative inquiry affects researchers and participants, and the knowledge produced through qualitative research affects our understanding of the human condition. Consequently, qualitative research is saturated with ethical issues. Obviously, this also goes for what I call qualitative inquiry in everyday life, where the researcher begins with events and cultural resources that already surround her when engaging in the research process. When researching human beings who are concerned with how their lives and experiences are described, conceptualised and analysed, it is impossible to separate completely the values and the facts, the ethical issues and the scientific issues.

In this chapter, I shall address some significant ethical issues that arise when conducting qualitative research in general and everyday life research in particular. I will do so from the premise that ethical issues are an intrinsic part of the research process throughout. In qualitative inquiry, we cannot predict and handle ethical issues completely before embarking on the research quest, e.g. by obtaining approval from an ethics committee. We must continually be aware of ethics as an ongoing reflection in the research process.

In qualitative research, ethical problems particularly arise because of the complexities of 'researching private lives and placing accounts in the public arena' (Birch, Miller, Mauther, & Jessop, 2002, p. 1). When we observe and talk to people, analyse what they do and say, and publish our interpretations to the larger public, we are engaged in a process with inescapable ethical aspects. Many ethical guidelines exist that are supposed to reduce the uncertainty that researchers may feel when confronted with moral issues. But rather than advancing an 'ethics of certainty', which often seems to be the goal in the current attempts to 'manualise' the ethical, I will in this chapter advocate an 'ethics of doubt' that puts emphasis on the researcher's ability to constantly remain open to and accepting of the dilemmas that arise.

Ethical guidelines and fields of uncertainty

Ethical issues are involved in the ends as well as the means of qualitative research. There is always an ethical *why* in research, related to the *ends* of the research activity: *Why* is it valuable to pursue this investigation? Who gains (if anyone) and who loses (if anyone) as a result of the investigation? Will it benefit the participants involved, yourself or the larger public? And if not, what warrants working further with this research question? There is always also an ethical *how* in research, related to the *means* of the research activity: *How* is the most responsible way of conducting my research? How will I ensure that no one is harmed? Is it enough to obtain approval for my research project by a research ethics committee and be nice to people, or are there more complex ethical issues at stake?

In what follows, I address four of the fields that are traditionally discussed in ethical guidelines for researchers: informed consent, confidentiality, consequences, and the role of the researcher (see also Kvale & Brinkmann, 2008). Rather than seeing these fields as entailing questions that can be settled once and for all in advance of the research project, I conceptualise them as *fields of uncertainty*, i.e., problem areas that should continually be addressed and reflected upon. Rather than attempting to 'solve' the issues of consent, confidentiality etc. once and for all, qualitative researchers researching everyday life work in an area where it often is more important to remain *open* to conflicts, dilemmas, and ambivalences that are bound to arise throughout the research process.

Ethical questions at the start of a qualitative research project

In Box 3.1 some of the questions that are raised by common ethical guidelines are outlined. Even if we cannot as qualitative researchers settle the issues once and for all, we should nonetheless ask ourselves such questions before embarking on a research project.

─────────────── BOX 3.1 ───────────────

Ethical questions at the start of a research project

What are the *beneficial* consequences of the study?

How can the study contribute to enhancing the situation of the participants? Of the group they represent? Of the human condition? Even though this book addresses small-scale research centred on the researcher's everyday life, there is always a chance that the study can improve the world, however little this may be. It is ethically wise to ask oneself about the motive for doing the study: Is it to understand something that is worth understanding, to critically throw light on social justice issues (both of which are laudable aims) or rather (and less honourable) to get revenge by writing about something (or even someone) that has upset you (which, alas, is a possible motive in everyday life research). If the latter is the case, it is better to solve the problem by other means.

How can the *informed consent* of the participants be obtained?

If you do everyday life research and write about other people, how can you make sure that the people involved agree to take part in your project? What if you are using observations of people on the bus or at work?

How much information about the study needs to be given in advance to participants, and what information can wait until a later debriefing?

Who should give the consent – the participants or their superiors?

How can the *confidentiality* of the participants be protected?

How important is it that the participants remain anonymous?

How can the identity of the participants be disguised?

Who will have access to the interviews and other materials that you include in your analyses?

Can legal problems concerning protection of the participants' anonymity be expected?

What are the *consequences* of the study for the participants?

Will any potential harm to the participants be outweighed by potential benefits?

When publishing the study, what consequences can be anticipated for the participants – including you – and for the groups they represent?

How will the *researcher's role* affect the study?

How can you as an everyday life researcher counteract over-identification with the field and participants, thereby losing critical perspective on the knowledge obtained?

I shall now turn to more specific discussions of ethical principles concerning informed consent, confidentiality, consequences and the role of the researcher. I will also depict the fields of uncertainty that these principles may disclose.

Informed consent

Informed consent entails informing the research participants about the overall purpose of the investigation and the main features of the design, as well as of any possible risks and benefits from participation in the research project. Informed consent further involves obtaining the voluntary participation of the people involved, and informing them of their right to withdraw from the study at any time. The demand for informed consent is sometimes not a problem in everyday life research, e.g. when the researcher utilises objects (e.g. novels, newspaper stories or television programmes) that are publicly available.

In other cases, there are particular problems associated with this kind of research, since everyday life researchers may write about people with whom they interact without knowing at the time of interaction that a meeting will become part of a research project. In such cases, it should be carefully considered whether the materials can be used, and, if the researcher decides to do so, special attention should be given to issues of anonymity. When conducting more formal research interviews as part of the research project (as reported in Chapter 5), the participants should be informed about the purpose and the procedure of the research project. This should include information about confidentiality and who will have access to the interview or other materials, the researcher's right to publish the whole interview or parts of it, and the participant's possible access to the transcription and the analysis of the qualitative data.

This ethical field of uncertainty thematises the question of how informed consent can be handled in exploratory everyday life studies where the researchers themselves have little advance knowledge of how the interviews and observations will proceed.

Confidentiality

Confidentiality in research implies that private data identifying the participants will not be reported. If a study will publish information potentially recognisable to others, the participants often need to agree to the release of identifiable information. The principle of the research participants' right to privacy is not without ethical and scientific dilemmas. There is thus a concern about what information should be available to whom. Should, for example, conversations with children be available to their parents and teachers? Protecting confidentiality can in extreme cases raise serious legal problems, such as in cases when a researcher – through the promise of confidentiality and the trust of the relationship – has obtained knowledge of mistreatment, malpractice, child abuse, the use of drugs, or other criminal behaviours either by the participants or others.

Confidentiality as an ethical field of uncertainty relates to the issue that, on the one hand, anonymity can protect the participants and is thus an ethical demand, but, on the other hand, it can serve as an alibi for the researchers, potentially enabling them to interpret the statements of others without being gainsaid. Anonymity can protect the participants, but it can also deny them 'the very voice in the research that might originally have been claimed as its aim' (Parker, 2005, p. 17). We should also note that participants, who have spent their time and provided valuable information to the researcher, might wish in some cases, as in a journalistic interview, to be credited with their full name.

Consequences

The consequences of a qualitative study need to be addressed with respect to possible harm to the participants as well as to the expected benefits of participating in the study. The ethical principle of *beneficence* means that the risk of harm to a participant should be the least possible. From a utilitarian ethical perspective, the sum of potential benefits to the people involved and the importance of the knowledge gained should outweigh the risk of harm and thus warrant a decision to carry out the study. This involves a researcher's responsibility to reflect on the possible consequences not only for the persons taking part in the study, but also for the larger group they represent. The researcher should be aware that the openness and intimacy of much qualitative research may be seductive and can lead participants to disclose information they may later regret.

The field of uncertainty that opens up when we consider the consequences of qualitative research is perhaps the most complex one because of its unpredictability. Given the open-endedness of human social life, it is not possible to calculate the consequences of one's actions with certainty, which is why researchers must display continuous openness and flexibility.

The role of the researcher

The researcher as a person is critical for the quality of everyday life studies as suggested in the present book. When 'the person is the research instrument', as Jean Lave pointed out in the previous chapter, morally responsible research behaviour becomes more than abstract ethical knowledge and cognitive choices; it involves the moral integrity of the researcher, his or her sensitivity and commitment to moral issues and action. Being familiar with value issues, ethical guidelines, and ethical theories may help in choices that weigh ethical versus epistemic concerns in a study. In the end, however, the integrity of the researcher – his or her knowledge, experience, honesty, and fairness – is the decisive factor. Given this dependence on the ethical judgements of the researcher, it becomes very important to foster the ethical skills of qualitative researchers, e.g. by discussing difficult cases with colleagues and peers. Reading fiction may also enhance one's understanding of the particularities of human ethical life (Nussbaum, 1986).

The field of uncertainty that is disclosed when reflecting on the role of the researcher can involve a tension between a professional distance and a personal friendship. Thus in the context of a feminist, caring, committed ethic, the qualitative researcher has been conceived as a friend, a warm and caring researcher. This, perhaps naïve, conception of the researcher as a caring friend has been criticised from a feminist standpoint. Duncombe and Jessop (2002) point out that a researcher's show of intimacy and empathy may involve a faking of friendship and commodification of rapport, sanitised of any concern with broader ethical issues (see also Burman, 1997). When under pressure to deliver results, whether to a commercial employer or to their own research publications, researchers' show of empathy may become a means to circumvent the participant's informed consent and persuade informants to disclose experiences and emotions which they later may have preferred to keep to themselves or even 'not know'. With an expression from a therapist-researcher (Fog, 2004), an experienced researcher's knowledge of how to create rapport and get through a participant's defences may serve as a 'Trojan horse' to get inside areas of a person's life where they were not invited. The use of such indirect techniques, e.g. in interviews and other research conversations, which are ethically legitimate within the joint interest of therapeutic relations, become ethically questionable when applied to research purposes. People may have very good reasons not to 'tell the whole story', perhaps because they have never made clear to themselves before what 'their story' is, and it is not necessarily the researcher's job to act as a quasi-therapist in facilitating the telling of a story that may do more harm than good.

Thinking through a brief example

To illustrate how these questions may play a role in a concrete example, we may refer to the idea for a research project that I articulated in this book's first chapter. The example was based on a breakdown in my understanding of the practices at my son's school that seemed to work counter-productively to segregate boys and girls and actually reinforce gender stereotypes. Already saying this much, and using the example in this way, has demanded considerable ethical reflection on my part, for I know and respect the teachers and pedagogues at the school and would not want to expose them as unprofessional. Here, it is thus very relevant to consider the ethics of confidentiality. Should readers really want to locate the school, it would be possible, and the people working at the school are likely to recognise their workplace, should they stumble upon my analysis. If I were to develop this project further, I would be very careful not to write anything that could be identified with particular persons or write anything that I would not in principle want to say to the people involved. The situation would be quite different if I chose to seek the participants' informed consent (which I have not done). Were I to collect further materials about the school, and perhaps supplement my initial everyday observations with more structured ones (which could include interviews with other parents and maybe also children), I should surely present this more formally as a research project to the people involved and get their approval before continuing.

It is not easy to say when one's everyday observations end and more traditional and structured research observations begin. Here, the researcher must use her powers of judgement and ask what she would think had someone based a research project on a practice where she was involved. In many cases, most of us would want to know if we provide materials for a research project, but, on the other hand, I believe a researcher can safely find inspiration in conversations with people on the bus or in the supermarket without informing them that they are now part of a research project. We should, on the one hand, be ethically sensitive, but we should, on the other hand, not let ethical worries paralyse us. My argument in this book is that being alive as a human being among other human beings is an interpretative process of inquiry, or, in other words, a research project, and this inevitably creates a dilemma about how much of people's lives should be involved before we should formally seek informed consent as researchers.

Following from this, I doubt that it is fruitful to speak of research ethics as something special. There are ethical demands in *all* human encounters and activities, and these pertain to everyday living as much as to research practices. As the Danish moral philosopher K.E. Løgstrup (1956) tried to show in his phenomenological ethics, our lives are always 'delivered over' to one another, and we never deal with each other without holding something of the life of the other in our hands. This is the fundamental and inescapable human condition: 'it is impossible to avoid having power over the person with whom we associate' (p. 53), and it is this that grounds our ethical obligations. We cannot *not* have power over the people that we deal with. It may be a little, e.g. in relation to the person at the check-out desk in the supermarket, or it may be a lot, e.g. in the case of one's children. The case of researchers and researched in qualitative inquiry probably fall somewhere in between these extremes (see also Brinkmann, 2007c).

According to Løgstrup, there are ethical demands only because people have the power to affect and ultimately destroy the lives of others: 'Because power is involved in every human relationship, we are always in advance compelled to decide whether to use our power over the other person for serving him or her or for serving ourselves' (Løgstrup, 1956, p. 53). And this gives rise to what Løgstrup called the universal ethical demand: to handle with care those aspects of the other person's life that are in our hands. How to specify this demand concretely, however, cannot be stated in universal terms, but rests on an informed judgement of the situation.

If we return to the example, it seems very difficult to predict the consequences of the study. Will it lead to increased awareness of the school practices, among teachers, parents and children, or will it lead to resistance and hostility? Would the analysis be able to say anything general that might be of interest at other schools, perhaps in society at large? Such questions may seem megalomaniac, but one need only think of Young's analysis referred to earlier to appreciate that qualitative studies of everyday life phenomena may have societal impact. Researchers cannot – and probably should not wish to – control how their reports are received and used, but there is still an ethical imperative only to write things that one is actually willing to defend.

Finally, the ethical question about the role of the researcher is difficult in this kind of everyday life inquiry, for one is always already a committed insider as a researcher. People are doing this kind of research because something is at stake for them, even if this may 'only' be a certain bewilderment that they wish to resolve. The key question becomes how to look at one's everyday life, with its characters, objects and events, in a way that is both enlightening (which sometimes demands distancing oneself from its immediacy, e.g. with the help of theoretical concepts), but at the same time maintaining positive relationships with the people that are part of one's life.

Ethical theories as tools to think with

This book has a crafts approach to inquiry, arguing that theories should be conceived as tools for thinking, understanding and writing. This also goes for ethical theories. We should therefore not necessarily reject guidelines and theories as such, but reconceptualise them as tools to think with. Moral rules may still be useful as rules of thumb, as 'descriptive summaries of good judgments [...] valid only insofar as they transmit in economical form the normative force of good concrete decisions of the wise person' (Nussbaum, 1986, p. 299). If true, it means that there is a primacy of the concrete and the particular in ethical reasoning. Although ethics committees work on the basis of abstract ethical principles, it is noteworthy that Stephen Toulmin (1981), himself a former member of such committees, recounts that committee members could very often reach consensus on what to do in specific cases, but very rarely on which ethical theories and principles should be brought forth to back their practical judgements.

The view that ethical theories and principles are tools to think with rather than ethical authorities was also articulated by Dewey, whom we met in the previous chapter. Dewey warned against reducing our moral experience to anything that a single theory about it or a set of rules could capture. As he said: 'a man's duty is never to obey certain rules; his duty is always to respond to the nature of the actual demands which he finds made upon him – demands which do not proceed from abstract rules, nor from ideals, however awe-inspiring and exalted, but from the concrete relations to men and things in which he finds himself' (Dewey, 1891, pp. 199–200). Here, the ethical burden is shifted from theories and rules to the person in everyday life contexts, who interprets and applies the rules in relation to these contexts. Thus, the virtues and capacities of the researcher come into focus, and also the standards of the research community of which the researcher is a part. Notably, the intellectual virtue that Aristotle called *phronesis* becomes important as the capacity to determine how to act well in concrete situations, and to decide which rules, if any, to apply (see Flyvbjerg, 2001, for a theory of phronesis-based research).

Micro and macro ethical issues

Ethical issues in qualitative research tend to be discussed in relation to the personal implications for the participants, which have also been in focus above, whereas the wider social consequences of the inquiries rarely receive attention. In order to grasp the ethical intricacies of qualitative research in the wider cultural context, a distinction between micro and macro ethics is relevant (Brinkmann & Kvale, 2008). Micro ethics is the ethics of the concrete research situation and relates to issues like consent and confidentiality. Macro ethics, on the other hand, is concerned with what happens when the methodologies and knowledge produced circulate in the wider culture and affect humans and society.

Ethical issues may differ when viewed from micro and macro perspectives respectively. A participant may experience the concrete interaction between researcher and researched in qualitative studies positively, when a researcher shows a strong interest in what he or she has to say. The wider social consequences of the knowledge produced in such studies may, however, in some cases be problematic. A case in point is qualitative market research, which today is perhaps the most extended and influential qualitative research practice. Consumer interviews as individual motivational interviews or as focus groups may well follow standard ethical guidelines and also be enjoyable to the participants. On a macro level, however, the consequences may be more questionable. Focus group interviews about teenager attitudes to smoking may provide knowledge for improving the effectiveness of cigarette advertisements to teenagers, or the knowledge produced may be used in health campaigns to prevent smoking. In today's consumer society it is likely that there will be more funding available for producing and using knowledge on smoking attitudes for the tobacco industry's advertisements to increase tobacco consumption than for public campaigns seeking to decrease it (Brinkmann & Kvale, 2008).

Ethical tensions between micro and macro levels may not just concern macro ethical problems in research that is micro ethically spotless. A classical case of the reverse problem is the study on anti-Semitism, *The Authoritarian Personality*, by Adorno and co-workers (Adorno, Frenkel-Brunswik, Levinson, & Sanford, 1950). In the wake of the Second World War the researchers investigated a possible relation of anti-Semitism to an authoritarian upbringing. An important part of the study consisted of therapeutically inspired interviews, where the researchers used therapeutic techniques to circumvent their participants' defences in order to learn about their prejudices and authoritarian personality traits. In the psychoanalytically inspired interviews, the freedom of expression offered to the interview person was seen as the best way to obtain an adequate view of the whole person, as it permitted inferences of the deeper layers of the participants' personalities behind the anti-democratic ideology. On a micro level, this research clearly violated the ethical principle of informed consent, whereas on a macro level the knowledge obtained of the roots of anti-Semitism could have beneficial social consequences.

Ideally, ethical issues on a macro level can be approached by public discussion of the social consequences and uses of the knowledge produced. This has been exemplified by the large-scale interview study by Bellah and co-workers (Bellah, Madsen, Sullivan, Swidler & Tipton, 1985) about individualism in America. The researchers saw the very aim of doing social science as a public philosophy, to engage in debate with the public about the goals and values of society:

> When data from such interviews are well presented, they stimulate the reader to enter the conversation, to argue with what is being said. Curiously, such interviews stimulate something that could be called public opinion, opinion tested in the arena of open discussion. (Bellah et al., 1985, p. 305)

Even though qualitative inquiry in everyday life as presented in this book will normally be on a much smaller scale, it may nonetheless be possible to stimulate the kind of public conversation addressed by Bellah. There is no reason why this cannot be done from an everyday life, first-person perspective, and thinking about how to present ones research and enter the public conversation demands macro ethical reflections in addition to the standard micro ethical ones.

Concluding comments: Towards an ethics of doubt

In this chapter I have addressed ethical concerns in the practice of qualitative inquiry in everyday life. I have attempted to go beyond research ethics as mainly following rules for ethical behaviour and emphasised the researcher's integrity, his or her ability to sense, judge and act in ethically committed ways. The shift of emphasis from a strict formal rules ethics to the situated ethical judgements of the researcher should, though, avoid individualising ethics in qualitative research to being mainly a concern for the participants and the integrity of the qualitative researcher. All in all, I believe we need to be much more open to our ethical doubts and ambivalences than the common guidelines encourage us to be. These typically advocate an ethics of certainty, according to which ethics can be formalised and perhaps even mathematised (as in some forms of utilitarianism). 'If two duties contradict each other, one of them is not your duty' – so goes a Kantian dictum, but this kind of ethical certainty is surely illusory. And the first step towards ethically responsible research behaviour seems to be, almost logically, that one is willing to doubt one's own actions and motivations. The first step towards becoming moral must be to admit that we are not perfect. In qualitative inquiry, we have the chance of writing about our moral ambivalences, of turning them into research texts that are honest and display our doubts and vulnerabilities, and this, I believe, is often a sign of ethical responsibility in itself.

EXERCISE

Reflect on the following ethical questions. Write a page or two about each and discuss your answers with friends or colleagues (writing is also a method of *ethical* inquiry).

- It is a common experience in qualitative interviewing that the conversation can suddenly come to touch sensitive issues. When the dialogue takes a turn that obviously moves the participant, how should the researcher react? Is it always good to pursue these issues in a quasi-therapeutic vein in order to help the participant (and perhaps obtain important knowledge as a 'side effect')? Or does this imply a risk of ethically transgressing the participant's intimate sphere? What kinds of situations could legitimately afford choosing one or the other conversational direction? Can the different ethical theories help in this regard – and how?
- Most of the cultural situations, resources and objects that comprise our everyday lives have been made by others (music, films, television, books). In your opinion, are there limits to how we may analyse the products of others? And what about the informal conversations we have with others – are these freely available for analysis, or are there ethical limits? Who can claim ownership to the meanings of what has been said and done in everyday life?

PART II

FOUR

Self observation

As living human beings, we all have the capacities for self observation. As language users, we also have the capacity to conceptualise and reflect upon the ways we observe ourselves, and we can communicate our self observations to others. Artists and human and social scientists alike make use of these capacities. Great novelists have provided us with detailed accounts based on self observation, and a systematic use of the capacities for self observation is central to many disciplines in the human and social sciences. Obviously, it is also central to everyday life research as conceived in this book. This chapter addresses the practice of self observation by taking a phenomenological perspective in a broad sense. We thus begin in the phenomenological leg of the triangle in Figure 2.1, but I shall also broaden the phenomenological scope to include other aspects as well.

The chapter addresses the subject or the self that is engaged in everyday life analyses by tackling issues about the *what*, the *who*, and the *how* of self observation. Concerning the *what*, it is crucial for an understanding of self observation to make clear what one wants to observe. Obviously, self observation involves an observation of the self. All empirical sciences from astronomy to sociology involve observing selves, i.e., scientists who observe processes and properties of the world. Essential to self observation, however, is the fact that the self is both subject and object in the process of observation. Thus, the self that observes is also the self that is observed. This, evidently, has generated a lot of discussion and critique of self observational methods in the history of psychology and other social sciences, mainly under the heading of introspection. Can reports based on self observation be reliable and valid? The main methodological problems in introspection are twofold: first, there is the problem of intersubjectivity (how can other people know and check that the introspective person reports correctly?); and, second, there is what we may call the problem of mediation (doesn't the activity of introspection itself unavoidably mediate and thereby change the psychological reality that is observed?).

The discussion of these questions, however relevant they are, has led to a neglect of a more fundamental issue, which may, incidentally, lead us to a clearer view of these other problems. This is the question of the self as such. What is the self that observes and is observed in self observation? This is the first and most fundamental question to be addressed below, and this discussion represents a bridge between the philosophical anthropology of the knower that was developed in previous chapters and the more empirical chapters that follow. The other questions that I shall address concern *who* observes in self observation, where a relevant distinction emerges between direct and indirect self observation, and, finally, *how* one proceeds in practice to conduct research based on self observations. Unlike later chapters, this one also gives an introduction to more mainstream methodologies of self observation that are related to the interpretative-pragmatic approach of the present book.

The phenomenological traditions

Before moving on to these sets of questions, I shall begin by explaining how this chapter relates to the phenomenological traditions. According to Amedeo Giorgi, a leading phenomenological psychologist, phenomenology is 'the study of the structure, and the variations of structure, of the consciousness to which any thing, event, or person appears' (Giorgi, 1975, p. 83). Phenomenology was founded as a philosophy by Edmund Husserl around 1900 and further developed as an existential philosophy by Martin Heidegger, and then in an existential and dialectical direction by Jean-Paul Sartre and Maurice Merleau-Ponty. The subject matter of phenomenology began with consciousness and experience, was expanded to include the human life world, and to take account of the body and human action in historical contexts by Merleau-Ponty and Sartre. The goal in Husserlian phenomenology was to arrive at an investigation of essences, i.e., to describe the essential structures of human experience from a first-person perspective. Phenomenology was then a strict descriptive philosophy, employing the technique of *reduction*, which means to suspend one's judgement as to the existence or non-existence of the content of an experience. The reduction is often pictured as a 'bracketing', an attempt to place the common sense and scientific foreknowledge about the phenomena within parentheses in order to arrive at an unprejudiced description of the essence of the phenomena (Kvale & Brinkmann, 2008, p. 27). So, a phenomenologist can study the experience of shame (which I shall use as a recurrent example in this chapter) without taking a stand on the issue whether there is a reason to feel shame in a given situation, or whether shame is correlated with this or that neurochemical process or physiological response. The subject's experience is the important phenomenological reality.

The concept of the life world eventually became central to Husserl. He introduced the concept in 1936 in *The Crisis of the European Sciences* (Husserl, 1954) to refer to the shared and intersubjective meaningful world in which humans conduct their lives and experience significant phenomena. It is a pre-reflective and pre-theorised world in which shame is a way of being-in-the-world, a meaningful response to certain events, *before* it (shame) may be explained with reference to its neurochemical correlates or by other objectifying means. If shame did not appear to human beings as an *experienced phenomenon*, a meaningful, yet painful, phenomenon in their life world, there would be no reason to investigate it scientifically, for there would in a sense be nothing to investigate. There is thus a primacy of the life world as experienced since this is prior to the scientific theories we may formulate about it. This was well expressed by Merleau-Ponty:

> All my knowledge of the world, even my scientific knowledge, is gained from my own particular point of view, or from some experience of the world without which the symbols of science would be meaningless. The whole universe of science is built upon the world as directly experienced, and if we want to subject science itself to rigorous scrutiny and arrive at a precise assessment of its meaning and scope, we must begin by re-awakening the basic experiences of the world of which science is the second order expression. (Merleau-Ponty, 1945, p. ix)

Using a metaphor, we can say that when we are concerned with how humans live their everyday lives, the sciences may give us maps, but the world of everyday life is the territory or the geography of our lives. Maps make sense only on the background of the territory, where human beings act and live, and should not be confused with it. Phenomenologists are not against scientific abstractions or 'maps', but they insist on the primacy of concrete descriptions of experience – of that which is prior to maps and analytic abstractions. This means that self observation comes to matter not simply as some additional peripheral methodology, but rather as one of the central means of accessing the lived territory of everyday life. The only instrument that is sensitive enough to grasp the intersubjective and meaningful realm of the life world is an observing self that must itself be understood as a part of what is observed and described.

What initially looks like a paradox – that the self that observes is the self that is observed – turns out to be a precondition for knowledge of the life world, since the life world can only be known 'from within', by a participating self. How can one understand the experience of shame, to stay with this example, without understanding the existential situations in which the self is painfully revealed to the gazes of others – e.g. when one is caught looking through a keyhole? The answer is that no scientific perspective that transcends the life world and the first-person perspectives within it (e.g. from the neurosciences) can ever grasp the *experience* of shame. Surely, we can study the level of stress in situations of shame by measuring hormone levels in the blood, for example, but this does not tell us what shame is as a meaningful, experienced phenomenon in the life world. Shame and other such human phenomena can only be understood from an immanent position within 'the whole hurly-burly of human actions', as Wittgenstein once put it (1981, no. 567), and this is where self observation turns out to be not only legitimate, but likely the only adequate method of inquiry.

The self that is observed

I shall now address the *what* of self observation: What is the object of self observation? In a sense, the answer is obvious: It is the self, but what is this? When one observes oneself in introspective studies, the self is often implicitly seen as something 'inner', as an inner experiential realm or a 'Cartesian theatre' in which mental objects appear. Costall (2007) has criticised this conception as a 'windowless room', which is part of a more comprehensive epistemology, according to which we cannot be in direct contact with our surroundings. According to the alternative view to be presented below, we – including our 'selves' – are indeed both in and of the world, and self observation is just as much a matter of observing ourselves acting, living and interacting as it is a matter of inwards introspection.

Rom Harré's (1998) distinction between three uses of the concept of self is helpful in outlining the *what* of self observation. First, we can think of the self as a standpoint from which one observes. Harré calls this Self 1. Secondly, we can conceive of the self as the totality of attributes of a person, which includes ideas about what sort of person one is, and this – Self 2 – can also be radicalised by following William James's perspective on the self as *'the sum total of all that* [someone] *CAN call his'* (James, 1890, p. 279), which, for James, includes clothes, family, friends, reputation, and material objects. From this perspective, self observation includes a careful study of the symbolic *and* material resources that make up the self. Thirdly, we can approach the self in line with the pragmatist G.H. Mead as an interactional self, or a Self 3. Here, self observation is primarily concerned with observing the self in social interaction guided by norms, and recording one's own reactions (this method has been used, for example, by Stanley Milgram and Harold Garfinkel, as we shall see below). I shall say a few words about each self conception in turn, as they are not just relevant to self observation in the narrow sense, but also to wider issues relating to qualitative inquiry in everyday life, and I return to them later in the book.

Self 1

Harré's notion of Self 1 is close to the phenomenological understanding of the consciousness of the first-person perspective. Harré writes that to have a sense of self 'is to have a sense of one's location, as a person, in each of the several arrays of other beings, relevant to personhood' (1998, p. 4). This sense of location relates fundamentally to occupying a location in space from which one perceives and acts in the material environment, but I believe that it can also refer more broadly to one's sense of being someone in a *social* environment. When someone describes what it feels like to be ashamed (e.g. that it feels like shrinking and being naked in the presence of others), then she is articulating that description from a Self 1 perspective, i.e., from the perspective of someone who experiences the world from this specific standpoint. Self 1 is also close to the pragmatists' (James, Mead) idea of the I, the self as subject, i.e., the impulsive, agentive side of the self as something other than the Me, the self as object.

Self 2

Self 2 is close to James's and Mead's notion of the Me, i.e., that phase of the individual's life process that occurs when the self appears as an object to itself with certain properties. Self 2 is the totality of attributes of a person, including that person's beliefs about herself. This is often conceptualised as the self-concept in psychology. Mead was clear that the self, as that which can be an object to itself, is a social entity arising in social experience (Mead, 1962, p. 140). A person can only have beliefs about herself because she has acquired the capacity to look at herself from the outside, which is a capacity that develops in social situations. We learn to objectify ourselves by taking the attitudes of others towards ourselves. And we need a language, itself a social tool, in order for us to entertain reflective beliefs about ourselves, so Self 2 is also a social product in this sense.

Self 2, as the beliefs one has about oneself, will often be articulated in narrative form, for the kind of self understanding that this sense of self implies manifests itself in the stories we tell about ourselves. Thus, someone does not think of herself as having done something shameful out of the blue, but there will always be a story to tell that frames a certain shameful incidence within a narrative structure with a plot. When such stories become particularly salient for an individual's self understanding, they may even constitute what narrative psychologists call a personal myth that make up a person's identity (McAdams, 1997). As part of Self 2, we should also include the material resources that are available to a person in her life and which enable her life processes. As I said with reference to James, this includes the sum total of all that someone can call his (or hers). We literally study ourselves when we begin to analyse the material objects that we possess. These are often extensions of the self's capabilities (glasses, computers, notebooks, etc.) or social identity (clothes, car, house) and are in that sense co-constitutive of the person's attributes. While Self 1 is phenomenological, related to the experience leg of the ontological triangle (Figure 2.1), Self 2 is related to the object leg of the triangle (see also Figure 4.1 below).

Self 3

The third use of the concept of self that is relevant for self observation refers to the sort of person that we are taken to be by others (Harré, 1998, p. 177). Although all self concepts have social aspects, this is therefore the most directly social side of the self, and we are here moving towards the discursive leg of Figure 2.1. There may be discrepancies between the self that I intend to make manifest in what I say and do, and the self that others see in my actions and speech. 'I am not crazy!' is a classic example of a sentence that may sound quite different to the person who utters it, and the psychiatrists who hear it, perhaps after having decided that the speaker is a psychotic patient. On a less dramatic note, people may interpret a person's reaction in a given situation as one of shame, whereas the person herself is unable to see anything shameful in the situation, but simply acts timidly – or vice versa. Obviously, there is also sometimes consistency between how a person understands herself and how she is taken up by others.

The point is here that the self – as Self 3 – is an interactional and conversational process. Like utterances, the self makes personal impressions on others, who then use these impressions to interpret the person and act in return. This process is dialogical in that each interpretation and act must be seen as a *response* to what went before in the process. There is a flow in our everyday lives that cannot be understood if we cut the episodes up into separate units. This notion of dialogical flow has methodological implications for self observation, since it underlines the importance of attending to the socio-temporal context within which something occurs or is done. It is not enough to observe something here and now without including the temporal background that enables something to appear in a certain way in the foreground. Again, as I argued in the first chapter, shame does not simply *happen*, but is *done* in dialogical encounters between persons in mundane social situations.

The three concepts of the self are included here to remind us that self observation can be many different things depending on which aspects of the self researchers intend to capture. They are included as legs in the ontological triangle in Figure 4.1 below. If we want to study how people experience shame as a life world phenomenon, we can try to describe as closely as possible what it feels like to experience this emotion from the first-person perspective as it happens (Self 1) (e.g. through the Experience Sampling Method to be addressed below). We can also ask people to look at themselves and inform us of situations in which they felt shame, i.e., we can get them to talk about their 'shameful selves' as quasi-objects with certain attributes (Self 2), which is what we often do in formal research interviewing. Alternatively, we can observe the social-discursive negotiations of emotions like shame in everyday life (Self 3) by studying how others ascribe this emotion to people (e.g. to ourselves as researchers) or how people refuse to accept some incidence as shameful. It is perfectly legitimate to combine these approaches in

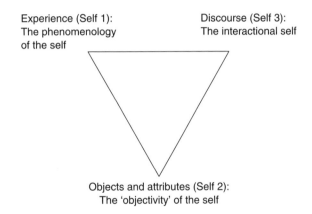

Figure 4.1   The ontological triangle of the self

qualitative research projects in everyday life, and I even think that an argument can be made that the most comprehensive understanding of some life world phenomenon (such as shame) would include perspectives from all three angles on the self. In relation to shame, three guiding questions would then be:

- Self 1: How does shame *feel*, how is it experienced? (This is the experience leg.)
- Self 2: How is shame *understood* by people, e.g. how does shame enter their self-defining stories? (This is the object leg concerned with the self-concept.)
- Self 3: How are people *taken up by others* as shameful, how is shame negotiated discursively? (This is the discourse leg.)

I have now introduced a distinction between different ways of answering the 'what' question in self observation studies of everyday life. The 'what' that is observed (oneself) may be conceived as one's consciousness, location or point of view (Self 1), one's sense of having a set of attributes, including self conceptions and belongings (Self 2), or one's participation in conversations and practices where the self is constituted by the impressions that one person makes on another (Self 3). The data in self observation studies can come from all three sources.

Who observes in self observation?

The next question to address is the 'who' in self observation. Who should observe? Here, we can distinguish between direct and indirect self observation. Direct self observation is when the researcher takes her own self and experiences as subject matter. This is foundational for the idea of qualitative inquiry in everyday life as presented in this book. Because the other chapters do not address issues that have to do with recruiting other research participants and using their observations, I shall say a little bit in this chapter about indirect self observation.

Indirect self observation

Indirect self observation is when informants (e.g. assistants, students, or others) are recruited as self observers. Observers may be trained or not, depending on the kind of reports that the researcher is interested in. A significant historical instance of a large self observation study with non-trained participants is the Mass-Observation Archive established in Britain in 1937, intended to create a 'people's anthropology', where several hundred ordinary people from Britain volunteered to keep daily diaries about their everyday lives (see Zittoun & Gillespie, 2010, for a description of this archive and an analysis based on a close reading of one diarist).

Indirect self observation is advocated in a number of methodologies, where the idea is to accumulate data from a representative sample (Hektner, Schmidt, & Csikszentmihalyi, 2007; Rodriguez & Ryave, 2002). If we want to know how young people *in general* feel during a day at school, how their moods and motivations fluctuate, or when they feel shame, and if we are interested in charting possible common patterns in these fluctuations, then it is necessary to recruit a number of participants that are representative of this part of the population.

When one uses participants, it is important to instruct them in how to observe. If they have been told to observe specific events or processes in their everyday lives, then they should try as much as possible to go about their daily lives without acting differently because of the assignment (Rodriguez & Ryave, 2002, p. 16). It is also a good idea to instruct participants not to judge (e.g. morally) the phenomenon that one is interested in as it occurs. Needless to say, this may be artificial and cannot always be maintained without destroying the phenomenon itself (it is hard *not* to judge oneself when feeling shame, for example, since a certain form of judgemental relation to oneself seems to be intrinsic to this emotion). Still, Ryave and Rodriguez recommend that participants are told something like the following: '*Once you notice it* [the topic] *is happening: do not judge it, do not slow down, do not speed up, do not change it, do not question it – just observe it*' (pp. 16–17). Hence, participants should try to be as descriptive (rather than analytical) as possible when reporting their self observations (e.g. on a report sheet), and the idea is to make them write the report immediately after a relevant event. Researchers can favourably prepare participants with training exercises.

Direct self observation

Direct or researcher-based self observation has a long history in psychology and the social sciences, ranging from early introspective studies to more recent studies of driving to work (Anthony Wallace), daydreams (Jerome Singer), playing jazz piano (David Sudnow) and other forms of systematic sociological introspection, as Carolyn Ellis calls them (Ellis, 1991) (see Rodriguez & Ryave, 2002, for these and more references to self observation studies). The studies cited here are relatively unobtrusive in people's everyday lives, but some researchers have also developed ways of intervening quasi-experimentally in social life, acting as their own subjects. The most famous of these is Harold Garfinkel, who developed the so-called 'breaching experiments' as part of his ethnomethodological investigations. In one variety of these, Garfinkel asked his students (here acting as researchers) to engage in ordinary conversations and insist that the person clarify the sense of commonplace remarks:

(S) Hi, Ray. How is your girl friend feeling?
(E) What do you mean, 'How is she feeling?' Do you mean physical or mental?
(S) I mean how is she feeling? What's the matter with you? (He looked peeved.)
(E) Nothing. Just explain a little clearer what do you mean?
(S) Skip it. How are your Med School applications coming?
(E) What do you mean, 'How are they?'
(S) You know what I mean.
(E) I really don't.
(S) What's the matter with you? Are you sick? (Garfinkel, 1967, pp. 42–43)

'S' is the subject and 'E' is the 'experimenter', deliberately breaching the ordinary production of social order in this piece of everyday interaction with the aim of understanding the normativities that are tacitly taken for granted (until they are broken). Such conversational experiments highlight the background expectancies that are rarely thematised in everyday life, and a typical result of Garfinkel's breaches was bewilderment, unease, anxiety, and even anger on behalf of the conversationalists, including the researcher.

It is perhaps less known that Stanley Milgram (famous for his psychological obedience experiments) conducted similar experiments in the 1970s, e.g. in a New York subway car, where he would ask another passenger for his seat in order to study the maintenance of social norms. Milgram recorded the number of passengers who gave him their seats (for no reason other than being asked), but his qualitative self observations are equally important. This is seen in the following account by Milgram:

I approached a seated passenger and was about to utter the magical phrase. But the words seemed lodged in my trachea and would simply not emerge. I stood there frozen, then retreated, the mission unfulfilled. My student observer urged me to try again, but I was overwhelmed by paralyzing inhibition. I argued to myself: 'What kind of craven coward are you? You told your class to do it. How can you go back to them without carrying out your own assignment?' Finally, after several unsuccessful tries, I went up to a passenger and choked out the request, 'Excuse me sir, may I have your seat?' A moment of stark anomic panic overcame me. But the man got right up and gave me the seat. A second blow was yet to come. Taking the man's seat, I was overwhelmed by the need to behave in a way that would justify my request. My head sank between my knees, and I could feel my face blanching. I was not role-playing, I actually felt as if I were going to perish. Then the third discovery: as soon as I got off the train, at the next station, all the tension disappeared. (Milgram, 1992, p. xxiv)

This wonderful phenomenologically precise and evocative passage has also been analysed by Valsiner (2006), and it is a good example of a self observation report that captures many aspects of the self in a 'breaching' everyday life situation. Few people would find a reason to argue against the trustworthiness and merit of such an account. Just as it is relevant to recruit and train participants for specific purposes (to do with representativeness) in some projects, it is equally relevant for other purposes to develop one's own skills of self observation and reporting as a researcher in order to attain a level of clarity and precision like Milgram's. This is particularly the case when it is analytic depth (rather than representative breadth) that one is after as researcher. It is difficult to imagine that participants, who are not researchers, could approach the level of precision and theoretical relevance that Milgram demonstrates in the quote above.

How does one practise self observation?

I will now introduce three more specific ways of answering the 'how' question in different approaches to self observation that have been cultivated in different methodologies. These are:

- ESM (Experience Sampling Method): A systematic phenomenology of the stream of consciousness in everyday life, which is meant to be suitable for quantification.
- SSO (Systematic Self-Observation): Useful for depicting the self in hidden and elusive social situations, primarily based on narrative reports.
- CAP (Creative Analytical Practices): An impressionistic and artful approach to self observation with a focus on autoethnography and writing as a method of inquiry.

CAP is closest to this book's general philosophy, and SSO may also be useful for researchers who are looking for ways of studying their lives in a social world. ESM, by contrast, is much closer to what we may call mainstream social science, and I have included it here to demonstrate one possible bridge between qualitative inquiry and quantification. CAP represents the least mechanised 'how' of self observation, which I return to in different ways in later chapters (particularly Chapter 8), while ESM is extremely standardised in comparison, and SSO falls somewhere in between. ESM is useful primarily in relation to Self 1 studies, while SSO is most useful concerning Self 2 and Self 3. CAP approaches can be more freely used for a number of purposes in qualitative inquiry in everyday life.

The Experience Sampling Method

The Experience Sampling Method (ESM) has been developed and practised since the 1970s by Mihalyi Csikszentmihalyi and co-workers. In a recent comprehensive book on the method, they describe it as a 'systematic phenomenology' (Hektner, Schmidt, & Csikszentmihalyi, 2007, p. 4). Building on Husserl's 'pure phenomenology', they use the tools of mainstream psychological investigations, including technologies (such as signalling devices), research designs and statistics, to develop ESM. This systematic phenomenology is meant to capture the events occurring in the stream of consciousness over time, and, with its focus on Self 1 – the contents of consciousness – it departs from the focus on the self in social situations (Self 2 and 3) that we find in Systematic Self-Observation (to be addressed below). The idea is to achieve the highest degree of immediacy possible by asking people (normally recruited participants who are non-researchers) to provide written responses to a set of questions at several random points throughout each day of a week (p. 6). The self observer is prompted to provide the response by a signalling device (e.g. a pager), and experience is thus ideally sampled the moment it occurs. Thereby, the proponents of the method argue that the distortions of experience associated with the use of retrospective accounts (e.g. the diaries used by CAP researchers) are avoided.

ESM studies are particularly well suited to investigate daily fluctuations in motivations, moods or subjective well-being, and can thus be used to identify the typologies of experience that arise during the day. One can say that the Husserlian life world is captured in bits and pieces throughout a number of days in a person's life. ESM scholars argue that the rather time-consuming work that is needed to build a good database will quickly pay off, as one can continually go back to the data and find new and surprising structures in them for years. And even small studies with five or ten participants may prove sufficient to be used reliably in simple statistical analyses.

How is an ESM study carried out in practice? Obviously, one should begin by considering whether one's research problem fits this methodology. ESM is designed to capture individuals' representations of experience as it occurs (Hektner, Schmidt, & Csikszentmihalyi, 2007, p. 32). It can favourably be used 'to measure dimensions of experience that are likely to be context-dependent' (p. 32) and that fluctuate over a day or a week. Questions such as 'How do you feel about yourself right now?' are highly relevant in ESM studies whereas questions like 'How do you generally feel about yourself?' are better suited to qualitative research interviewing, for example. It is important to consider the signalling schedule. Most ESM studies use signal-contingent sampling, where participants respond to a signal (often randomised). But it is also possible to use interval-contingent (responses are expected at the same time every day) or event-contingent (a self-report is completed following certain specified events) forms of sampling. It should normally not take participants more than one or two minutes to complete the form (p. 49).

When the data are in, they should be coded, and the authors recommend developing a codebook that targets both the external coordinates of experience (e.g. date, time, location) and the internal ones (here Likert scales are often used). Then the data should be analysed, and the analytic options are legion. Pure qualitative approaches can be used that focus on the life of a single respondent (or a single kind of situation found in the material), and statistical analyses can be used to calculate correlations between a number of variables. This, however, is hardly in line with the original phenomenological ambition to go to 'the things themselves' (one of Husserl's famous credos) rather than scientific abstractions. I will refer the reader to the ESM method book for details about different forms of analysis.

Kahneman and colleagues refer to ESM as the 'gold standard' in the field (Kahneman, Krueger, Schkade, Schwartz & Stone, 2004, p. 1777), and it is true that the use of ESM has resulted in interesting research reports. That said, however, I believe that ESM has drifted quite far away from its phenomenological background and its ambition to study 'the flow in everyday life' (Hektner, Schmidt & Csikszentmihalyi, 2007, p. 286). First, there is often (although not necessarily) a quantification of people's experiences built into the forms that are given to participants, which may not be true to the qualitative world of human experience. Consequently, most ESM studies proceed by studying statistical averages, which may give us fascinating demographical facts, but say little of human experience in the life world. When we are told, for example, that on average, close to a fourth of a person's waking hours are spent in solitude (p. 280), we do not know whether and how this applies to individual human beings or how it in fact is experienced. The problem is, in technical terms, that most social and psychological phenomena are *non-ergodic*; this means that the individual's variability of the psychological flow over time is *not* structurally identical to the inter-individual variation within a population (Salvatore & Valsiner, 2010, p. 821). The flow and flux of an individual life is simply of a different order from the flow and flux that pertains to inter-individual processes that can be captured statistically. The rather mechanical and quantitative approach of ESM may, however, have the advantage of persuading people to study experience in at least a quasi-phenomenological way which would otherwise not have been attracted to such a research method from fear that it would become too subjectivist.

Other problems of ESM include what could be called a 'fetishization of the present', as if human experience must be captured the moment it occurs in order to be valid, as purely and unmediated as possible, with the risk of overlooking the temporal and mediated nature of much, if not most, of our experience. ESM researchers are sceptical of the diary method, for example, but why should the mediated externalisation of thought processes in diaries be less true to human experience than the 'inner experience' reported in ESM forms? (On the use of diaries, see Zittoun & Gillespie, 2010.)

Finally, the implicit philosophical position in ESM seems to be rather mentalistic in the sense that its proponents typically address self observational data as 'contents of mind' (Hektner, Schmidt & Csikszentmihalyi, 2007, p. 6). The human mind is seen as a storehouse of mental phenomena, a Cartesian theatre or a 'windowless room' (Costall, 2007). ESM is thus designed to observe the mental entities that reside in the storehouse, theatre or room, but this spatial understanding of mental phenomena is far from the sophisticated approaches developed by Husserl, Heidegger and Merleau-Ponty, who stressed the inherent intentionality and world-directedness of the mind.

Systematic Self-Observation

Systematic Self-Observation (SSO) has been developed as a rigorous qualitative research methodology by Rodriguez and Ryave, mainly from a sociological perspective (Rodriguez & Ryave, 2002), and it is much closer to this book's interest in qualitative inquiry than ESM. SSO is particularly well suited to study hidden and elusive aspects of social life such as lies, the withholding of compliments, how individuals compare themselves to others, and how they experience shameful emotions like envy (p. 3). A SSO topic would preferably address a single, focused phenomenon of everyday life that is natural to a culture, and which is noticeable, intermittent, bounded in time and of relatively short duration (p. 5). As the examples testify, SSO has primarily been used to study the dimensions of the self that Harré called Self 2 and Self 3, perhaps due to the sociological background of this methodology (Goffman, Garfinkel and the symbolic interactionists are sources of inspiration). The goal of SSO is to generate field notes that are accurate descriptions of the participants' experience in social situations (and the participants may be the researchers themselves). Unlike ESM, SSO encourages participants to write *narrative* reports of their experiences immediately after they have occurred.

A SSO study normally proceeds according to the following sequence of tasks: (1) choose a subject matter appropriate to the methodology, (2) formulate the topic, (3) recruit informants, (4) guide the informants to understand the logic of social science, (5) teach informants to observe in a sensitive way, (6) teach them to report observations in a detailed and accurate manner, and (7) prepare the informants with training exercises (Rodriguez & Ryave, 2002, p. 10). A lot of emphasis is put on training informants from the conviction that good data are completely dependent on the informants' skills. When the qualitative researcher herself is also the informant, many of these steps will already have been taken; at least if the researcher has been educated in qualitative inquiry. After these steps, however, comes the process of reading the collected material analytically, ordering them, making typologies and choosing typical, critical or extreme cases to report, depending on one's research interests.

In many of the reported studies that use SSO, the data are in the form of short conversational sequences. In a study of lies in everyday life, an observed sequence can be reported like this:

First Instance
Place: In a parking lot outside a high school.
Who: Basketball friend and myself.
Situation: Standing by our cars talking about nothing.

Friend: We play tomorrow in Pacific Palisades. Why don't you come see us play?
Me: Oh really? What time do you play?
Friend: We play at 7:30 on Friday. You should come down if you get a chance.
Me: Okay, I'll be there [Lie]. (Rodriguez & Ryave, 2002, p. 30)

This is not the place to unfold the authors' specific findings concerning lies, but they argue rather convincingly that lying emerges primarily from the general features of everyday social interaction. All informants in the study lied, and most lies occurred spontaneously, and although this goes against our common-sense understanding of lies as immoral, lying often seemed to be a preferred action according to the normative conventions of social interaction. In short, lying was found to be a pervasive feature of our lives that often, and perhaps paradoxically, serves a moral function.

There is nothing in SSO studies that prevents researchers from counting and quantifying data (see Rodriguez & Ryave, 2002, for examples), but the methodology has its strength in the immediate qualitative descriptions, often in narrative form, that participants can construct. Unlike ESM, which often charts people's doings and sufferings in general during a day, week, month or so, SSO is rather more focused on specific issues, such as telling lies, name dropping, gossiping and other similar aspects of our conversational reality. With SSO we have a manageable method for social phenomenological studies of self observation, which is flexible enough to suit a number of different research purposes, but which is at the same time rigorous enough for researchers to communicate their findings in efficient ways to others who are familiar with the method.

Creative Analytical Practices

From a certain perspective, we are all engaged in self observation as we go about living our daily lives. All of us notice from time to time how we experience and act in the world. As language users, we not only live in the present, but we have the capacity to distance ourselves from the immediate impressions the world makes on us, and from the immediate impulses we have to act. This distancing involves self observation in a minimal sense and is enabled by our capacity to use language. Humans have also developed different cultural tools and practices that aid in the process of distancing one from oneself, ranging from simple note taking to psychotherapy. One helpful tool in self observation is the diary or journal, which has been advocated as a qualitative research instrument by Janesick (1999) and others who work creatively with self observation in everyday life (e.g. in autoethnography). Diaries are normally used rather unreflectively in people's lives, but a focused use of journal writing can refine the researcher's understanding of her role as a research instrument and also of the responses of participants (p. 506). Janesick describes how the making of lists, portraits, maps of consciousness, guided imagery, altered points of view, unsent letters and dialogues may facilitate the journal writer's phenomenological awareness (p. 519). Often, there is a short route from journal writing to actual self observation analyses.

Using personal journals in the way advocated by Janesick is related to the current interest in autoethnography (Ellis, Adams & Bochner, 2011) as the most visible of the Creative Analytical Practices (CAP) in qualitative inquiry to have emerged in recent years (some of the others are investigative poetry and performance ethnographies). Autoethnography seeks to describe and analyse (this is the 'graphy' aspect) personal experience (this is the 'auto' aspect) in order to understand cultural processes (this is the 'ethno' aspect) (p. 1). The goal is to craft aesthetic and evocative thick descriptions of experience with inspiration from the arts. Autoethnographers put emphasis on writing as a method of inquiry (Richardson & St. Pierre, 2005) and are generally sceptical of more standard methodological guidelines for analysis. Some favour the use of theoretical concepts to analyse experience – Ellis and colleagues thus refer to theoretical tools as those which make autoethnography potentially more valid than Oprah Winfrey's talk show, for example (Ellis, Adams & Bochner, 2011, p. 8) – while others prefer to write more descriptively, e.g. in the tradition of intimate journalism (Harrington, 1997) (see Chapter 8).

In any case, it is difficult to present guiding principles for how to work with self observation in CAP traditions (Richardson & St. Pierre, 2005). Richardson does, however, encourage researchers to do a number of specific things. Some of the most important ones are:

1 Join a writing group
2 Work through a creative writing guidebook
3 Enrol in a creative writing workshop
4 Use 'writing up' field notes to expand one's writing vocabulary
5 Write an autobiography (e.g. about how one learned to write)
6 Transform field notes into drama
7 Experiment with transforming an interview or an observation into a poem

Readers are encouraged to try one or more of these. Regardless of one's understanding of CAP inquiries, it is useful to regard writing as a mode of inquiry throughout a self observation study. Like Richardson, who reports having been taught 'not to write until I knew what I wanted to say' (Richardson & St. Pierre, 2005, p. 960), I believe that writing is a central way for qualitative researchers not just to report some findings, in the final instance, but also to experiment with analyses, different perspectives on the textual material, and ways of presenting, as a method of inquiry in its own right. Writing should thus be treated as an intrinsic part of the methodology of research – and not as a final 'postscript' added on (I return to this later in the book).

The main conclusion that emerges from these considerations is that different self observation approaches are suitable for different research questions. We should engage systematically *and* creatively in self observation and judge the different methodological perspectives pragmatically in light of the scientific results that ensue. CAP approaches, when done well, may give readers a deep understanding of possible human experiences, in most cases the researcher's own, whereas ESM and SSO approaches are better suited to studies on a larger scale that can throw light on different aspects of the self.

Beginning a project on self observation

Before moving on in the next chapters to more specific kinds of everyday life materials, I would like to conclude this chapter with a few exercises that may help you to get started on a project based on self observation. Since self observation is particularly well suited to study elusive and hidden aspects of our everyday lives, I will encourage you to work with topics like lies or shame. We shall go through the six steps that I presented in Chapter 1:

1 *Choose a topic.* You may choose lying or shame or something else, but it is important that the topic is something that you can in fact observe yourself doing or experiencing in your life. Some researchers estimate that people tell four lies on average every day (if we include such banalities as 'I'm fine'), and the experience of shame is also not uncommon. Before going further, write a few words about why your chosen topic is important. Think about the three aspects of self that were addressed above and decide whether you would like to focus on one of these in particular, or do self observation in a way that includes them all. Write a few words about your choice and your reasons for choosing it. Be sure to include reflections on the ethical questions that were raised in Chapter 3.

2 *Collect materials.* Buy a notebook that you can carry around. Choose a specific day or two as suitable for your research purpose. Depending on your choice of analytic awareness, use the notebook to describe the time, place, persons and social situations (when, where, who and what), whenever the phenomenon that you are interested in occurs. Work with a combination of short, descriptive sentences (e.g. of when, where and

with whom something happened) and longer narratives (typically of what happened). Experiment with dividing up the pages in your notebook, e.g. according to the distinction between short description and longer narration. You can use Milgram's description above as exemplary of how to draft a narrative. However, it should not take more than around five minutes whenever you write in the notebook. It may be awkward to write in the book immediately after something has occurred in a social situation, but you can go somewhere in private to collect your thoughts and make your notes. It is often helpful not just to write down what happened (e.g. when you told a lie or felt shame), but also your thoughts about what the study of the phenomenon contributed to your life. Did it somehow encourage lying that you had set yourself the task of observing your 'lying self'? Or were you able to more or less forget the task and act 'naturally'?

3 *Consult the literature.* After the days of self observation are over, read your notes carefully. You may already begin posing some analytic questions to your materials at this stage. What is interesting about the phenomena and situations? What is puzzling? Here, a kind of breakdown in understanding, or even 'mystery' (Alvesson & Kärreman, 2011), may occur, and you can try to make explicit what is mystifying about your notes, although this may be difficult at this stage. The idea is to let the breakdown, your confusion, surprise or wonder, direct the readings that you may do. Most often, researchers are already familiar with theoretical literature about the subject matter, and should think through how certain theories or paradigms would approach the phenomenon. If you know very little about lying or shame, try to simply browse through a textbook on social psychology (or something similar) to see if some of the discussions there can inspire you. You should also notice if something is lacking in the literature. Do your small examples thematise aspects that are not covered in the books?

4 *Continue collecting materials.* After having read about the topic of interest and juxtaposed the readings with your initial observations, choose another day or two and repeat the self observation process. Now, your way of observing and understanding may have changed because of the theoretical readings that may have sensitised you to other aspects of the situations. Do not think of this as a source of error, but rather as a new mediation of your experience.

5 *Do analytic writing.* Collect all your materials and use your theoretical tools to help you read and analyse. Do not wait to write until the analytic process is finished, but use writing as an analytic method of inquiry. It is not easy to explicate how to do this, but you may use the three strategies outlined in Chapter 1 as inspiration:

- Make the obvious obvious: Is there something about lying/shame (or whatever your topic is) that happens always or often, but which is so obvious that we rarely notice it? Try to think counter-factually to help you notice the obvious but unnoticed: What if your lie had been true, what if you had not felt shame, but pride in this situation? What if you had been one of the other participants in the situation – how do different perspectives matter?

- Make the hidden obvious: Try to ask Parker's (1996) question: What relationships and implicit theories of self must obtain for this material (situation) to make sense? What discourses and understandings of social life are working in the situation that made you feel shame or tell a lie?

- Make the obvious dubious: Try to read your materials with a destabilising intention. We think we know what a lie is, for example, but is it really that simple? Is it really lying to say that 'I'm fine', even if I don't feel too good? Doesn't this presuppose that there is some 'truth' about how one feels that only the speaker has access to and that she may intentionally conceal from others? What theory of subjectivity is involved in such a presupposition – and is there something in or about your observations that may challenge this?

6 *Publish your text.* If your text is an assignment, to publish just means to hand it in, and if it is something else, then show it to friends or colleagues and ask for their opinions. Make sure to notice their reactions without being defensive: if they like it, what is it about your analysis that resonates with them? And if they don't like it, you should try to understand if there is something about your analysis that is badly crafted, or if their criticism concerns basic paradigmatic differences. Perhaps they don't think that something like that can count as qualitative research? After listening carefully to the criticism, you may ask them why they are critical of this way of working, and it will often be possible to use their feedback when working further on the paper.

ALTERNATIVE EXERCISE

If the six steps above seem a little too much at this point, you may try a simpler observational exercise (and perhaps return to the exercise above after reading the rest of the book). Some helpful exercises are found in Janesick's book on '*Stretching Exercises' for Qualitative Researchers* (2004). Here is one variation on her exercise called 'Observation in the home or workplace':

- Purpose: To develop observation skills within a setting. Observe an area in your home or workplace.
- Problem: To see your own space – and yourself in it – as you never have before.
- Time: 30 minutes.
- Activity: Select an area to observe and describe which is part of your everyday life (home/work). Set aside 30 minutes for quiet time to describe your room or office. Initially, you should write without stopping or censoring yourself. Describe as many details of the room as possible, including your own presence in the room, both in the here-and-now (i.e. describe your perspective) but also historically (we see not just physical surfaces, but also something of the history of the person who has decorated the room, arranged the furniture, etc.). After taking notes, read them carefully, and consider how to edit the notes and possibly integrate them into an analytic text about your observation of being-in-a-room.
- Discussion: If you do this together with others (e.g. in class), compare and discuss your notes and possible analytic texts. Think about what the 30 minute timeframe meant for your activity. It is a luxury to have 30 minutes just to observe one thing, but there are still indefinitely many aspects and properties of the room – and you in it – that escaped notice. Think about how theories and concepts can help you notice some aspects and properties and exclude others.

FIVE

Conversations

Human beings are conversational creatures that live a dialogical and conversational life (Mulhall, 2007). From the earliest days of our lives, we are able to enter into proto-conversations with care-givers in ways that involve subtle forms of turn-taking and emotional resonance. The dyad in which proto-conversations occur from the first days of childhood is in a sense prior to the child's own sense of self. We are intersubjective and conversational creatures before we become subjective and monological ones (Trevarthen, 1993). We do learn to talk privately to ourselves, and hide our emotional lives from others, but this is possible only because there was first an intersubjective communicative dance that involved others. Any monological utterance is really just an element in a dialogue, as Bakhtin has taught us (see Holquist, 2002). This should be a significant addition to the philosophical anthropology that was developed in Chapter 2: the process of interpreting the world and inquiring into its situations and events is, by necessity, a *conversational* process. Knowing is dialogical. We use a language that was first acquired conversationally, and we try out our interpretations in dialogue with others and the world. Our very inquiring and interpreting selves are conversational at their core; they are constituted by the numerous relationships we have, and have had, with other people.

Unsurprisingly, conversations are therefore a rich source of knowledge about personal and social aspects of everyday life for human beings. In this chapter, I will show how we can use conversations as materials in qualitative analyses of everyday life to understand others, ourselves and the culture at large. I shall first address the role of conversations in human life a little bit more closely, before making a number of distinctions between different kinds of conversations that we may use for research purposes, some of them more formally set up as 'research interviews' and some less so. The chapter concludes with an example of a piece of everyday life research based on a conversation I had with a friend with whom I had lost contact because he joined a spiritual community (or a 'sect').

Conversational reality

In a philosophical sense, all human research is conversational, since we are linguistic creatures and language is best understood in terms of the figure of conversation (Mulhall, 2007). Since the late nineteenth century (in journalism) and the early twentieth century (in the social sciences), the conversational process of knowing has been conceptualised and refined under the name of *interviewing*. Like 'dialogue' and 'conversation', the very term 'interview' itself testifies to the dialogical and interactional nature of human life. An interview is literally an *inter-view*, an interchange of views between two persons, conversing about a theme of mutual interest. *Con-versation*, in its Latin root, means 'dwelling with someone' or 'wandering together with', and the root sense of *dia-logue* is that of talk (*logos*) that goes back and forth (*dia-*) between persons (Mannheim & Tedlock, 1995, p. 4). Thus conceived, the concept of conversation in the human and social sciences is much broader than simply referring to interviewing as yet another empirical method.

Conversations are indeed a set of techniques, but also a mode of knowing and a fundamental ontology of persons. As Rom Harré has put it: 'The primary human reality is persons in conversation' (Harré, 1983, p. 58). Cultures are constantly produced, reproduced, and revised in dialogues among their members (Mannheim & Tedlock, 1995, p. 2). Our everyday lives are conversational to their core. This also goes for the cultural investigation of cultural phenomena, or what we call social science. We should see language and culture as emergent properties of dialogues rather than the other way around. Conversations – dialogues – are not several monologues that are added together, but the basic, primordial, form of associated human life. In John Shotter's words:

> [W]e live our daily social lives within an ambience of conversation, discussion, argumentation, negotiation, criticism and justification; much of it to do with problems of intelligibility and the legitimation of claims to truth. (Shotter, 1993, p. 29)

Not just our interpersonal social reality is constituted by conversations. This also goes for the self. Charles Taylor argues that the self exists only within what he calls 'webs of interlocution' (Taylor, 1989, p. 36). We are selves only in relation to certain interlocutors with whom we are in conversation and from whom we acquire a language of self-understanding. In referring to Heidegger's concept of *Dasein* – or human existence – philosopher Stephen Mulhall, author of the aptly entitled book *The Conversation of Humanity*, states that '*Dasein* is not just the locus and the precondition for the conversation of humankind; it is itself, because humankind is, a kind of enacted conversation' (Mulhall, 2007, p. 58). We understand ourselves as well as others only because we can speak, and 'being able to speak involves being able to converse' (p. 26). Human reality is a conversational reality.

This means that the conversation is not only a specific empirical method in the form of research interviews; it also involves a view of the self and the human world. The phenomena of our lives must be seen as *responses* to people, situations, and events. As responses they are conversational and dialogical, for, to quote Alasdair MacIntyre, 'conversation, understood widely enough, is the form of human transactions in general' (MacIntyre, 1985, p. 211). When people are talking, e.g. in research interviews, they are not simply putting preconceived ideas into words, but are dialogically responding to each other's expressions and trying to make sense by using the narratives and discourses that are available (Shotter, 1993, p. 1). There is an element of collusion in this (McDermott & Tylbor, 1995), i.e., a kind of 'playing together' that is needed to uphold the conversational flow, which is a precondition for communication.

Traditional research interviews

It is common to distinguish between different kinds of research conversations or interviews, such as:

- *Structured interviews*: These are employed in surveys and are based on the same research logic as questionnaires: standardised ways of asking questions will lead to answers that can be compared across participants and possibly quantified. Although structured interviews are useful for some purposes, they do not take advantage of the dialogical potentials for knowledge production that are inherent in human conversations. They are passive recordings of people's opinions and attitudes, and often reveal more about the cultural conventions of how one should answer specific questions than about the conversational production of social life itself.
- *Semi-structured interviews*: These are planned, yet flexible, interviews with the purpose of obtaining descriptions of specific experiences of the interviewees, and which normally aim for some interpretation of the meaning of the described phenomena. Semi-structured interviews can make more use of the knowledge-producing potentials of dialogues by making much more leeway for following up on whatever angles are deemed important by the interviewee, and the interviewer has a greater chance of becoming visible as a knowledge-producing participant in the process itself, rather than hiding behind a preset interview guide.
- *Group interviews*: In the case of so-called 'focus groups', a moderator seeks to focus the group discussion on specific themes of research interest, and will often use the group dynamic instrumentally to include a number of different perspectives on some theme. Often, group interviews are the most flexible ones, which have the largest similarities to everyday discussions. They can be used, for example, when the researcher is not just interested in *reports* of what has happened, but in how participants give *accounts* of important issues in their lives.

In qualitative inquiry, semi-structured interviews are probably the most wide-spread approach. A rather formal, stage-wise approach to research interviewing is depicted in Box 5.1.

BOX 5.1

Seven stages of an interview inquiry

Kvale & Brinkmann (2008, p. 102) suggest that an interview inquiry may be broken down into the following steps:

1 *Thematising*: Formulate the purpose of an investigation and the conception of the theme to be investigated before the interviews start. Clarify *what* you will study before deciding on *how*.
2 *Designing*: When planning the study, take into consideration all stages of the investigation before interviewing.
3 *Interviewing*: Conduct the actual interviews based on a thematic interview guide.
4 *Transcribing*: Prepare the oral interview material for analysis in writing.
5 *Analysing*: Decide on a mode of analysis that is appropriate for the interviews and the knowledge you aim to produce. Modes of analysis range from strict forms of coding and content analysis to more holistic forms of narrative readings.
6 *Verifying*: Ascertain the validity (have you actually studied what you intended to study?), reliability (are your results consistent?) and generalisability (do your analyses apply to other contexts and populations?) of the interview findings.
7 *Reporting*: Communicate the findings of the study and the methods applied in a form that lives up to scientific criteria; takes the ethical aspects of the investigation into consideration; and results in a readable product.

If you know in advance what you will study quite specifically, or have a theoretical idea to test *deductively*, you may proceed along the lines described in the box. Or, if you are interested in gathering broad, *inductive* data in order to say something general about how something is experienced by members of a given population, you may also work according to the steps of Box 5.1. However, our everyday lives are full of conversational encounters that are not set up as formal research interviews, but which simply surprise us, or stick in our minds as significant, and these can be fertile soil in processes of *abductive* inquiry into the fabric of everyday life. In the latter case, it may be helpful to work according to the research logic of the present book. This logic says that conversational breakdowns in everyday life can be a springboard for entering into fruitful interpretations of significant cultural issues.

An everyday life conversation

In order to illustrate how a tiny bit of an ordinary conversation can be used to unpack larger social orders, I shall now introduce a much-discussed example that involves two (anonymous) characters that have come to be known as Sano (a healthy man) and Enfermada (a sick woman). The two of them are attending a conference in a strange city, and they are looking for a place to buy medicine for Enfermada. Sano enters a shop to make inquiries, but exits with the disheartening message that there are no pharmacies in the vicinities. The following, seemingly simple, exchange then takes place (from Davies & Harré, 1999, p. 47):

Sano: I am sorry to have dragged you all this way when you are not well.
Enfermada: You didn't drag me. I chose to come.

Bronwyn Davies and Rom Harré use this little example to demonstrate the analytic power of a certain discourse analytic theory known as *positioning theory*, designed specifically to study conversational episodes. We shall learn much more about this theory in Chapter 6. Here, I shall merely use the example to note how rich even such small excerpts from everyday life conversations can be. For Davies and Harré demonstrate how the two speakers can be seen to position each other in different ways through this micro exchange. Sano positions himself as having the duty to take care of Enfermada, presumably because of Enfermada's vulnerable situation as sick. Sano's initial apology ('I am sorry') positions him as having exercised a *right* he feels he has, as an active and capable person, to put Enfermada in the passive position of patient. The storyline that makes the exchange meaningful is thus one of carer and patient. This is a power relation that gives one party powers and duties (to act) and another party the right to be taken care of. But Enfermada interestingly resists this positioning move and puts herself in an active position by underlining that she *chose* to come. From her point of view, Sano did not *do* anything to her (drag her). She herself was the agent, and she may implicitly or subsequently (at least this is how Davies and Harré tell the story) position Sano as a male chauvinist, who thinks that he has the right and duty to take care of another person simply because this person is a woman (with a cold).

This little conversational interchange, the like of which we may all experience in our daily lives, thus makes sense only given very specific storylines, positions and beliefs about selves, rights and duties, which are immanent in the episode and can be unpacked to explain its meaning. As an aid in the process of unpacking, one can raise Parker's question that we learned of in Chapter 1: What relationships and theories of self must obtain for this material, this conversational episode, to make sense? What everyday life researchers can do is therefore defamiliarise themselves with such occurrences and use a form of abductive reasoning to interpret it: What must be the case in order for this to make sense? Can we destabilise (or deconstruct) the meanings that are normally taken for granted in such social episodes, or can we criticise the power relations that are at work? We should, as qualitative researchers, learn to become surprised by the obviousness of such conversations, write them down in our notebooks when we experience them, and use our theoretical knowledge to interpret them.

In addition, however, I believe that we can use conversations more consciously or even *instrumentally* (in Dewey's sense, as intellectual tools) for knowledge production in our everyday lives. The rest of this chapter introduces this idea and shows how it can be applied. I will thus focus on conversations that are conducted for a research purpose, rather than those that we simply stumble upon by chance, but I wish to develop an understanding of interviewing as something human beings may stage and enact in their *everyday* lives, where the interviewer, *together* with the conversation partner, appear in a knowledge-producing role.

Doxa and *episteme* in conversations

Conversations and interviews are many different things, and one goal of this chapter is to open up our minds so that we can think of – and practise – research conversations in many ways other than the traditional ones. Most research interviews today cast the interviewer in a specific role, namely that of a receptive questioner who asks questions without intervening much in the conversation with objections or confrontations. The knowledge sought in such conversations frequently, yet implicitly, concerns what the Greek philosophers called *doxa* (opinions, attitudes and the like). As an example, we may consult the following, more or less standardised, excerpt from a semi-structured qualitative interview:[2]

SK 1:	I want to first ask you a maybe difficult question. If you'll try to remember back when you went to primary school, are you able to remember the first time you ever had any grades?
Student 1:	I remember a time; but it might not have been the first time.
SK 2:	Let's take that time. Can you tell me what happened?
Student 2:	I did very well. I remember getting a red star on the top of my paper with 100; and that stands out in my memory as exciting and interesting.
SK 3:	Yes. Is it only the red star that stands out, or what happened around it?
Student 3:	[*laughter*] I remember the colour very very well. It was shining. I remember getting rewarded all the way around. I remember being honoured by my classmates and the teacher and my parents – them

---

[2]The interview is reported in full in Kvale & Brinkmann (2008, pp. 124–127), and Steinar Kvale is the interviewer (SK) while the interviewee is a student at a qualitative research course.

SK 4:	making a fuss. And some of the other kids not responding so well who didn't do so well. It was mixed emotions, but generally I remember the celebration aspect.
	You said mixed emotions. Are you able to describe them?
Student 4:	Well, at that time I was the teacher's pet and some people would say, 'Aha, maybe she didn't earn it, maybe it's just because the teacher likes her so well.' And some kind of stratification occurring because I was not only the teacher's pet but I was maybe getting better grades and it created some kind of dissonance within my classmates' experience of me socially.
SK 5:	Could you describe that dissonance?
Student 5:	Well, I think there's always some kind of demarcation between students who do well and students who don't do as well, and that's determined, especially in the primary grades, by the number that you get on top of your paper.
SK 6:	Was this early in school? Was it first grade?
Student 6:	Third grade.
SK 7:	Third grade. Well, that's a long time ago. Are you able to remember what they said? Or –
Student 7:	No; it was more feeling –
SK 8:	The feeling –
Student 8:	Yeah, it was the feeling of, I'd put some space between me and the peer group –
SK 9:	Because of your good grades –
Student 9:	Yeah.

The interviewer does not object to or contradict the interviewee; he more or less acts as a neutral mirror of whatever emerges in the narrative of the interviewee, simply facilitating the process of telling the story of this experience. Looking at Figure 5.1, which is meant to map different approaches to interviewing on two axes (assertive versus receptive conversational styles and *doxa* versus *episteme* as knowledge ideal), the interview above – like most interviews today – can be characterised as receptive and doxastic, i.e., it belongs in the lower left quadrant (Brinkmann, 2007a).

This style of interviewing definitely has its merits, and my discussion here is not meant to discredit it, but rather to show that other styles have other knowledge-producing potentials that are often not taken advantage of. The specific style in the lower left quadrant goes back to Carl Rogers' classic 'non-directive method as a technique for social research', as a very clear example of the doxastic approach (Rogers, 1945). As Rogers explained, the goal of this kind of therapy/research is to sample the respondent's attitudes towards herself: 'Through the non-directive interview we have an unbiased method by which we may plumb these private thoughts and perceptions of the individual' (p. 282). Although often framed in different terms, I believe that many contemporary interview researchers conceptualise the research interview in line with Rogers' humanistic, non-directive approach, valorising the respondents' private experiences, narratives,

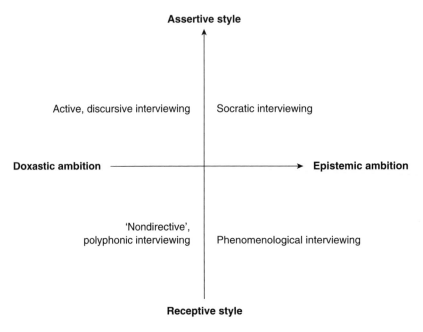

Figure 5.1   Different conceptions of interviewing

opinions, beliefs and attitudes, which can be captured with the concept of *doxa*. 'Empathetic interviewing' (Fontana & Frey, 2005), for example, involves taking a stance in favour of the persons being studied, not unlike the positive regard displayed by Rogerian therapists, and the approach is depicted as at once a 'method of friendship' and a humanistic 'method of morality because it attempts to restore the sacredness of humans before addressing any theoretical or methodological concerns' (p. 697).

Interviews can also be receptive, but with an epistemic ambition (the right quadrant at the bottom). The method of interviewing developed in empirical phenomenology is one example (Giorgi & Giorgi, 2003). Giorgi's starting point is in the respondents' experiences, the *doxa*, but the goal of phenomenological interviewing is to arrive at general knowledge in the sense of *episteme*. The point is, however, that the central part of the process of reaching *episteme* is confined to what happens after the interview conversation, when the interviewer can engage in scientific analysis of the material (by employing the phenomenological reduction and the *epoché*, as described in the previous chapter).

Perspectives on interviewing also exist that put emphasis on a more assertive stance, but still employ a doxastic style. An example here could be Holstein and Gubrium, who have long argued that interviews are interpretatively active, meaning-making practices (Holstein & Gubrium, 1995). They are still doxastic, however, in the sense that they work with respondents' experience conveyed 'more on, if not in, their own terms' (Holstein & Gubrium, 2003, p. 20). There is no questioning of experience in the process of interviewing (only later on, in the post-interviewing phase of analysis). Discourse analysts such as Potter and Wetherell can also be placed in the upper left quadrant. In a classic text, they describe the active, constructive role of the interview researcher and summarise discourse analytic interviewing as follows:

> First, variation in response is as important as consistency. Second, techniques, which allow diversity rather than those which eliminate it are emphasized, resulting in more informal conversational exchanges, and third, interviewers are seen as active participants rather than like speaking questionnaires. (Potter & Wetherell, 1987, p. 165)

Variation, diversity, informality, and an active interviewer are the key words, but the process is nonetheless seen as resulting in *doxa*, e.g. in articulations of the 'interpretative repertoires' of the interviewees, but without the interviewer necessarily investigating the legitimacy of these repertoires in the interview situation or the respondent's ways of justifying them.

In what follows, I shall look in another direction and develop the potentials of one specific knowledge-producing form of conversation, which I call epistemic interviewing. The greatest epistemic interviewer in history was Socrates, who will serve as a main inspiration for how to use conversations to produce knowledge. Socrates used his conversational skills in his life to ask questions that were existentially important to himself and also to his fellow citizens in Athens. In this sense, he used conversations as a tool for solving everyday life problems about justice, love and beauty (and many other important issues) in the community and for interpreting the human condition. I will not argue that doxastic or receptive approaches are misguided, but I wish to advocate the Socratic approach more positively as it represents a promising approach to qualitative research in everyday life.

On the epistemic in human conversations

As we saw in Chapter 2, the term 'knowledge' is immensely complex, and the search for necessary and sufficient conditions for knowing is probably futile. Yet, as we also saw, an essential normativity runs through the processes and activities that we refer to as *knowing*. When we characterise an episode or a state as that of knowing, philosopher Wilfrid Sellars argued, 'we are not giving an empirical description of that episode or state; we are placing it in the logical space of reasons, of justifying and being able to justify what one says' (Sellars, 1997, p. 76).

Thus, when we talk about an episode as one of knowing, we necessarily raise the issue of its normative status: in order for something to count as knowledge, we have to be able to justify what we think we know. That a belief is true is not enough for it to count as knowledge, for example, for the true belief may be the result of a lucky guess. So saying that something is knowledge does not involve describing it empirically, or placing it in what Sellars called 'the space of causation'. A belief may be caused by many different processes in my brain, my mind, or my social group, but when we call it 'knowledge' we are not talking about what caused it empirically, but whether it can be justified normatively. That is, we place it in what Sellars called 'the logical space of reasons' – a space of justification and accounting practices. This connects to what I argued in Chapter 2 that knowing is something humans do; it is a 'success term' and not something that simply happens as a causal process.

Plato's dialogues, in which Socrates figured as the main protagonist, were precisely designed as ways of testing whether the conversation partners have knowledge (*episteme*) in this normative sense, i.e., whether they are capable of adequately justifying their beliefs, and if they cannot (which is normally the case), if their beliefs are *unwarranted*, the dialogues unfold as dialectical processes of refining their beliefs – their *doxa* – in light of good reasons, in order to approach *episteme*. In order to illustrate this more concretely, I shall give a simple and very short example from Plato's *The Republic*. It very elegantly demonstrates epistemically that no moral rules are self-applying and self-interpreting, but must always be understood contextually. This is very useful knowledge, produced conversationally. In the example, Socrates talks with Cephalus, who believes that justice (*dikaiosune*) – here 'doing right' – can be stated in universal rules, such as 'tell the truth' and 'return borrowed items':

> 'That's fair enough, Cephalus,' I [Socrates] said. 'But are we really to say that doing right consists simply and solely in truthfulness and returning anything we have borrowed? Are those not actions that can be sometimes right and sometimes wrong? For instance, if one borrowed a weapon from a friend who subsequently went out of his mind and then asked for it back, surely it would be generally agreed that one ought not to return it, and that it would not be right to do so, not to consent to tell the strict truth to a madman?'
> 'That is true,' he [Cephalus] replied.
> 'Well then,' I [Socrates] said, 'telling the truth and returning what we have borrowed is not the definition of doing right.' (Plato, 1987, pp. 65–66)

Here, the conversation is interrupted by Polemarchus who disagrees with Socrates' preliminary conclusion, and Cephalus quickly leaves in order to go to a sacrifice. Then Polemarchus takes Cephalus's position as Socrates' discussion partner and the conversation continues as if no substitution had happened.

Initially, as a contrast to conventional (doxastic and receptive) research interviews, we may notice that Socrates violates almost every standard principle of qualitative research interviewing. First, we can see that he talks much more than his respondent. There is some variety across the dialogues concerning how much Socrates talks in comparison with the other participants, but the example given here, where Socrates develops an absurd conclusion from the initial belief voiced by Cephalus, is not unusual, although the balance is much more equal in other places. Secondly, Socrates has not asked Cephalus to 'describe a situation in which he has experienced justice' or 'tell a story about doing right from his own experience' or a similar concretely descriptive question, probing for 'lived experience'. Instead, they are talking about the definition of an important general concept that does indeed play a role in their everyday life. Thirdly, Socrates contradicts and challenges his respondent's view. He is not a warm and caring conversationalist, although he respects the conversational powers of Cephalus. Fourthly, there is no debriefing or attempt to make sure that the interaction was a 'pleasant experience' for Cephalus. Fifthly, the interview is conducted in public rather than private, as an episode in their everyday lives, and the topic is not private experiences or biographical details, but justice, a theme of common human interest, at least of interest to all citizens of Athens.

In relation to the general approach of this book, where inquiry is seen as often beginning with a breakdown in understanding, we can notice that Socrates is *intentionally introducing a breakdown* by contradicting the conversation partner. Hesitation, confusion and tension may arise, but as something productive, akin to the idea of 'mystery' articulated by Alvesson and Kärreman (2011). We can say that the epistemic conversation is meant to create a dialogical breakdown that the conversation partners then have to work out together with the goal of understanding their lives better in the process. This cannot be depicted as a mechanical method, but is something much more hermeneutical and existential.

Also, the hermeneutic philosopher Gadamer drew inspiration from the Socratic art of asking questions. We begin to question, Gadamer argued, not simply for fun, but when:

> … we are shocked by things that do not accord with our expectations. Thus questioning too is more a passion than an action. A question presses itself on us; we can no longer avoid it and persist in our accustomed opinion. (Gadamer, 1960, p. 366)

We use conversations exactly to *move away* from mere opinion to arrive at something more trustworthy that may pave the way for better understandings, and, ultimately, better forms of action in our communities.

A few researchers have used the Socratic approach in modern social science. What Bellah and co-workers (1985) refer to as 'active interviews' in their *Habits of the Heart* correspond quite well to epistemic interviews, and they represent one worked-out alternative to the standard doxastic interviews that probe for private meanings and opinions. Such active interviews do not necessarily aim for agreement between interviewer and interviewee, and the interviewer is allowed to question and challenge what the interviewee says, which we see in the example below where the interviewer, Steven Tipton, tries to discover at what point the respondent would take responsibility for another human being:

> Q: So what are you responsible for?
> A: I'm responsible for my acts and for what I do.
> Q: Does that mean you're responsible for others, too?
> A: No.
> Q: Are you your sister's keeper?
> A: No.
> Q: Your brother's keeper?
> A: No.
> Q: Are you responsible for your husband?
> A: I'm not. He makes his own decisions. He is his own person. He acts his own acts. I can agree with them or I can disagree with them. If I ever find them nauseous enough, I have a responsibility to leave and not deal with it any more.
> Q: What about children?
> A: I... I would say I have a legal responsibility for them, but in a sense I think they in turn are responsible for their own acts. (Bellah, Madsen, Sullivan, Swidler, & Tipton, 1985, p. 304)

In the example, Tipton repeatedly challenges the respondent's claim of not being responsible for other human beings. With Socrates in mind, we can see the interviewer pressing for a contradiction between the respondent's definition of responsibility, involving the idea that she is only responsible for herself, and her likely feeling of at least some (legal) responsibility for her children. The individualist notion of responsibility is almost driven *ad absurdum*, but the definition apparently plays such a central role in the person's life that she is unwilling to give it up. The authors of *Habits of the Heart* conclude that unlike 'poll data' generated by fixed questions that 'sum up the *private* opinions', active (epistemic) interviews 'create the possibility of *public* conversation and argument' (Bellah, Madsen, Sullivan, Swidler, & Tipton, 1985, p. 305). We are far away from the traditional doxastic view of social science interviews, portraying these as ways of understanding what people privately think, feel and want.

Postsecular lessons: An example

The remainder of this chapter recounts an attempt made by myself to use an everyday conversational encounter – somewhat inspired by Socrates – to better understand religion and spirituality. It is also the story of an attempt to re-establish a friendship that waned after I graduated as a psychologist and my friend joined a spiritual community. Now, almost ten years later, I have visited my friend and tried to learn about and understand how someone can take a spiritual cosmology seriously. I call the text 'postsecular lessons', and, after presenting it as an example, I return to some general issues about conversations in everyday life.

The text begins with an autoethnographic element (see Chapter 4). I insert myself into the text with all my doubts and desires to know about certain dimensions of human life, namely those that have to do with basic worldviews, metaphysics and religious beliefs. Often, qualitative inquiry in everyday life will develop from a personal experience, from something that struck the researcher as particularly interesting, strange or salient (the 'breakdown'). As I argued in Chapter 2, most (if not all) significant inquiry actually functions like this, but a unique feature of qualitative inquiry is that these personal aspects can be brought forth, described and discussed as noteworthy constituents in the research process. In this case, I did not stick to the personal intersection of biography and the social world (as in autoethnography), but approached a former friend in order to develop knowledge about the theme that interested me. And I tried to use the Socratic potentials in human conversations as a way of reaching this goal. In this sense, the example of qualitative inquiry in everyday life that follows can perhaps be conceived as a piece of 'Socratic autoethnography'.

Preface: The making of a secularist psychologist

I grew up in an atheist family in Denmark, arguably the most secularised country in the world (Zuckerman, 2008). It was simply assumed that any reference to the supernatural, the transcendent, was foolish; nothing more than a childish idea that modern science had completely dismantled. At my school, this was confirmed: most of my teachers were left-wingers, some of them quite radically so. My teachers taught me the Marxian lesson that religion is opium for the people. But they also instilled in me an idea of progress: from its dark past of superstition and oppression, humanity would emerge as a self-confident species without the need for transcendent or metaphysical guarantees. Religion was to be thought of as a cultural artefact, something that belonged in museums. Instead, we would have psychology and other sciences with which to understand the world.

At the age of thirteen, however, most of us went to the local church for 'confirmation', a Lutheran practice of affirming baptism, but, as I recall, none of us took it very seriously. We had to go to weekly sessions with the priest, and we more or less competed in the art of messing things up and making the poor priest look like a fool. I remember asking dumb questions like 'Are there pizzas in heaven?' In hindsight, I probably shouldn't have been there, but, as is widespread in Danish families, religious practices are repeated although they are often emptied of contents, and Christian holidays are celebrated, but without much faith in the metaphysics of Christianity.

In spite of my secular everyday life, I had all the philosophical questions of childhood in me; questions that are traditionally answered by religious systems: What happens when we die? Why are we here? Why is there something rather than nothing? Why should we behave well (if there is no God to punish us)? One of my earliest childhood memories (but, as a psychologist, I am aware of the extreme untrustworthiness of these things) is of me sitting on the sofa with my mother, when I am suddenly struck by death anxiety. I must have been around five or six years old, and I clearly remember the downright physical presence of finitude I felt when pondering the idea of mortality. I told my mother that if we are all going to die, then nothing is significant. I don't remember her answer, but I know now what I would have liked her to answer: 'If we are all going to die, then *everything* that we do in this life is significant.'

This is what I tell my children now. I have three kids and two of them are old enough to be asking me these questions. And they do. In particular the older brother, now eight, who has had these questions from a very early age. He has learned that 'Daddy doesn't believe in God, but Mom does', but he is relentless in his quest for answers. As a father, however, it has occurred to me that I have very little to offer him concerning metaphysical ideas. I really have no cosmology to give him. How can a disenchanted view of the universe provide the grounds for an edifying socialisation? How can it inspire hope and courage? The experience of being paralysed when confronted with existential questions from my children provides some of the impetus behind the present exploration of life under post-secular conditions.

Scholars today talk about a postsecular turn in social theory (McLennan, 2010). No one believes any longer that the world, not even the West, is on its way to eliminating faith and religion. A new consensus is emerging that religion is and will remain important. Only a few societies were ever secular (Western Europe, Canada and New Zealand come to mind), but in all of these we witness an increased presence of religious discussions. This is confusing for a secularist such as myself. Ten or fifteen years ago, I had it all figured out. The battle cry of the French revolution, calling for *liberté*, *egalité* and *fraternité*, seemed to be able to provide a firm ground on which to build free, democratic societies – however utopian they otherwise appeared. Spirituality, religion and faith were not part of the revolutionary trinity upon which European societies had modelled themselves. Was this a mistake?

As a qualitative researcher, I have decided to try to use my confusion and worries concerning these matters productively. We do research, inquiry, exactly when we are unsure about what something means or about what to do. As a secularist, I am mystified and fascinated by people's unyielding religious convictions, in particular by the postmodern bricolage that occurs when people construct their own religious worldviews and cosmologies, borrowing creatively from a number of sometimes unlikely religious sources. How can someone do this seriously? How can someone use the symbolic resources (Zittoun, 2006) of widely different religious systems to construct a sense of identity – and do this without a gist of postmodern irony? If qualitative inquiry is to be good for anything, it should surely assist in making us understand that which initially baffles us. So I recently decided that I had to study these things and confront my own secularist biases.

The making of a spiritual snow leopard

I was a psychology student from 1997 to 2002. To wit, I am still a psychology student today, but, as a professor, I have the privilege of being paid for my studies! One of the best friends I made as a student was Thomas. Like me, Thomas had a background in another discipline before he came to psychology. He came from journalism, I came from philosophy. In Danish psychology departments, the large majority of the student population is female, so the few male students quickly form friendships based on soccer, beer, and sometimes also academic interests (this was before any of us had read feminist literature). I don't remember exactly how Thomas and I met, but our relationship quickly evolved into a musical one. We spent many hours making electronic music together on our computers, and we even performed once at a student party.

Thomas lived in a small room in a dormitory. His room was always extremely messy and rather filthy and testified to what I saw as his laissez-faire lifestyle. If he felt like it, he would fart in public. Being a more controlled type myself, I secretly admired his free modes of expression and sometimes even tried to copy them. Towards the end of our student years, however, Thomas and I began to drift apart. I became a father and graduated in 2002, and by that time Thomas's life had taken a completely different direction. He had met a girl, who became his girlfriend, and who told him about a spiritual community she had begun to visit. He went to this community in 2000, and this changed his life. He soon moved south, to the town of the community, and joined them. They think of themselves as a spiritual community; others would call them a sect. In any case, I was extremely baffled and could not fathom that my friend Thomas, a beer-drinking anarchist, music maker, and lover of large breasts, was now living in a spiritual community. With his postsecularism, he seemed to have betrayed what I admired most about him: his anti-authoritarian and rebellious attitude.

For eight years or so, I had no contact with Thomas. I did do some internet stalking, and I could see on his website that he now referred to himself as a snow leopard and offered courses in spirituality and Tantra. I heard from some of our common friends that he had become the tantric lover of the spiritual leader in the community: a woman in her mid-fifties, almost twenty years older than Thomas. After the emergence of the social networking sites, we became Facebook friends but did not correspond. I could see that his relationship with the spiritual leader had ended, for he had married someone else from the community and had had a daughter with her. One day in August 2010, I decided to contact Thomas. I wanted to meet him because I wanted to know what had happened to him. I also wanted to learn about his spiritual worldviews. In short, I wanted him to give me a postsecular lesson.

He reacted very positively to my email and we quickly arranged a meeting. I went to his newly acquired house, located just next to the buildings of the community, and we talked for four hours. The community buildings and the nearby garden are beautiful, and a lot of work has gone into constructing them by the community members. During my visit, I also had a chance to meet his wife, his daughter, and his spiritual teacher and former lover. It was an intense conversation and a challenge for me as interviewer, wavering between the roles of friend and researcher. I recorded the conversation on my sound recorder, and below follows my account of (aspects of) what happened. I decided before the interview that I wanted to be honest with Thomas and tell him about my scepticism concerning his worldviews. I also decided that I would freely contradict his utterances whenever I disagreed with them during our conversation.

As an author of literature on qualitative research interviewing, I have been interested in developing interviewing in a more confrontational direction than the warm and harmonious style of most conventional interviews (Brinkmann, 2007a; Brinkmann & Kvale, 2005) – for do we often not learn exactly from contradictions and confrontations? Do we not need, like Socrates, to subject our claims to knowledge to courts of public criticism? And why cannot conversations conducted for research purposes serve as such a court? But I obviously also wanted to be respectful towards Thomas's choices and ideas, even if I did not agree with them. I wanted to learn about a form of postsecularism that I didn't understand. I would work not with interviewing as a method of friendship (Fontana & Frey, 2005), but rather with friendship as a method of interviewing. That is, I would not use our friendship, or whatever was left of it, as a way of acquiring private and hidden information, but I would rather use the interview, and my research project, as a way of trying to re-establish a friendship. The friendship wasn't instrumental in the research process – which I find ethically problematic (see also Duncombe & Jessop, 2002) – but doing research was instrumental in reconstructing a relationship. Researching postsecularism from my qualitative everyday life perspective, and making Thomas part of this, was the excuse I needed to re-establish contact with him. Thomas has seen the draft of what follows and has sent me corrections of some misunderstandings, which I have tried to incorporate into my initial writings.

Spirituality in Tiger's Nest

Thomas spent about an hour and a half telling me about the history and beliefs of the spiritual community. It was founded under another name in 1988 by the current leader, Anne Sophie, and her husband at the time. They divorced ten years later, and he founded a new, but similar, community in another part of the country. After the break-up, the community was renamed Tiger's Nest. This name is similar to the famous Buddhist monastery in Bhutan, Taktsang Dzong, or the Tiger's Nest (constructed in 1692 and famously located on a spectacular cliffside), but it was important to Thomas to stress that Anne Sophie did not as such name the community after this monastery, but simply felt that this was the proper name.

There are around 80 people who live permanently in the village and many other people visit frequently at weekends, but do not live there. Anne Sophie is the main figure in the community. She 'sees things' and informs the residents about her visions. This sometimes sets the life of the community on a new path, as when she saw, about ten years ago, that they should incorporate Tantra as a central component in their religious system. Before this, they mainly practised meditation, but without the tantric element, which includes ideas about sex and nature. Thomas makes clear that Anne Sophie does not give orders about what the members of the community should believe or do. The students of her teachings are supposed to feel by themselves that her visions are true.

The Tigers (as they call themselves) borrow creatively from Buddhist and Christian sources, but it is important for Thomas that they put these things together themselves. They do not simply repeat old doctrines, but create their own ones. I make clear to Thomas that this form of metaphysics is completely alien to me, and I ask him how he knows that it is true. How does he know, for example, that his dreams are proof that he has lived past lives in Bhutan (as he claims) and therefore is a key person in the spiritual life of the community?

> 'I have had lots of dreams about it', Thomas says. 'Also in other places. Well, most recently in the East, but before that in India and I have also had something in Mexico. I still don't understand that.'
>
> 'But the fact that you have these dreams', I object, 'is that enough for you to believe? People dream all sorts of things…'
>
> 'That's right. Good positive dreams, they mean something, and negative dreams don't mean anything!' We laugh at his irony like we used to when sitting in his dorm room. And he continues: 'That's our intuitive way of interpreting dreams.' But then he gets serious: 'No, well, one has to be able to distinguish between things in dreams. You can practise this… You know, there is some knowledge about dreams that is good to have: to be able to distinguish between things and recognise different symbols, to be able to interpret… You know, the classic case is when I dream about you, it isn't really about you. If I have a dream that you are dead, then you are not really dead. It is not a

warning that... Then it is something that you symbolise. It's the same with everything that takes place in a dream. Roughly speaking. Things symbolise other things...'

Having heard nothing about such aspects of dreams in scientific psychology, I keep pressing on and pose a new sceptical question: 'How would you answer the question: How do you know that those things do symbolise something? How do you know that because you have a dream that you have lived before, that this is actually the case?' Thomas looks me directly in the eyes and quickly says: 'Then I would pose the mean counter-question: How do you know that you love your children? This isn't written down anywhere. Basically. How do you know it? That kind of love cannot be put into a test tube and be measured. But you know that it's there and how big it is.'

I think about this, and sense some kind of faulty logic, but before I can reply he continues: 'Well, in fact my best answer is not this counter-question, but it is: because I *feel* it. I am never 100 per cent sure, right, about how to understand or feel a dream. And you are never 100 per cent sure about how you feel. But you can be fairly sure that something means one thing or another.'

This, I think while we are talking, confirms one of my main objections to spirituality: things are taken as true because people *feel* that they are true. It seems to me that this could license all sorts of strange, irrational or unethical beliefs and could justify just about anything. This becomes a recurring theme in our conversation, for example when Thomas later tells me about Tantra and two cosmic axes that structure his metaphysics (a horizontal one between 'romance' and 'pornography' and another vertical one between the 'beastly' and the 'angelic' – to use his own words).

'How do you know that this is what the world looks like?' I ask him.

'It boils down to feeling it', he answers, 'I feel that it's right. And those things on the top [on the angelic end of the axis], I feel a longing for them.'

We keep talking about metaphysics, including his theory that each human being has a prescribed 'assignment', as he says – some job in our life that we need to do. This is totally alien to my much more existentialist leanings – that we create our own lives together. But in spite of my reservations, I am also struck by ambivalence, since there is a certain aesthetic appeal to the cosmology described by Thomas. It is an enchanted cosmology of energies, past lives and symbols that depicts the world as an exciting, vibrant and multi-layered reality. But I am notably struck by the fact that an educated person, a psychologist who once thought otherwise, can believe in these things, and not just as a hobby, but as something that structures his everyday existence and has become perhaps the most important thing in his life. How did this happen?

A personal process of development

In the final half of our conversation, we move from metaphysical and religious issues to more personal issues that have to do with Thomas's personal process of development. I try to formulate my understanding of him as in some respects the same person that I knew and at the same time as someone who has changed fundamentally.

'One of the things that are fascinating to me about your situation', I say, 'is that – and I may be very wrong here – but at least before I came here, it seemed to me that the world of Tiger's Nest is a world of systems, among other things. That there are some beliefs, some things that you have to agree with. That you are not supposed to rebel against.'

'Right.'

'There are some articles of faith, there are different rituals, and what do I know? Some things that you ought to do, *must* do and so on. And I cannot reconcile this with...', I hesitate and try to find the proper way of saying it.

'With me?', Thomas helps out.

'Yes, with you as the rather rebellious anarchist who just does what he feels like doing.'

Thomas thinks for a second and replies in a perfectly logical manner: 'Yes, but it can be reconciled through the fact that it has turned out, for ten years now, that this is what I have felt like doing the whole time. If some day, I don't want to do it anymore, I am out of here, you know. But this goes deep into me that it's, well, it's really a feeling of coming home. So it probably won't happen. Then it would have to be because I moved away from home, so to speak. But I feel that I have come home where I belong. In that way, I don't have to change in relation to being rebellious and intuitive... Because I feel like this all the time. It feels intuitively right. I have merged with it.'

'Can you describe your own development?' I ask. 'I mean, what has happened to you? From then to now?'

'Right, in those ten years?'

'Yes.'

'Yes. Mmm.' Thomas changes position on his sofa before continuing. 'A huge, significant, central thing in the development process is that, shortly after I came here, moved here in 2001, and it could be seen already in the first course I took, there were some signs... It was the fact that I began as Tantra partner with Anne Sophie, who runs this place.'

'Yes...', I respond, practising the non-directional style of interviewing to the best of my abilities...

'I began doing this in 2001, when I moved here. I had no idea. When I came here. That I was going to be *that*. That it was in the air. It's like when you don't know that there is someone that you are in love with. And then we started doing that, and it lasted for four and a half years, and so many things happened in that period, which are still in a sense the primary things in my life, mmm, in my process.'

'Yes.'

'And it lasted for four and a half years until 2005 and then we stopped, and shortly after I began with Astrid [his current wife]. And then a different life began. And this is the life I still live. But you can say that it is basically still centred on the first one, with Anne Sophie, and the relationship I had with her. The contact we built then... in many ways it is that contact that I still live on or use or... It is what I realise. And you can say that the tantric relationship with

Anne Sophie, which lasted around half the time I have been here, right, in that phase it was the inner that was put into place. That became realised or opened. That was found. And now it is the outer.'

I am intrigued by this love story and ask about how it ended.

'It stopped', Thomas explains, 'because our relationship was like a process that played out *through* us. A little bit like what I said before about a plan that I hadn't written down myself. So there were some things that we had to go through. That's what we felt. And the only thing we could do was destroying the process. Those learning processes that I had to go through, and that she had to go through, they were shared. And all processes have endings. If not, they are not processes. I believe.' He smiles and adds that the teacher–student relationship has continued, 'Just not as physically close. But it simply ended when the assignment was completed.'

Thomas describes his meeting with Anne Sophie as a defining moment in his life. It is what Denzin (following James Joyce) calls an epiphany (see e.g. Denzin, 2001a), an existential moment or turning point in a life. In such moments, Denzin tells us, 'personal character is manifested and made apparent' (p. 34). Thomas's description is strong and vivid, but my trouble as we talk is related to the fact that the epiphany implied a certain submissive attitude that I found hard to associate with Thomas as I knew him. I felt, perhaps, that he had betrayed, through this submission, what I admired most about him. When listening to the conversation and reading the transcript now, I see that I clearly struggle to find remnants of his rebellious attitude to life in him, and it is obvious from the conversation that I try to invite him into a specific self-understanding, which he himself has worked to leave behind for several years. He has been in a 'process' (a word that he is using consistently throughout our conversation to refer to the task of self-development in a certain direction) for years, which has transformed him on the inside as well as on the outside (to use his preferred terminology). He describes this process in terms of a preordained plan, which he simply had to follow. This, I find, is very different from my own philosophy of existence, but I cannot avoid feeling a little bit envious of someone who is able to interpret his life in this way.

Interpreting a life

My psychologically informed interpretation of Thomas's life, as he articulates it in our conversation, is one of a young man in search of a worthwhile direction in life, who came across a system of symbolic resources that afforded a certain kind of self-interpretation, with a community and a number of collective social practices attached. Anne Sophie's charismatic personality and the appealing metaphysics of Tiger's Nest made possible a life that was at once exciting and quite well-ordered. What many of us are looking for today, I conjecture, are

symbolic resources that enable us to distinguish between more and less important moments in our lives. Symbolic resources are cultural elements (like pictures,
books and films) that are part of symbolic systems. Traditionally, these have been
handed down from one generation to the next, particularly as part of religious
traditions and practices (e.g. as crystallised in the Bible), but in today's post-
traditional social reality, people must to some extent act as bricoleurs and construct their own identity on the basis of the resources they can find and put
together. Even if they, like Thomas, experience things as happening according to
a plan that they did not design for themselves.

In a well-known analysis, MacIntyre (1985) has described this situation specifically with regard to morality, which he sees as collapsing into emotivism. MacIntyre
depicted an emotivist self that can only evaluate life possibilities on the basis of
feelings. In some ways, I interpret Thomas's self-descriptions as emotivist, since his
choices, on the face of it, are guided explicitly (and solely) by what he feels is right
for him. On this interpretation, the solidity of his conduct rests only on the perma-
nence of his feelings. His life has woven together themes from religion, spirituality,
and also psychology. In one way, Thomas has resisted the disenchanting 'everywher-
eness of psychology' (Jarzombek, 2000) by making use of spirituality and the transcendent in leading his life. Yet, in another way, the spirituality of Tiger's Nest – if
stripped of its metaphysics – comes very close to the psychologies of self-realisation
and human potential movements as found, for example, at the Esalen Institute in
California (where the idea of being 'in process' is also emphasised).

Nevertheless, my secularist and psychological interpretation is, of course, quite
at odds with his own. According to Thomas, he has simply come home. There
is something he is meant to do in this life, and his assignment became obvious
to him upon first meeting the teacher and later tantric partner, Anne Sophie.
Our different interpretations converge, however, on the issue that the way he
lives his life now answers to a need for something. But while Thomas will invoke
the transcendent in order to explain this need, I have resorted to psychological explanations about a need for meaning and community. Who has the best
account? It seems impossible to say, since we do not look at life from the same
set of premises. What is frustrating to me is that ten years ago, we seemed to
share such premises, perspectives and vocabularies. A lesson to learn from this,
I believe, is that we should stop looking for *one* correct interpretation – in life as
well as in qualitative inquiry (which are two sides of the same coin anyway, at
least according to the philosophy of the present book). Instead, and in a more
pragmatic spirit, we should ask what kinds of experiences and possibilities for
action are opened up if we choose to conduct our lives based on one rather than
another interpretation of existence.

Needless to say, this is a lesson that hermeneutic philosophy has long been
trying to teach us, but it remains difficult to practise in one's own life. From a

methodological viewpoint, I believe that engaging in the conversation with Thomas, and deliberately allowing myself a confrontational style as interviewer–friend, was helpful concerning knowledge production. Contra the established 'wisdom' in much qualitative psychology and research interviewing, I made my own views obvious to him. I did not try to fake an understanding of something that I didn't understand or act as a neutral mirror of his narratives and descriptions. Rather than visiting the community with a silent, accepting attitude – only to objectify and dissect their beliefs and practices later in an analytic process – I have made my own reservations and criticisms clear in the conversational process itself, objecting to his ideas whenever I found it necessary. Returning to Figure 5.1, my conversational role was thus more on the assertive side, with some kind of epistemic ambition. I hope that this made the process ethically sound, and, in any case, I am certain that it facilitated the dialogue and gave it a Socratic edge, which implied examining and testing our views.

Like the conversation partners in many Platonic dialogues, however, the dialogue ended without any final, unarguable agreement or shared definitions. This lack of resolution – *aporia* in Greek – should not be lamented, but can be interpreted as illustrating the open-ended character of human social and historical life, including the open-ended character of the discursively produced knowledge of life generated by qualitative inquiry. To use the popular terms of social constructionist metatheory, the goal is not to end the conversation in a settled and frozen account, but to 'continue the conversation'. Such conversation is also with oneself, as a writer. In writing this piece, I have chosen to insert my own writing self into the text. This explains the rather confessional beginning, which I believe is important in order to understand where I am coming from in asking my questions. Interviews are literally inter-views (between views) and we have to address both sides of the between-views in order to understand the conversational process.

Concluding comments on the conversation

So what have I learned from my postsecular lesson? I have not acquired an enchanted metaphysics that I can teach my children. I still believe that talk of reincarnation, cosmic energy and healing is strange and something from which I am deeply alienated. But I have come some way towards understanding how someone I knew and liked a lot could acquire a spiritual worldview and lifestyle. Upon seeing Thomas with his wife and daughter, I am reminded of the pragmatist dictum that there cannot *be* a difference that doesn't *make* a difference. We hold different beliefs, but I am not so sure that they make much of a difference to how we live our lives. For his life – I mean what he does, how he relates to his wife and daughter, etc. – seems not so different from mine, in spite of our different beliefs.

Concluding comments on the chapter

In this chapter, I have described different ways of thinking about the research interview. These may inspire us to think anew about how to use some of the conversations we conduct in our everyday life as knowledge-producing activities. I have advocated in particular a Socratic mode of conversation, given the idea that knowing is a dialogical activity that involves objections, confrontations and sometimes outright disagreement. These often spring from breakdowns in understanding. I have tried to illustrate these ideas with the example of my conversation with my friend. It is impossible to say whether this was a conversation among friends about existential issues or a research interview, and this is precisely the point of everyday life research – that there is no sharp line between life and research.

The project in this chapter of developing the epistemic potentials of conversations in everyday life is allied, I believe, with other recent explorations of alternative interview forms, for example Norman Denzin's (2001b) idea of performance interviews in the 'cinematic-interview society'. Denzin formulates 'a utopian project', searching for a new form of the interview, which he calls 'the reflexive, dialogic, or performative interview' (p. 24). Qualitative researchers are increasingly becoming aware that interviewing, as Charles Briggs (2003, p. 497) has argued, is 'a "technology" that invents both notions of individual subjectivities and collective social and political patterns'. Different conversational practices, including research interviews, produce and activate different forms of subjectivity. Thus, ethico-political issues are always internal to practices of interviewing. Epistemic conversations in everyday life position the conversation partners as accountable, responsible citizens, which can be presented as an alternative to experience-focused, psychologised research interviews that position respondents more as clients or patients.

I have argued that knowledge is a normative concept and that a basic interpersonal attitude in human encounters is one of meeting others as accountable agents that can give reasons for their actions, feelings, and beliefs. Not that people can always do so, of course (often we have trouble coming up with reasons for our beliefs), but most people have at least the important ethical and political potential to engage in such conversations. I tried to practise this in the encounter with Thomas. In what I have called epistemic conversations, the analysis is in principle carried out *in* the conversation, together with the accountable respondents involved, since the analysis mainly consists of testing, questioning and justifying what people say. This also explains why I have reported rather long extracts from the conversation without many analytic interjections. Epistemic conversations involve a co-construction of conversational reality *in situ*. Also in this regard, Socrates is my source of inspiration, and the classical dialogues with him are reported without Plato's interjections. If I should depict my encounter with Thomas in terms of the six steps that I have formulated in this book, it would look something like this:

1 *Choose a topic.* I chose religion and spirituality because I experienced a breakdown in my secular understanding of these phenomena. How can we understand the cultural conditions of postsecularism?
2 *Collect materials.* My contact with Thomas, and the conversation we had, became my way of collecting empirical materials. I recorded about two hours on my sound recorder and transcribed most of the conversation that we conducted.
3 *Consult the literature.* I read about postsecularism, but also a little bit about the religious traditions that inspire Thomas's religious community. These readings enabled me to focus on particular issues in our conversation.
4 *Continue collecting materials.* I sent my preliminary analyses to Thomas, who gave his comments, and these comments influenced the way I continued analysing.
5 *Do analytic writing.* This consisted in particular of writing myself into the text. In order to understand why the issue of secularism and spirituality was pressing for me, and led to a breakdown in understanding, I had to include my own biography. This topic thus presented itself as a chance to use Mills' sociological imagination to understand what is happening in 'the intersections of biography and history within society' (Mills, 1959, p. 7). In terms of analytic strategy, what I did come closest to was making the obvious dubious. It was obvious to me that spirituality was foolish. Could an epistemic encounter with a spiritual person challenge this obviousness? And could I challenge Thomas's choices in life? I did not want to deconstruct Thomas's choices, or interpret them in light of psychoanalytic theory, for example, but rather to question his and my own worldviews dialectically, which involved revealing my own vulnerabilities and insecurities concerning what to believe and do in this life.
6 *Publish your text.* This I have done in the present book, but I am also in the process of developing the piece into a journal article. Writing, like life itself, is a continuous process that comes in many versions.

EXERCISE

Clearly, there is no 'method' as such in using everyday conversations for research purposes (just as there is no 'method' for how to conduct a conversation with your friends). Qualitative researchers should be alert to details of the conversations that they participate in (cf. the Sano and Enfermada example), but they could also intentionally create conversational situations of inquiry (cf. my meeting with Thomas).

Some suggestions for how to proceed in this vein are brought forth in the following exercise:

- Think of a problem that bothers you. It may have to do with racism, how to raise a child, procrastination or whatever. Find someone who has experienced what you are interested in and ask if they can help you learn more about the problem so that you can find your way about.
- Then use your conversational capabilities to inquire into the issue. You may record the conversation, transcribe it, and work analytically as in standard research interviews. Or you may stick to taking notes. After the conversation, write a summary (and perhaps transcribe the words) of what happened. Try out different ways of interpreting the text, using any conceptual or theoretical resource you think is relevant.
- You should then show your preliminary analysis to your conversation partner and listen carefully to her reaction. You may choose to construct a co-authored text, or you may stick to taking the conversation partner's comments into account when finalising the piece. After this, show your analysis to colleagues and friends, revise and possibly submit it to a journal that is known to be open to this way of working.
- Alternatively, you can think of a conversation that stuck in your mind. It could be a conversation that changed your life (an epiphany) or just something that bothered you without you knowing why (e.g. 'why was I offended by that remark?'). Ask yourself what made what happened possible. What historical, discursive and cultural practices were necessary for this event to occur? What biographical backgrounds can be invoked to explain the event? What are the general – human, social – features of the event?

SIX
Media materials

Like many other people in the Western world, I'm a news junkie. As I write these words, there has recently been a tsunami and a nuclear disaster in Japan, there are riots in many North African countries, and fighter jets from my own country (Denmark) have just gone to war against Gaddafi in Libya. I have Japanese friends on Facebook, who inform me of the latest developments in their country, and I am capable of reaching people I know in many parts of the world through the internet. Major events, like those I just described, may warrant spending time watching news on television, listening to news on the radio and constantly searching the internet for updates on my favourite blogs and news sites, but my habits are more or less the same even when the news is not full of such dramatic stories. And I suspect that things are similar for many others. We consume media stories like never before, and the enormous quantity of media continuously compete for our attention.

We can add to this that many modern media not only present news to consumers, unilaterally, but also invite people into participating in discussions about what happens in the world, locally, nationally and internationally, and how we should react to, and think about, whatever happens. In short, the media have become interactive. And they are not just interactive in the sense that messages go back and forth between users and media, or between user and user mediated by internet sites, but they are more properly designated as *transactional* (Dewey & Bentley, 1949), which means that all parties are affected in the process. Print newspapers have always had sections of letters to the editor, but this is radicalised on the internet media where consumers of media stories presumably are always right and are given voices (but, alas, often lack what is called 'netiquette' or internet etiquette). These voices shape the stories that are subsequently publicised in quasi-democratic fashion (consumerist democracy), and the people who comment are presumably influenced by what they read and write.

Different social media, such as Facebook (a social networking site) or *Second Life* (a simulated reality), are also used by millions of people every day. It is estimated that Facebook has around 800 million users worldwide (as of November 2011), which is more than a tenth of the planet's total population. The new social media have transformed our everyday lives: human relationships, how we fall in love (through the numerous dating sites), how we work (e.g. when people work from home – as I often do – connected to colleagues and others through the media) and how we acquire knowledge (think of the importance of Wikis and Google for our knowledge of so many things – and of how the media shape *how* we come to know them). Some people act as if the only kind of knowledge that exists is textual knowledge, as represented on the internet, and this even sometimes goes for self-knowledge, resulting in what sociologist Eva Illouz has called a 'textualization of subjectivity': 'a mode of self-apprehension in which the self is externalized and objectified through visual means of representations and language' (Illouz, 2007, p. 78). Just think of how we construct ourselves through the information we write about who we are on Facebook or dating sites. This, unsurprisingly, is a favourite research topic among my students.

The internet tends to make the self into a commodity on public display (Illouz, 2007, p. 79), resulting in selves that are quite literally materialised and amenable to analysis in the shape of what was called Self 2 in Chapter 4, the self as an object, but also as Self 3, the self as taken up by others. For who we are on the internet is to a very large extent determined by how others react to us. If the dramaturgical perspective of Goffman is suitable for analysing human life and interactions as lived on a stage, it is less useful for studying the human world as a library, gallery or exhibition (Horgan, 2010). And this is how the self is often constructed on the internet: as a kind of exhibition, an artefact that is the result not of a live performance, but of a past construction. What Horgan calls 'the self as exhibition' is still a form of presentation of self (along the lines described by Goffman), but it is one that understands the agent more as a *curator* than as an *actor*.

It is reasonable to conclude from these scattered descriptions that media in many forms are omnipresent in our everyday lives. Much of our everyday life is lived on the screen (Turkle, 1997), and it is necessary to turn this central aspect of humanity into an object in qualitative studies if one wants a full understanding of everyday life (Markham, 2005). In our medialised world, human experience is co-constructed through the stories that circulate in the different media and by the symbolic resources that are offered there, which afford certain kinds of self-interpretation. The mass media have the power to focus our attention on specific topics rather than others, and they can even be involved in large-scale political changes, as we witnessed early in 2011 in several North African and Arab countries (although the exact impact of social media have been questioned in this context). The mass media should consequently be an object of attention for all qualitative researchers (and not just media researchers). Through the media, our social imaginaries are formed, and it is often through media stories that we are socialised into specific patterns of thinking and feeling (Brinkmann, 2010).

In this chapter, I will first give an introduction to the mass media and how to conduct qualitative analyses of the media materials that saturate our everyday lives. Then I will look specifically at the internet and consider some ways of doing qualitative inquiry that addresses this form of medialised reality. Finally, I will present a piece of everyday life research that addresses a news story that caught my attention a couple of years ago, and which was much discussed in Denmark. This was the public confession of the former elite cyclist Bjarne Riis that he had used performance-enhancing drugs in his career, and I will use this to discuss what we can learn about everyday life issues related to guilt and shame if we focus on medialised constructions of such emotions.

The mass media

A medium is 'any social or technological procedure or device that is used for the selection, transmission, and reception of information' (Altheide, 2003, p. 657). All cultures employ media to store and transmit information, but the main media of the modern world are newspapers, radio, television and the internet. These are all *mass* media since they permit communication to large audiences that can be said to make up a public sphere. I will address television more specifically in the next chapter on audiovisual materials, and in this chapter I will concentrate on news media, including internet media. With the mass media, people are able to communicate with others around the globe, at least those of us who have access to the relevant technologies, and we should always bear in mind that there are many people in the world who do not have access to the electronic media.

From a critical interpretative perspective, Denzin has outlined four goals of the mass media as an entire complex in our culture:

> The prime goals of the mass media complex are fourfold, to create audiences who (1) become consumers of the products advertised in the media, while (2) engaging in consumption practices that conform to the norms of possessive individualism endorsed by the capitalist political system, and (3) adhering to a public opinion that is supportive of the strategic policies of the state [...]. The fourth goal of the media is clear, to do everything it can to make consumers as audience members think they are not commodities. (Denzin, 2003, pp. 1000–1001)

According to this critical perspective, the mass media work by subjectifying people as consumers and even commodities, while simultaneously covering over this very function by making people believe that they are free to choose. Denzin seems to think that a form of possessive individualism is built into the mass media, and although this may be a valid analysis in some cases, I believe it is too general. I have already mentioned the fact that mass media can, in certain cases, be used for political purposes that clearly serve functions other than supporting an ideology of possessive individualism. In my view, the mass media serve as many different functions as human interaction and communication themselves do. For all communication is mediated, whether it be by spoken or written language or sign language. And it is surely an impossible task to make an exhaustive list of the functions of human communication since interaction and communication make up the very fabric of our social life.

On a more theoretical note, communication can be considered as the mediating link between human minds and the material world. This was spelled out by C. Wright Mills, who argued as follows:

> The consciousness of human beings does not determine their existence; nor does their existence determine their consciousness. Between the human consciousness and material existence stand communications, and designs, patterns, and values which influence decisively such consciousness as they have. (Mills, 1963, p. 375)

Following Mills, Denzin (2003) approaches the mass media as having the task of making this 'second-hand world' of communications, values, etc. natural, but also invisible, to its participants. This invisibility makes it highly relevant to employ the strategies of making the obvious obvious, the hidden obvious, or the obvious dubious (cf. Chapter 1).

Like never before in history, humans are now capable of accessing and negotiating the symbolic resources that affect their lives when they circulate in the media. Bearing the ontological triangle in mind (cf. Figure 2.1), the media are of course *experienced* and can be studied as such (there is a kind of lived experience to 'life on the screen', for example), but they also represent spheres of *discourse* that are extremely important in today's world, and the symbolic resources that they contain (e.g. a profile on Facebook) represent some of the most significant *objects* in the self-understanding of many of us. As always, researching everyday life using media materials can be approached from any of the legs in the ontological triangle. Like postmodern life itself, our medialised world is a chaotic, heterogeneous and fascinating web of symbols and stories without a centre. If the human world once had a centre in premodern times (e.g. a deity) and also in modern times (the human mind or rationality), any conception of a centre must be given up today, and instead we must think of the social as a set of networks and practices with the mass media as arguably its most important materialisation. These networks criss-cross in any individual's everyday life and can be researched from within the first-person everyday life perspective.

How does one study such chaotic processes? One option is to follow standard methodological guidelines such as those articulated by the media scholar David Altheide (1996). I have summarised his step-wise approach in Box 6.1.

BOX 6.1

A standard procedure in media research

Altheide (1996) suggests breaking down the research process into discrete steps: (1) pursue a specific problem to be investigated, (2) become familiar with the process and context of the information source (e.g. newspapers), (3) become familiar with several examples of relevant documents (perhaps six to ten), (4) draw a list of categories – a protocol – that will guide your data collection, (5) test the protocol by collecting data from several documents, (6) revise the protocol, (7) arrive at a sampling strategy, (8) do the actual data collection, using preset codes, (9) perform data analysis, including conceptual refinement and data coding, (10) write summaries of data for each category and do comparisons, e.g. between 'extremes', within the pool of data, (11) combine these summaries with examples of typical as well as extreme instances, (12) integrate findings, interpretations and key concepts in a draft text – and then you should be ready to publish!

Readers who are interested in representative large-scale studies of how a given phenomenon is represented in the mass media would be wise to follow something like the procedure made explicit by Altheide. But, as should be clear by now, the present book advocates a different approach, namely one that begins not with 'a specific problem' that can be made explicit, but rather with a breakdown in one's understanding of something in everyday life. If, for example, you stumble on a news story that surprises you, but you do not know exactly why, then you could proceed according to the approach suggested in this book. Personally, I was puzzled upon witnessing the confession of Bjarne Riis that he had used drugs as an active cyclist (to be analysed below). It surprised me that this event became one of the biggest news stories in Denmark in 2007, and I also found my own fascination with the story curious. Why did it catch everyone's attention – including mine? This prompted me to take a closer look at what this was all about, and you can read the resulting analysis in the final part of this chapter.

In general, using media materials rather than other kinds of everyday life materials that are addressed in this book does not demand specific research procedures. Of course, there are some unique properties of media materials, but the ways of interpreting and analysing the materials are similar. One advantage of using media materials, especially those found on the internet, is that they are

---

often very easy to capture and store (e.g. on a computer). The internet presents qualitative researchers with fascinating opportunities to seek 'unsolicited narratives' and other kinds of data that can easily be found on web pages, blogs or online newspapers (Evans, Elford, & Wiggins, 2008). On the other hand, however, there are also unique ethical challenges related to using such unsolicited materials for one's research purposes, for how does one obtain informed consent and how does one, as a researcher, respect people's privacy? These questions should, in my view, be carefully considered, and just because something has been made public on the internet does not, as I see it, give researchers *carte blanche* to do whatever they want with the materials. In the next section, I look more specifically at how to use the internet in qualitative everyday life inquiries.

The internet and social media

A couple of years ago, when the virtual world of *Second Life* was being hyped by numerous internet experts, I supervised a Master's student in psychology, Maria Virhøj Madsen, who did an online autoethnography in this virtual world. At the time, I was new to both internet-based research and also authoethnography, so it was a significant learning experience for me. Some of Maria's research is summarised in Box 6.2.

BOX 6.2

Second Life – an online autoethnography

When Maria did her research, it was estimated that *Second Life* had at least 7 million 'inhabitants' in the form of so-called avatars that are controlled by users. Avatars can move about, interact with others, chat and join different communities. Maria did her research in *Second Life* as she would have done in any other ethnographic setting. She did participant observation and recorded a large number of interviews with other individuals. She had had no particular experiences with online communities beforehand, so she chose to use techniques from autoethnography, which meant writing from her own perspective and depicting her own experiences.

In the course of her online fieldwork, Maria very much grew into her virtual character, the avatar. She describes, for example, how she began to take her avatar and made it hide behind a tree or a house whenever she wanted to change the clothes of the avatar (Madsen, 2007, p. 38). She discovers that a certain natural shyness is conferred on to her virtual self, even if she has no real status to lose in *Second Life* and is unacquainted with the 'real selves' of the other avatars. Some of her

---

interviews with others indicate that this experience is shared by others (in the quote below, SL means *Second Life*, RL is Real Life and 'an av' is an avatar):

Maria: Funny that an av can be shy
Ashton nods
Ashton: I'm afraid to dance, even on SL
Maria: Really? Well, I'm still nervous about what to wear
Ashton: Even crowds still scare me [chuckles]
Maria: It's not 100% possible to escape from RL
Ashton smiles
Ashton: Yeah, but I think that is a good thing
Ashton: People would lose their humanity I think
Maria: Absolutely!
Ashton: Funny, this coming from a furry;)

Ashton is a furry, which is a kind of avatar that was quite popular and was characterised by a mix of human and animal qualities.

Maria developed quite close relationships with her key informants and, as a future psychologist, she was interested in the psychological dynamics of *Second Life*. Among other things, she participated in (virtual) group therapies and discovered that many people seemed to benefit from living much of their life through *Second Life*, in particular people who are shy or even suffer from social phobia, but also deaf people and people with cerebral palsy.

The study that I have briefly described in Box 6.2 is an example of everyday life research that has been successfully carried out. I consider this an example of this book's approach, since Maria would likely have joined *Second Life* anyway, as many other young people did at the time, and she was courageous enough to turn her initiation into this world into a research project. She found inspiration in the literature on autoethnography and her careful descriptions of the experiences she had with others in this world are well worth reading, and although they are based on a single person's voice and perspective, they nonetheless give a very useful general sense of what *Second Life* is and what possibilities and problems this virtual world contains.

If we are looking for more specific advice on how to do internet research than what we can find in the general literature on fieldwork and autoethnography, we may consult Annette Markham on online ethnography (Markham, 2005). Markham argues that a number of issues that are specifically relevant in online research must be considered (pp. 801–808):

- One should be particularly careful to define the boundaries of the field. Unlike normal ethnographic work, where one can normally draw a boundary quite easily, whether we are talking about an organisation or a tribe, it is difficult to determine boundaries online. We must go from geographic to discursive boundaries. The internet is a 'hyperlinked' world, where it is tempting to constantly expand the intertextual field, as it is often quite easy to see which other texts a given text draws upon (and it may even be marked with a concrete hyperlink). Using the internet, then, demands a certain kind of discipline and a skill of knowing when to stop the intertextual description.

- One should also be careful in determining what constitutes one's data. The computer-mediated communication that is taking place with research participants through the internet tends to separate the wholeness of a person into parts, and this may be useful for some research purposes but less so for others.
- Following from this, one should reflect on what it means that we are interpreting others through their text, as we can read it on the screen. In internet research we are often confronted with a textualisation of subjectivity in a very concrete sense. The sense of being with others and experiencing through joint action with others is severely diminished and disembodied. However, there can also be advantages in escaping the confines of embodied social markers, to engage in a form of 'meeting of the minds' (Markham, 2005, p. 808). Such issues cannot be resolved once and for all, but it is important that one considers the 'stuff', the relationships and the material and semiotic resources that enable specific events and materials to appear online.

Empirical example: A confession in the mass media

To illustrate how one can work with a very small amount of empirical media materials and still say something topical about the social world, I will now turn to an example. It has been published as a journal article (Brinkmann, 2010), and is an analysis of the medialised confession of the 1996 winner of the Tour de France, Bjarne Riis, that he had used performance-enhancing drugs as an active cyclist. This is a piece of everyday life research in the sense that I witnessed the actual event on television and later acquired the transcribed confessional speech, which together constitute the materials that I analysed. My main interest concerns human emotions, in particular guilt, and its status in a postmodern culture. I thus begin with some remarks about guilt as an emotion before moving on to the mass media event itself.

Guilt and the emotional landscape of postmodernity

According to the leading sociologist of postmodernity, Zygmunt Bauman (2007), the culture of contemporary Western societies leads to a diminishing importance of guilt as an emotion. Bauman argues that this is due to some recent changes in how we evaluate different life strategies. In the past, he claims, we evaluated life strategies in relation to an antinomy of the allowed and the forbidden, whereas we now tend to orient ourselves according to an opposition between the possible and the impossible (p. 94). When considering how we ought to live our lives, the primary question is no longer 'What *ought* I to do in order to live up to the norms?' but rather 'What *possibilities* do I have of realising my preferences?'

Bauman relates this change in mentality to society's change from industrial society to consumer society. In consumer society, rules, norms, and values have become *fluid* or *liquid* (to use Bauman's favourite metaphor), which makes it difficult to determine when they are broken. Almost by definition, one cannot break what is fluid. In earlier times, rules, norms, and values were more solid, and only things of some solidity can be broken. According to Bauman, the change from solidity to fluidity has given us new dominant pathologies: 'human sufferings nowadays tend to grow from a surfeit of *possibilities*, rather than from a profusion of *prohibitions*, as they used to in the past' (Bauman, 2007, p. 94; italics in original). This has consequences for our understandings of guilt. For it means:

> that depression arising from the terror of *inadequacy* will replace the neurosis caused by the horror of *guilt* (that is, of the charge of *nonconformity* that might follow a breach in the rules) as the most characteristic and widespread psychological affliction of the denizens of the society of consumers. (Bauman, 2007, p. 94; italics in original)

Consequently, 'I cannot keep up' is replacing 'I want too much' as a central life problem. Exhaustion is replacing guilt, fear of inadequacy is replacing fear of non-conformity, and depression is replacing neuroses as a dominant social pathology. Unsurprisingly, this is also reflected in our (applied) psychologies, where cognitive therapy and stress management are to a large extent replacing psychoanalysis as iconic therapies. Psychoanalysis would help you *adjust* – cognitive therapy (stress management, coaching, etc.) will help you *keep up*.

Guilt as an emotion is interesting in this context for at least two reasons. First, it seems pertinent to ask if Bauman's diagnosis is really correct. Is guilt really losing in importance and is it possibly even withering away in favour of a feeling of inadequacy (leading to depression)? Are Western societies no longer dominated by a 'culture of guilt' (Benedict, 1946)? An answer to these questions can help us assess just how fluidly postmodern we have become. Secondly, by definition, guilt is connected to a breach (real or imagined) in shared norms and rules, and this means that investigating guilt as an emotion can be a significant probe into the moral order of a culture. How does this emotion manifest itself, and what are people's grounds for feeling guilty today? Answers to such questions can surely be approached from within our everyday lives, and yet inform us of larger social processes. For the feeling of guilt is arguably the most central criterion that one has transgressed the moral order, and, if so, the experience of guilt can serve to mark the morality of a culture.

Emotions in general can be said to embody the moral values, thoughts and judgements of a culture, which is why emotions represent an excellent source of knowledge about larger social wholes:

> most emotions reflect – to a greater or lesser extent – the thought of an epoch, the secret of a civilization. It follows that to understand the meaning of an

emotion is to understand the relevant aspects of the sociocultural systems of which the emotion is a part. (Averill, 1982, p. 24)

And conversely, moral values and ideals can only be upheld in a culture if they resonate emotionally in individuals. Emotions, ideals, and the moral order are deeply interrelated. Guilt plays a central role here, since it is something one can feel if one has the experience of being the source of some wrongdoing, relative to a local moral order. Guilt need not ensue in such situations (there is no direct, mechanical link involved), but there is at least a normative reason to feel guilt. Other emotions can also accompany the experience of having acted wrongly. One can be angry with oneself, be embarrassed, or shameful. But I believe that guilt is primary, for if one becomes angry with oneself in such a situation, it is *because* one did something that elicited guilt, and not the other way around (unless, of course, it was the very display of anger that constituted a breach in the shared norms).

Most (if not all) of us know what it is like to feel guilt. The phenomenology of guilt involves a combination of an empathic, distressful condition, where one shares the discomfort or suffering of another, with an attribution of the responsibility for the discomfort or suffering to oneself (Baumeister, Stillwell, & Heatherton, 1994). Thus, if my friend is suffering from the consequences of a divorce, I may feel compassion (indeed, I have a *reason* to feel compassion), but if the divorce was the result of my extramarital affair with my friend's wife, I have in addition a reason to feel guilt. Guilt is rooted in human connectedness, and feeling and expressing guilt is a way of manifesting care for others and an attempt to restore interpersonal bonds that may have been broken. If guilt is connected to moral transgressions, we can approach this emotion as perhaps the most significant probe into the moral experiences that are prevalent in a culture. I shall do so in what follows through the theoretical lenses of positioning theory that I have explicated in Box 6.3. We met positioning theory in the previous chapter, but in this context it will operate more systematically as a toolkit of theoretical concepts that are supposed to sensitise the researcher to certain aspects of the social process (this toolkit can also be applied to many other human and social phenomena, including some of those that are addressed in other ways in this book).

BOX 6.3

Positioning theory

Positioning theory is a recent variety of discursive psychology that was originally developed as a dynamic alternative to sociological theories that stress roles and rules (Davies & Harré, 1999). Rather than invoking static roles that determine how

---

individuals act, positioning theory argues that the concept of positioning can bring forth the dynamic and changeable aspects of social life, where discourses are seen as offering subject positions that individuals may take up – or may be forced into. Instead of reified social structures or transcendent rules allegedly governing social life, positioning theory argues that 'rules are explicit formulations of the normative order which is immanent in concrete human productions' (p. 33). Humans may act in ways that can often be described by rules, but, according to positioning theorists (who follow Wittgenstein on this point), this does not mean that they follow rules in acting (Brinkmann, 2007b).

A particularly clear account of its main tenets is given by Harré and Moghaddam (2003), often summarized as 'the positioning triangle' of (1) position, (2) storyline, and (3) acts:

1 A *position* is defined as 'a cluster of rights and duties to perform certain actions with a certain significance as acts, but which also may include prohibitions or denials of access to some of the local repertoire of meaningful acts' (Harré & Moghaddam, 2003, pp. 5–6). In every social context, practice or situation, there exists a realm of positions in which people are located, and such positions are inescapably moral (Harré & van Langenhove, 1999), in the sense of involving 'oughts'. If I am positioned as the leader of the expedition, I *ought* to guide the participants to the best of my abilities. This is what it means to lead the expedition. Positions consist of rights to do certain things, to act in specific ways, and also of (moral) duties to be taken up and acted upon in specific ways. In virtue of his or her position, a teacher will normally be positioned as someone with a duty to arrange situations that will help pupils or students learn and develop. Learners, conversely, and in virtue of their respective positions, can be said to have a right to be taught, and a duty to respect the institution of schooling.

2 Positioning theorists argue that social life displays an order that can be described by norms and established patterns of development, and such patterns have come to be known as *storylines*, typically 'expressible in a loose cluster of narrative conventions' (Harré & Moghaddam, 2003, p. 6). Sometimes participants in a social episode disagree on which storyline is unfolding. If a man is opening a door for a woman, the man may interpret the event according to a storyline of gentlemanly behaviour and civility, whereas the woman may interpret the event as one involving male chauvinism that positions the woman as weak and in need of male protection. Like other forms of social constructionism, positioning theory emphasises the vague, ambiguous, and negotiable nature of social reality (cf. the example of Sano and Enfermada in the previous chapter).

3 Every socially significant action, including speech, as Harré & Moghaddam point out, must be interpreted as an *act*; that is, not just as an intended action (e.g. a handshake), but as an intelligible and meaningful performance (the handshake can be a greeting, a farewell, a seal, etc.). An action is given meaning within social practices and as part of an unfolding narrative, and once it is interpreted within a given social episode, it is subject to norms of correctness. Like our thoughts and behaviours, emotions are subject to normative appraisal in our everyday lives, and they are constantly evaluated as warranted or unwarranted, suitable or unsuitable. Identifying acts, including emotional acts, presupposes that we identify the

reasons on which they are based, and this in turn involves an understanding of the social episodes and practices in which reasons exist. That is, in order to identify some emotional phenomenon as anger, fear, or guilt, for example, it is not enough to introspect or consider ongoing bodily perturbations. Such emotions are responses to objects and situations: anger can result when one's rights have been violated, fear may occur when one has been threatened, and guilt may ensue when one judges oneself to have violated a moral norm. Different situations give us different *reasons* to be angry, frightened, or guilty.

Positioning and the emotions

W. Gerrod Parrott (2003) has linked positioning theory closely with a study of the emotions, and this comprised my main theoretical resource for analysing the case that follows. Gerrod Parrott describes how emotions can play different roles in positioning. One way of positioning *oneself* 'is to display the emotions that are characteristic of one's position' (p. 29), and a way of positioning one's *opponents* 'is to state what emotions they ought to be feeling and to characterise as inappropriate the emotions they are feeling' (p. 29). Thus, ascribing emotions to oneself and to others is a central aspect of social life. It is also a significant part of human socialisation, where parents and educators consistently attempt to position children by stating which specific emotions they should appropriately feel. We say such things as 'Aren't you happy?', 'You should be ashamed of yourself!', and 'There is nothing to be afraid of!'. If emotions were pure, causally induced states in organisms that were suffered in a passive, mechanical way, such forms of normative emotional positioning would be unintelligible.

A distinction can be drawn between 'counter-emotions' and 're-labelled emotions'. Counter-emotions are emotional expressions that contradict a positioning that was inherent in a preceding emotional expression (Gerrod Parrott, 2003, p. 33). If A is angry at B, for example, then B is positioned as blameworthy, for anger is legitimately felt in response to experienced wrongdoings. Thus, according to the conventional choreography of emotional episodes, B ought in such a case to express the emotion of guilt and perhaps offer an apology. B is here positioned as guilty, but B may also react by re-positioning A through expressing a counter-emotion, for example anger. This would position A as the wrongdoer in the sense of having felt *unwarranted* anger. An alternative option for B would be to accept responsibility for the action that made A angry, but at the same time maintain that the action was justified, and perhaps express pride rather than guilt. Re-labelled emotions are often found in political contexts, when the anger expressed by one group is re-labelled as envy by another group ('the protesters have no right to be angry – they must really be envious of us'). We can see the same (paternalistic) process of re-labelling occurring when parents are positioning misbehaving children as tired. Re-labelling the emotions of others is a very powerful way of positioning them, e.g. as immature or uncontrollable, and it clearly illustrates the power relations that are present in social episodes.

Another form of re-labelling concerns one's own emotions. We can use the example of irritation and anger (Gerrod Parrott, 2003, p. 35). Anger is often legitimate in the case of a perceived moral transgression, whereas irritation has much of the same phenomenology but without implying a clear moral transgression. If someone then labels my emotion as irritation, he or she may thereby imply that I do not have a blameworthy target object of my emotion, and it can be pertinent for me to re-label my emotion as anger to assert that there is in fact a socially sanctioned basis for my emotional exclamation. We shall see many of these processes played out in the following example, where I shall analyse one recent and major public event in the Danish society.

A public confession

The event that caught my attention was a press conference held on 25 May 2007, by Bjarne Riis, but in order to understand this specific episode, I will first have to provide some background information. Bjarne Riis is a very famous public figure in Denmark. He was a successful professional cyclist and managed to win the Tour de France, arguably the most prestigious race for any cyclist, in 1996. Riis, a quiet, shy and determined man from the completely flat mainland of Denmark, was nicknamed 'The Eagle from Herning' (Herning being his hometown), due to his surprising skills in climbing mountains on his bike. After his 1996 victory, he was given an exceptional reception by hundreds of thousands of people in Copenhagen, the capital of Denmark, where he was taken through the city in an open car and welcomed by the prime minister in the Tivoli. The day before there had been a similar reception in the German capital (Riis was then part of a German cycling team), where chancellor Kohl received him. This testifies to a tremendous public outburst of positive emotions in celebrating Riis, who became an idol for large parts of the Danish society, across age groups, classes and sexes. I had personally followed Riis's career since the early 1990s, when he was much lower in the cycling hierarchy, acting as Laurent Fignon's helper, and my claim to fame as a school boy concerned the fact that I once celebrated New Year's Eve with him (as his parents-in-law at the time were friends with my parents!).

Since Riis's retirement as an active cyclist in 1999, he has owned and managed a professional cycling team, which in recent years has become among the top teams in the world. Like many other professional cyclists, however, Riis was accused by journalists of having used performance-enhancing drugs while he was active, but he repeatedly denied having done so. In 1998, Riis gave an interview on Danish television where he responded to the interviewer's question asking if he had ever used the illegal drugs with a sentence that has since become famous in Denmark: 'I have never been tested positive'. Riis thus did not directly deny that he had used drugs, which caused quite an uproar in Denmark. As a result, Riis subsequently had to state on public television that he had never used performance-enhancing drugs in his career, but to many people's minds, this came across as untrustworthy (and it turned out to be a lie).

Discussions about cycling, drugs, and especially Riis's actions as an active cyclist, were prominent and widespread in Denmark in the latter half of the 1990s. Cycling is a very popular sport in Denmark, and following the three-week Tour de France on television during the summer holiday is a favourite pastime of many Danes, including me, and some even spend their holiday going to France to follow the Tour on location (I have tried this myself a couple of times). It is a sign of the popularity of the Tour de France that the two TV reporters (Jørn Mader and Jørgen Leth), who covered it for many years, achieved cult status in Denmark, and one of them (Leth) is also a famous film director and poet, whose commentaries gave cycling a poetic, aesthetic, and indeed existential dimension in many people's lives. This also added to the heroic and mythical status of Bjarne Riis. It is no exaggeration to say that the Tour de France as a cultural event became akin to a symbolic resource (Zittoun, 2006) that people in Denmark used to navigate moral and existential issues in their lives. What Bauman (2007) calls consumer society is also an experience society, where elite sport ranks among the most popular experiential commodities, affecting not just individuals, but also whole nations such as Denmark.

During 2007, a number of confessions from cyclists who admitted having used drugs in their careers began to emerge. These involved some of Riis's earlier teammates, such as the Germans Rolf Aldag and Erik Zabel. Zabel broke down in tears during a televised confession in Germany on 24 May, and generally, the majority of confessing cyclists expressed guilt and regret. There was consequently a pressure on Riis to confess as well, and finally, the next day, on 25 May, Riis held a press conference in Denmark with extreme media coverage. During this conference, Riis read a statement that had been prepared in advance, and he admitted that he had used performance-enhancing drugs as an active cyclist from 1993 to 1998. Many discussions and consequences followed this event in Denmark. Among other consequences, Riis was removed from the official canon of elite sports people in Denmark, and the minister of culture declared that Riis's actions were unethical. Commentators both in Denmark and abroad quickly accused Riis of being opportunistic, without conscience, and a fraud, and leading experts on public relations argued that Riis ought to retire completely from his current team (Ekelund, 2007). This, however, has not happened.

What can this event teach us about guilt today? First, I believe a case can be made that public media events such as Riis's confession represent a crystallisation of moral debates in a culture, at least in modern consumer societies where the public sphere is primarily constituted by media, i.e., mediated by information technologies. Such events are significant for social scientists, who are interested in understanding the moral order of a culture and how this moral order is created, upheld and developed. Major public events, for example Princess Diana's death (which has been analysed by Gerrod Parrott & Harré, 2001), function to focus cultural attention on issues that have to do with values, ideals, and other normativities. They are significant moments in the cultural construction of emotions and proper emotional responses that enable us to chart the 'emotionology' of a culture and understand the 'oughtness' of social life.

If we approach the event with positioning theoretical tools as laid out in Box 6.3 (position, storyline, act), we can see that the storyline unfolding is clearly one of *confession*. The confession is a well-established practice in Christian cultures such as Denmark, and although confessions traditionally took place in secluded dyads, modern medialised confessions have inherited much that is associated with traditional confessions. In Riis's statement, he began by saying (having welcomed those attending and having expressed pride in his results):

> Today, as I approach you as Bjarne Riis, the private person, I do so to put the past behind me and to ensure that all the good work I do with my team today is not obstructed. [...] I have never felt a need to confess anything, and I do understand that people have had difficulties in accepting this. [...] Now the time has come to put all the cards on the table.[3]

When introducing the meeting, Riis mentions the confession as a practice himself, although he denies having a need to confess anything. He states all this before actually admitting having taken drugs (EPO) and having lied about this to others 'and in a way also to myself'. Later on during the press conference, he returns to the confession as a theme and says:

> One thing is absolutely clear: I must admit that I do not at all respect confessions that are either prompted by personal gains or by a need to place the blame on others for mistakes that they have committed themselves.

There is thus much ambivalence towards the confession as storyline in the statements, but not towards taking responsibility. Here, and throughout his speech, Riis puts all responsibility on his own shoulders ('I take the full responsibility. I bought it myself and took it myself'). Although he previously denied that his act was confessional, the storyline unfolding clearly borrows from a confessional narrative, and there is an interesting contradiction between what Riis does

---

[3]This and the following quotes are from the verbatim transcription (in my own translation from Danish) retrieved from www.berlingske.dk/article/20070525/sport/105251196/

(confesses) and the fact that he distances himself from the confession. This con-tradiction is also reflected in the very *act* that is performed, namely that of taking responsibility. This is an important moral speech act in Western culture, and in Riis's case it is coupled with an apology:

> When all is said and done, it is you as a cyclist who is responsible for saying yes or no [to drugs]. It is our own responsibility, no one else's. I have lied about some things, to others and in a way also to myself. I have always believed that the past was the past, but it is no longer so, and that is perhaps a good thing. On that level, I wish, of course, to say that I am sorry.

It is not entirely clear what 'that level' refers to, but one interpretation that seems valid from reading the entire transcript is that Riis is sorry that he has lied, but not (at least not so much) about having used drugs in his active career. Drug-taking seems to have been very widespread among elite cyclists, perhaps even the norm. In Riis's statements, the speech act of taking moral responsibility is coupled with a more strategic concern for the survival of his cycling team (in March 2008, the main sponsor of the team announced that they would terminate their sponsor-ship at the end of 2008). This represents a significant tension (between moral and strategic dimensions of the act) in the whole episode, and this tension probably contributed to the considerable public anger directed at Riis which followed.

Significantly, Riis tries to take responsibility, but *without* expressing guilt. Instead, he claims to be 'happy and proud' concerning his professional results. According to Gerrod Parrott's (2003) analysis, this is a way of positioning oneself as having done something that can be justified. Those who observed Riis during the press conference could also note a conspicuous absence of the standard emotional signs of guilt and remorse. Unlike his former colleagues, who confessed the previous day in Germany, Riis did not break down and cry. Instead, he upheld a stone face and spoke in a rather flat voice. The public opinion about drugs in cycling would posi-tion Riis as guilty, but he did not display the emotions characteristic of this posi-tion. One could say that the very emotional performance by Riis (or perhaps the *lack* of the proper emotional performance) involved an attempt at re-positioning himself as having acted properly, perhaps not according to public morality, but rather according to the local moral order of professional cycling.

The anger directed at Riis afterwards showed that the public did not accept his attempt at emotional re-positioning. We may speculate that much would have been different if Riis had in fact displayed the emotion of guilt. This would have been an implicit acknowledgement that he had been involved in a moral trans-gression, and the public would thus have been offered a chance to forgive him. When one refuses to take up the position as guilty – but at the same time takes responsibility for an act – the storyline that one projects into the future does not afford forgiveness from others, but rather anger and resentment. Riis's act in the situation is interesting because it revealed the cultural normativity of feeling guilty by breaking the norm of proper emotional display, which prompted a public reaction (no doubt intensified by the previous heroic status of the perpetrator and the general high status of cycling as a cultural phenomenon in Denmark).

In addition to accepting responsibility and expressing pride (thereby positioning himself as having acted in ways that can be justified), Riis used the press conference to express anger at the press. He accused them of only being interested in the sensational rather than the sport as such. By expressing anger at the journalists, who had tried to expose the use of illegal drugs that had taken place in cycling for many years, Riis attempted to position someone else as being guilty (the press), which is an example of a counter-emotion, implicitly asserting that his former acts were justified.

Concluding comments about the episode

I have provided an analysis of one of the most heavily covered mass media events in Denmark in 2007. This event has attracted my attention because it contained a social episode where the main actor did not perform the emotion (guilt) that many people had expected, and thus did not react in a normatively proper way – at least as seen from the perspective of the 'public opinion'. The conspicuous absence of guilt as an emotion in this case indicates that Bauman (2007) might be wrong when he claims that guilt is losing importance in the fluid, postmodern moral order. The expectancies of a 'guilt performance' that people had *vis-à-vis* this confession were not fulfilled, which reveals that guilt is still sometimes seen as a warranted and proper emotion. People still expect others to feel guilt when they have transgressed the moral order, and we see this most clearly when the norms are broken (Garfinkel, 1967). On the other hand, Riis's attempts at re-positioning the event by expressing other emotions, pride (in his results) and anger (at the press), rather than guilt, shows that there may also be some truth to Bauman's analysis. Riis did not see himself as having broken or transgressed the moral order, and this is why the whole meeting appears as a strategic performance, intended to save the reputation of the team and the sport as such. Thus we may conclude that guilt is still a relevant emotion, but that it has acquired a more complex status in the fluid, postmodern culture.

Concluding comments on the chapter

In this chapter, I have approached the role of the mass media in constructing our everyday lives in general and our emotions more specifically. I have looked briefly at the internet, but concentrated on news mass media, and my empirical example was a televised press conference that had also been transcribed and was freely available for analysis on the internet. The example was chosen because the lack of guilt displayed was surprising and thus constituted a kind of break-down in my understanding. At the same time, it was easy to gain access to the material and it was of personal interest to me, but I also sensed that it had wider cultural implications. To help in the analytic process, I used positioning theory. My analysis employed different strategies: to make the obvious obvious (e.g. by attempting to describe carefully what is actually going on in a social episode – which *acts* are performed?), to make the hidden obvious (e.g. by revealing which storylines are at work 'below the surface', in this case the confession, although Riis explicitly denied this), and to make the obvious dubious (e.g. by analysing the episode not as an apology, but rather as a strategic performance). Trying to understand the role of guilt and confession today was interesting, and has since made me think about how the medialised public has replaced God as that in rela-tion to which one needs to confess (more about this in the following chapter).

Using media in qualitative inquiry

What I did in this case can also be spelled out using my general scheme:

1 *Choose a topic.* I chose the topic, simply because it interested me and had a surprising element, which is often significant in driving good analyses. It also seemed to be a test case for some of the more theoretical literature I was reading (on topics such as emo-tions and positioning theory). It is frequently fruitful to try out one's theoretical tools by applying them to concrete instances.
2 *Collect materials.* The materials were collected as I chose the topic. I was watching the press conference on television and would then discuss the episode with friends and colleagues, read analyses in newspapers and on the internet, and ultimately analyse the transcript itself. This was one continuous process.
3 *Consult the literature.* I mainly used three kinds of literature. First, sociological analy-ses of the emotional landscape of postmodern society, represented in particular by Bauman. Secondly, psychological analysis of emotions, especially guilt, and, thirdly, positioning theory. I had not decided to bring these three together before, but they seemed to supplement each other nicely, and enabled me to understand the phenom-enon better. Positioning theory in particular served as a theoretical toolkit that enabled me to understand the episode in question.
4 *Continue collecting materials.* I went back and forth from theoretical readings and searched for more material on the episode that interested me until I had achieved what I thought was a nice balance of theoretical and empirical analyses.
5 *Do analytic writing.* Positioning theory in particular served me well as a toolkit of con-cepts that enabled me to understand the episode in writing. I gradually understood more of it as I wrote about it. I did not have the whole analysis in my head before

writing it down, but my readings of positioning theory inspired me to analyse the episode as I was writing.

6 *Publish your text.* It was not difficult to find a journal that was willing to publish the text (*Culture & Psychology*).

EXERCISE

An endless variety of topics can be investigated by studying media materials. Many of us 'swim in media' like fish swim in water, which often makes it difficult to discover just how pervasive medialised stories and discourses are in our everyday lives. This emphasises the need for a thorough defamiliarisation with the obviousness of media impact. Theoretical tools are often very helpful in this regard, as they invite the analyst into a very specific way of looking at the world (cf. positioning theory, for example), and can open up to new angles and questions. It is important to keep questioning the seemingly trivial, and I believe that the following exercise may help.

- Obtain a copy of today's newspaper. Locate the most significant headline. Read it carefully along with its article.
- Ask Parker's question that we have met in an earlier chapter: What relationships and theories of self must obtain for this piece of text to make sense?
- Ask yourself the question: What is the problem of the article represented to be (Bacchi, 2009)? Why is the given problem (if a problem is represented) problematic? To whom? And why? To whom may the problem represented *not* be a problem – and perhaps not even news?
- Consider how the reader is addressed and positioned? As someone who should be frightened, worried, surprised, indignant or pleased? And why?
- Write a page or two, trying to provide answers to these questions. Think about how the topic covered in the news story is related to your own life and the larger social world, and make an attempt to make the biographical and social meet in your analysis.

SEVEN

Movies, images and television

We live in a visual culture, constantly surrounded by images, some of which are still (pictures) and some of which are moving (films, television). I have, for example, more than 500 pictures on my smartphone. Like many others in this rich part of the world where I live, I can take a picture whenever I feel like it, share it with friends and family, or even upload it to the internet, e.g. a social networking site like Facebook. I also have collections of albums with developed pictures from my childhood, which can be used to elicit memories and uphold a sense of personal identity across time. My children have similar albums, which assist in constructing their identities. We talk about the pictures and remember significant details from the past, which help us create a sense of who we are. In many ways, our selves, particularly what was called Self 2 in Chapter 4, are constructed by visual means today.

Furthermore, many of us spend a considerable amount of time watching moving images on television. We use television as a news source, as entertainment and also to learn about the world around us. We learn much about our existence (and basic human phenomena like love, hate, morality, community, individuality, etc.) through the visual, movies and television. Movies, in particular, are a prime source of knowledge for human beings in what Norman Denzin has called the 'cinematic society' (Denzin, 1995). Thus, the impact of these kinds of visual materials on our lives deserves to be analysed by qualitative researchers.

In this chapter, I will address how we can use visual and audiovisual materials from our everyday lives to research our personal and social worlds. The idea is to use movies, images or television programmes that we would watch or look at anyway, with the intention of learning something important about human life in the process. In this chapter, I thus approach social life from the object pole of the ontological triangle. I realise that there are huge differences between the various materials that I shall include (e.g. family photos versus Hollywood blockbusters), but I have chosen to group them together in this chapter because of their shared visual qualities. I will begin by providing an overview of different kinds of visual and audiovisual materials that are conventionally included in human and social science research projects. The chapter concludes with an example, namely an analysis of the television programme series *Paradise Hotel*, which is extremely popular among (mainly) young people in Scandinavia.[4]

Why use visual materials?

There are several reasons why visual and audiovisual materials are worth including in qualitative studies of everyday life. First, as I have already indicated, our everyday lives are saturated with images and films, so the visual offers a window into cultural processes that seems almost indispensable if we want to understand human experience in our visually oriented culture. The modern world is very much a 'seen phenomenon' (Banks, 2007, p. 40), ordered, stabilised and articulated through images, pictures and (more recently) films and television as media. We very much subscribe to 'an epistemology of the eye' in the West (Brinkmann & Tanggaard, 2010), according to which knowledge is modelled on vision: we know something when confronted with it visually. But, as scholars like Foucault have argued, there is nothing neutral and objective about the visual as such, and vision can certainly become a tool by which power is exercised (Banks, 2007, p. 14). Foucault showed this most famously in his analyses of the gaze and the panopticon (a prison structure designed by Jeremy Bentham, which enabled a single guard to monitor a large number of prisoners). A critical reflection on what has been called 'ocularcentrism' (the privileging of vision in Western society, which often hides its power relations) must accompany qualitative analyses that make use of visual materials.

Secondly, when constructed by either researchers or research participants, photographs and film recordings are capable of capturing real-world, real-time actions and events (Loizos, 2000). They cannot capture 'everything', and they are not necessarily more 'objective' than other means of framing and freezing social processes, but they are definitely capable of capturing other features of the world than sound recordings or documents, for example. All data, all everyday life materials, allow for many possible readings, but visual materials probably do so to a larger extent than other kinds of material. Some refer to this as 'the polyvocality of images', which is their ability to permit multiple readings and interpretations (Banks, 2007, p. 10). Visual materials are seemingly inexhaustible in terms of their

[4]This analysis has been carried out together with Ole Jacob Madsen from Norway, who should be considered first author of the text that comprises the empirical example. I thank Ole Jacob for allowing me to use the example in the present context.

'interpretability'. There is a saying that 'a picture is worth a thousand words', implying that we can communicate something very economically and efficiently with the use of pictures, but it is equally true that a picture normally opens up for more potential readings than a piece of prose. We still analyse and interpret the drawings from the Lascaux caves that were made around 15,000 years ago, and it is unlikely that we will ever establish their 'true meaning' (whatever one could mean by this).

There are two main strands in the social scientific study of visual materials: (1) the use of images to study society and (2) the sociological study of images (Banks, 2007, p. 7). The first one involves visual materials constructed by the researcher, such as photographs taken by the researcher herself or by research participants instructed by the researcher, and also the making of ethnographic films, for example. The use of films or photographs in eliciting responses from research participants in research interviews also belongs in this category. The second strand focuses on what I shall here (somewhat misleadingly) refer to as naturalistic materials, by which I mean visual and audiovisual materials that are part of the everyday life of cultural members, including the researcher herself (which is what I concentrate on in the present book). Naturalistic visual materials are thus considered as cultural or symbolic resources that humans use in living their everyday lives. The term 'naturalistic' should be taken with a pinch of salt, however, since these materials can indeed be created by the researcher. Thus, if I choose to analyse my holiday photographs as materials in a qualitative study, I am analysing something that would have been there anyway (and is thus 'naturalistic'), even if I took the photographs myself.

This chapter primarily deals with audiovisual materials in line with the second strand, as a qualitative study of everyday images, movies and television. I concentrate on visual materials that are already a part of the researcher's everyday life. I will thus primarily address visual objects as resources that are used by individuals and groups to construct social practices, identities and negotiate important existential issues. And, as always, this goes in both directions at the same time, for specific objects for visual consumption are also produced because of certain social practices, identities and existential concerns, which means that we can study these by looking at images, films and television. Visual materials are co-constitutive of 'who we are' in a visually oriented culture, and 'who we are' is simultaneously expressed through visual media – the images and films that we create.

Materials constructed for a research purpose

I shall here present a loose taxonomy of audiovisual materials by making two distinctions. First, between different *histories* of the emergence of the materials (constructed versus naturalistic materials) across the board, and, secondly, between different *kinds* of materials (images, films and television). I shall first briefly describe visual materials that are constructed by researchers, before going into greater detail concerning naturalistic materials, where I will also include a number of empirical examples.

Images

It is quite common in qualitative inquiry to use images as a supplement to textual description. In ethnography and sociology, for example, we often find 'illustrated research articles' (Harper, 2005), where images help to put faces on the textual narratives or the statistical data. Visual documentation, Harper argues, can here become a part of research triangulation, confirming theories by using different kinds of data. In this role, images are not analysed in great detail, but are used by researchers to 'tell more' than words alone can convey. Although pictures can be important in this role, they are nonetheless secondary to the text.

Another role of constructed images in qualitative inquiry is as elicitation methods. Harper (2005) gives an example from his own research on the historical transformation of agriculture and the consequences for those involved. In order to facilitate conversation with research participants, Harper showed photographs from the 1940s to elderly farmers and asked them to remember stories and events brought to mind by the photos. In this case, the researcher constructs a situation of remembering by using evocative artefacts. This method can work very well in oral history projects, but also in other kinds of projects that are oriented to participants' biographies, where images can elicit recollections of the past. In other kinds of research projects, research participants can be instructed by the researcher to take pictures or make films (e.g. a video diary), which then make up the corpus of empirical data to be analysed.

Films

Like still images, films have quite a long history in the social sciences. Ethnographers have long used the camera to visually capture the cultures, practices and people that they have studied. If ethnographers are interested in communicating a sense of 'being there', there is little doubt that films can be highly valuable in this regard. Ethnographic films differ concerning the extent to which they are edited or directed by the researcher. Some early ethnographic films were heavily directed, e.g. Robert Flaherty's famous *Nanook of the North* from 1922, a portrait of the Inuit people, which involved actors that were instructed to act, whereas other films try to document events as they unfold. There is no clear line between ethnographic films and more regular documentaries that are sometimes hard to distinguish from social science, communicated through the audiovisual, in so far as they aim to document a certain part of the social process.

Naturalistic materials

As I pointed out above, what I refer to as naturalistic materials can be constructed either by research participants or the researcher (they can be one's own photographs or recorded films, for example), but the point is that they have not primarily been made for a research purpose, but for 'life purposes'. In this sense, they are everyday life materials that would have been there anyway. Of course, there can be cases when it is difficult to draw a line between what is constructed for a research purpose and what would have been there anyway in the researcher's life. But this is exactly one of this book's main points: that there is no sharp distinction to be made between living a life and doing qualitative inquiry.

Images

Images (pictures, paintings, photos) can be used to learn more about a group of people, a culture or an epoch. Visual materials are articulations of human experience in specific times and places and represent a significant materialisation of the norms and concerns of people. Loizos refers to Aries' now classic study of childhood as a clear example. Aries used paintings from pre-industrial Europe that depicted children dressed in the same clothes as adults, and with similar facial expressions etc., using this to argue that the idea of childhood as a special period in a person's life is a much more recent invention than one should think (Loizos, 2000, p. 95).

If we jump to our own times, and my own place of living (Denmark, Scandinavia), we can look at a completely different image, reproduced below, and attempt to read the image with the intention of understanding something about contemporary cultural experience. The image is taken from the sixth season of the Danish reality television show called *Paradise Hotel*, and I shall use this image at this stage to illustrate different analytic approaches to visual materials.

Paradise Hotel centres on a group of single women and men who live together in a luxurious resort to see who can stay in the hotel for the longest time. Couples must pair off and share a room together, and when a person is left alone, he or she must check out of the hotel. New guests arrive regularly during the show, and losing contestants are occasionally allowed to check back in. Finally, the last couple left standing receives the prize money – $250,000 in the American original – which they then have to decide whether to share with their partner or not, running the risk of being left out by their trusted partner. A much more

Figure 7.1   Contestants from Denmark's *Paradise Hotel*, 2010 (photo courtesy of TV3/Lemche & Serup)

elaborate reading of the show as a whole is offered below. At this stage, I shall merely use the picture as an example. How does one analyse or interpret such a picture? How does one get started? One way is to use the three analytic strategies from Chapter 1.

- *Make the obvious obvious*: This entails describing what is there to be seen in the picture. We see ten people standing in a shallow water swimming pool. They wear bathing suits, according to the norms of Western culture. Thus, the five young men have naked upper bodes, but wear long swimming trunks, and the five young women wear varieties of female swimsuits. One of the women wears a swimsuit that covers only some of the abdomen, but reveals much of the breasts, whereas the four other women wear rather small bikinis. The women stand in front of the men, thus revealing more of their bodies than the men, and all women are smaller than the men. The women each rest one arm on the hip (the arm that is closest to the viewer), while the men's arms simply hang down. This indicates (as does the picture as a whole) that it was arranged for this occasion. A couple of the women seem to raise one of their shoulders, while the men's shoulders hang down like their arms. The ten people are all slim, tanned and athletic. The women have long hair, while the men have rather short haircuts. All women smile, three of them showing their teeth, whereas only one of the men is clearly smiling (the one furthest to the right). Two of the men are quite expressionless, while two others (furthest to the left) display a rather ambiguous smile.

Although this is seemingly a very simple picture, the description could go on and on like this. Images are indeed polyvocal and inexhaustible. What one might gain from describing a picture very closely, and describing the obviousnesses like this, is a sense of the details that normally escape us when we browse through a magazine with pictures such as this one, in our everyday lives. There is so much that is taken for granted in our visual culture, which we can only see by forcing ourselves to keep looking and keep describing. What is made obvious through careful description of this specific photo can be summarised in many ways, depending on one's analytic focus, but what strikes me are the heteronormativity and gender stereotypes that this picture affirms. The differences between men and women are emphasised in everything from their respective positions in the picture, different body postures, clothes and expressions. The men seem to incarnate a very masculine habitus of strength and emotional control, while the women appear 'sweeter' and rather seductive. Evidently, this is a reading of the picture that depends on my own standpoint and attunement to young adults, and something is obvious only (and can only be *made* obvious) given a certain standpoint that should be made visible to some extent in one's interpretation of any piece of visual material.

- *Make the hidden obvious*: What is hidden in this picture? A question that is always relevant to pose about visual materials is 'What is absent?' Numerous kinds of people are absent that one could reasonably expect to find in a photograph of ten young adults, had these simply been randomly chosen. There are no persons of colour in the picture, no (visibly) disabled persons, no overweight persons… and the list could go on. The people in the swimming pool are all model-like and conform to the reigning norms of beauty in the Western world. We can also ask about the history of this picture. How was it constructed? How was it arranged? How did these people end up together in a swimming pool, posing for a huge national audience? Who told them to undress and wear swimming outfits? Did they have a choice? The history of the picture is in a way hidden in the picture itself, but could be uncovered were we to gather more information about *Paradise Hotel*. The young people are probably not there, for example, because they compose a group of friends that enjoy each other's company as such, but rather because there is a monetary reward in sight for one (or two) of them, inviting them into a strategic game of manipulation through a display of emotions and sex (more on this below). The contestants use sex and intimacy instrumentally in order to win the prize, so there is a constant ambivalence, which I find is reflected in this picture, about authenticity. Are they – their smiles, poses and expressions – real? And what does real even mean in this constructed paradise?

A critical reading of the picture can thus reveal hidden or absent features. What are the conditions of existence of this picture that are not directly visible in the picture itself? Asking this question enables one to go beyond the surface, and although my short readings here are fairly neutral concerning theoretical paradigms, theoretical concepts are often helpful when one is trying to make the hidden obvious. The picture could thus be read through psychoanalysis, Marxism, feminism, post-structuralism, etc.

- *Make the obvious dubious*: How can we destabilise the obviousnesses of an image? I have already raised some questions that may help us do so, for example about the absences in the picture. Absences stabilise meanings just as much as presences. But we can go further along this line and imagine alternative renderings of the picture: What if the women had been standing behind the men? What if the picture had depicted ten obese teenagers – or ten seniors – in swimming outfits? What if all the men had been black and all the women white – or vice versa? What if the men had been wearing female swimsuits – or vice versa? Asking these kinds of questions might enable us to confront cultural stereotypes and biases, but obviously also our own. What would we think in these cases? And what do our ways of thinking about these questions tell us about why we find the actual picture trivial at first sight (if we do so)? Why have our eyes become accustomed to this kind of visual arrangement of persons – and not to others like those just mentioned? What does this tell us about current cultural practices and norms?

Reading images with the intention of making the obvious dubious can make us address the issue of why certain cultural practices, involving the two genders as represented in frozen form in this image, have become ordinary and expected. Things could have been otherwise, and a deconstructive look at images may force us into productive reflections about why they are not.

Films

There is a significant tradition in Cultural Studies of using films to understand the culture in which they are created. We live in a 'cinematic society' that knows itself through reflections produced by the movie industry (Denzin, 1995). A classic example of the use of films to analyse cultural processes is the work of Siegfried Kracauer, who studied German cinema from 1918 to 1933 (and published immediately after the war) in order to understand the culture in which Nazism emerged. Philosophers have also begun to focus on films. Stanley Cavell is a pioneer, using American cinema of the so-called Golden Age of Hollywood (the 1930s and 1940s) to tackle philosophical issues (Cavell, 2004). Stephen Mulhall has more recently devoted a book to the *Alien* quartet, not in order to read the films as a reflection of postmodern society or something like that, but rather to bring out the more perennial philosophical questions that these films articulate in their own dramatic ways. There is an existential intensity to the *Alien* films, as they present us with 'small, isolated groups of human beings framed most immediately against the infinity of the cosmos' (Mulhall, 2002, p. 8). The films essentially give us what I would call an 'existential laboratory', where existential issues about finitude, vulnerability and the bodily basis of human identity appear in a particular salient form. Mulhall argues that the films are not simply ornamentation for philosophical discussions, but instead represent 'film as philosophizing' (p. 2). Films can thus invite analyses of specific cultural processes as well as more universal philosophising.

Television

In the lives of most of us, television plays a large role – at least in pure quantitative terms – and much larger than cinema. Watching television takes up about 25 per cent of all home time and 40 per cent of all leisure time in the USA (Hektner, Schmidt, & Csikszentmihalyi, 2007, p. 130), and the figures are probably similar in other countries. This means that daily life for most of us is accompanied by television, and TV affects, reflects and co-constitutes our everyday lives. Below, I shall analyse a specific television series (the aforementioned *Paradise Hotel*) in greater detail as an example of qualitative inquiry in everyday life, but readers who are interested in more standardised ways of analysing television can consult the methodology developed by Diana Rose (2000). This methodology puts great emphasis on how to sample materials. Rose recommends doing a broad sweep of prime-time coverage and picking out the topic of interest. Transcription is also underlined, with a focus on choosing units of analysis and a relevant coding frame. A short example of a transcription from Rose's work is given in Figure 7.2.

This transcription is from a study of how madness is represented on television, and some codes have been inserted into this segment. CU means close up, MCU means medium close up and ECU means extreme close up. Obviously, it is very time consuming to transcribe and code large bodies of data in this way, but it is crucial for certain purposes, e.g. if one wants an overview of how madness is represented on the BBC in general. In this case, a valid *inductive* analysis presupposes

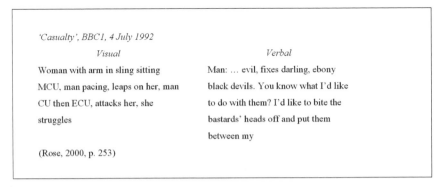

'Casualty', BBC1, 4 July 1992

Visual	*Verbal*
Woman with arm in sling sitting	Man: … evil, fixes darling, ebony
MCU, man pacing, leaps on her, man	black devils. You know what I'd like
CU then ECU, attacks her, she	to do with them? I'd like to bite the
struggles	bastards' heads off and put them
	between my

(Rose, 2000, p. 253)

Figure 7.2   Representation of madness on television

careful sampling and coding, but the kind of *abductive* interpretative analysis advocated in this book implies a much more in-depth hermeneutic reading of more specific cultural objects. Rose also puts emphasis on quantification of the data (she advocates the construction of tables of frequencies), which makes sense in her case, since she is interested in how often madness is associated with such aspects as danger and distress, for example.

An analytic reading of *Paradise Hotel* as a showcase of shamelessness

I shall now leave the general issues about qualitative studies of visual materials and focus on one particular example. What follows is a study of the Norwegian and Danish versions of the reality television series *Paradise Hotel*. We met a few of its contestants in the photo above, and they are invited by the show to live in a nameless exotic location, where they are encouraged to do nothing but enjoy and expose themselves to the viewers and each other.

In contrast to similar television series, *Paradise Hotel* does not have a linear storyline or a clear goal with traditional winners and losers, but is staged more like a biblical scene that warrants the demonstration of shamelessness as a kind of late modern cultural ideal. This is the reading we shall attempt below. We argue that some of the guests (predominantly male in line with prevailing gender norms) in *Paradise Hotel* may truly qualify as shameless – after spells of physical and psychological revelations in front of the camera with no visible regrets – still the price is perhaps the loss rather than the gain of freedom. 'The shameless self' lives in a media event that only exists a few weeks or months, and demands the submission to strong criteria of bodily and emotional values, which only postpones most of the guests' shame and regrets until after the cameras are turned off. And this particular fall from grace may have unwanted personal consequences that lead to a spiral ascent crueller than Adam and Eve ever underwent.

About the show

Paradise Hotel is an American reality television programme that first aired on the Fox broadcast television network in 2003. The show belongs to the subgenre of 'gamedocs' that succeeded the earlier wave of 'docusoaps' from the mid-1990s. The gamedoc signals a shift in television towards a 'postdocumentary' culture, which involves a transformation of reality. Like other gamedocs, such as *Big Brother*, *Paradise Hotel* 'operates its claims to the real within a fully managed artificiality' (Corner, 2002, p. 256), where everything that happens is predicated on the presence of the camera. The concept was created by Mentorn, a UK independent production company, which has also produced various versions of the show around the world. Danish, Dutch and Swedish versions followed in 2005; an Israeli adaptation under the name *The Bay of Love* was launched in 2008. Norway became the most recent country to produce a version of *Paradise Hotel* in 2009. The American version of *Paradise Hotel* became something of a cult hit, but never quite took off on the TV ratings, and it was stalled until a sequel series was finally launched on the Fox Reality Channel in 2008, perhaps encouraged by the successes of the Scandinavian versions of *Paradise Hotel*. The Danish show gradually became one of Denmark's most popular series.

A sixth consecutive season of *Paradise Hotel* Denmark premièred in February 2010 (its contestants are portrayed in the photo above), and the final was the most watched final yet. As I write these words, there is great excitement among the many fans of the show, as the seventh season is about to commence. In Norway, *Paradise Hotel* became the most talked about reality show in 2009, and was commended for rejuvenating a genre that was beginning to look old. The show gathered an average of a quarter of a million viewers, a considerable share of the market in a country of just 4.9 million people. The show was particularly a hit among young viewers, especially female viewers in the 19–29 age group.

The postmodern ideal of paradise?

Paradise Hotel reads as an extreme version of postmodernity, as an epoch when everything is at stake. On the surface, the guests are exposed to a warm, *Club Tropicana*-esque atmosphere in a highly luxurious resort where the 'drinks are free' and 'strangers take you by the hand'. Nothing is really demanded from the participants; they might win a huge money prize, but most of them won't, of course. Still, they nonetheless get a free holiday and achieve national fame through their different publicised actions, at least for 15 minutes.

Even though the atmosphere may be nice and warm, the humane climate most definitely won't be. The whole set-up of the television show is meant to create intense human dramas under the stifling sun, echoing Thomas Hobbes' stark view of man's natural state of singular individuals in constant conflict in the absence of a Sovereign. The plot is created for the purpose of continuously singling someone out, which means that it is a game of survival, alliances and rivalry, where no one can really be trusted, and the level of conflict is guaranteed to be high. Also, the rules are constantly twisted, fluid or liquid in Bauman's (2007) terms, in order to keep up the interest among viewers. So even if the contestants succeed in creating a trusting, stable alliance, the producers who continuously monitor the plot will often make sure that it won't last.

Since *Paradise Hotel*, unlike most other reality shows, does not involve a contest of skills or talents (see below), the guests' primary assets are themselves, their own bodies and selves. This quickly creates a human market-like environment where sexual appeal becomes a tradable commodity. One of the Danish contestants described her breasts as her 'biggest assets', while another guest in the Danish version was promised sexual services from an exposed contestant, which led to a debate in the press of whether *Paradise Hotel* actually promoted prostitution.

Like fictional works of art, reality shows like *Paradise Hotel* both mimic the dominating ideas of the current epoch, and try to offer a therapeutic catharsis to the antagonisms of our allegedly fluid and guiltless, but (perhaps) shameful, backdrop of postmodern culture. Its allure is especially directed at young people and consists of inviting them 'back to paradise' to achieve not only guiltlessness, but ultimately shamelessness. *Paradise Hotel* thus offers us insight into the current conditions of selfhood, shame and the relations between them.

Theoretical framework: Return to Eden – shame and the self

The biblical analogies in *Paradise Hotel* are numerous. The contestants are invited to a luxurious resort far away, with a tempered climate that allows them to walk around wearing a minimum of clothes (see the photo above). The script of the show encourages them to 'do nothing' apart from sunbathing, drinking and partying, which of course easily gives the impression of them being in some sort of hedonistic paradise. Also, the archetypical man–woman alliance, and ultimately the fact that only one man and one woman can remain in the end, cut into these constant analogies to the origin of man (Book of Genesis). Dramaturgically, *Paradise Hotel* tells a story that inverts the biblical narrative of the banishment from Eden – in the televised paradise the contestants are gradually drawn back into Eden until only one Adam and one Eve are left.

The biblical myth of the Fall from Eden has been a source of inspiration for theoretical analyses of morality, emotions and the self at least since Kierkegaard's *The Concept of Anxiety* (Kierkegaard, 1844). Famously, Kierkegaard interprets the myth to be about the existential anxiety that humans feel in response to nothingness. It is anxiety that pulls humanity from innocence and into reflective, and thus potentially guilty and shameful, consciousness. Unlike fear, which has a concrete object, anxiety in the existential sense is directed at the possibility of freedom, which is nothing until it has been realised as a possibility. As creatures of body, mind and spirit, we are, Kierkegaard says, able to conceive of nothingness, of possibility in the sense of the not-yet-realised, which is at once a condition of freedom and at the same time the ground of anxiety. The sense of nothingness and anxiety are crystallised in the prohibition in Eden: How could Adam understand the prohibition of eating the fruit, when he had not yet acquired an understanding of good and evil? Without this understanding, the very idea of acting against God's command makes no sense and thus creates anxiety – but also evokes the possibility of freedom and non-innocence in Adam.

In Jack Katz's social psychological reading of Genesis, the story appears not just as a cosmological myth (about the creation of the world as such) but as 'an experiment in theoretical imagination that produces a highly compressed social psychology' (Katz, 1996, p. 557). Genesis is a social psychology about how the human self was born in guilt and shame, and it works as a social psychology 'to the extent that it is an economic description of the challenges that people face in their relations with others' (pp. 559–560). We learn from the myth that the self is born as a reflective and conversational process, involving an 'I' and a 'Me', to speak with Mead, when the person sees herself through the eyes of the other, which is a shameful incident. It is shameful because the first glimpse of self-reflection (thus of the self as such) appears the moment when Adam and Eve realise that they have done something wrong by violating God's command. They then see that they are naked and they must cover their bodies, assisted by God who gives them clothes.

Symbolically, Adam and Eve reach upwards, to the branches of the tree, lured by the earthly snake, to eat and acquire wisdom, and consequently understand the ideas of good and evil, right and wrong, and thus the concepts of guilt and shame. If we ask how Adam and Eve could have been guilty when their sense of good and evil only emerged with the eating itself, the answer seems to be that they could not. They become guilty only in retrospect, when they shamefully come to understand that their deed was wrong. And with this recognition emerges the self as a reflective process. The forbidden fruit, Katz concludes, is 'the very process of self-conscious reflection' (Katz, 1996, p. 549), and *shame* thereby becomes the fundamental emotion that gives birth to the self, to the person's relationship to community and to other moral emotions (p. 546).

When eating the fruit, Adam and Eve become like their creator. Eating the fruit, and breaking the command, is their first act of freedom and creativity, and they become agents who are not just created, but who can from then on create their own story and make their own history. Here, according to the myth, human history begins as something beyond our animalistic, natural and innocent history. Consequently, Adam and Eve are expelled from Eden. They must be expelled because they have attained the godly knowledge of good and evil, which puts them on a par with the legislator. And man must from then on exercise this knowledge on earth in mortal bodies, half godly, half beastly.

The myth seems to be valid as a condensed description of the emergence of the human self. It articulates the idea that the self is born in shame. This emotion is a sign that the self is revealed to the eyes of others. A paradigm of shame can be when someone is looking through a keyhole and discovers that she is being observed by others. The self is here painfully objectified, revealed, in the eyes of other subjects, and the person is unable to control the presentation of herself in relation to the community, which is a powerful mechanism of social control. Paradoxically, in this painful revelation of the self, it is simultaneously created as a reflective product. Through shame, the community emerges not merely as an abstraction (an 'imagined community'), but as a concretely-felt reality with basic norms that resonate in most of us when they are broken. Numerous questions can be raised: Does the cultural lack of shame, then, lead to the lack of self-hood? Is this something we find in a postmodern culture of shamelessness? Was Kierkegaard right that, without prohibitions, there can be no freedom? Could *Paradise Hotel* be a social psychological test case in this regard? And the contestants, who are living in such an experimental setting, are they absolutely free – or absolutely unfree?

Like Katz, who interprets the text of Genesis as a set of universal claims about human nature, we shall seek to understand *Paradise Hotel* as a set of claims about selfhood in late modernity. Our research interest in the Scandinavian versions of *Paradise Hotel* lies mainly in the category of shame among the younger generations of Scandinavians, which both occupy and follow the show in large numbers. We shall now examine aspects of the show with this aim in mind, and, like ethnographers confronted with a strange, and in this case televised, culture, single out a number of situations.

No competition – no rules?

An interesting design aspect of *Paradise Hotel* is that unlike its many predecessors in the genre of reality television, its contestations do not really compete in anything. For instance, comparable reality shows in tropical surroundings, such as the Swedish *Expedition Robinson* and the American *Survivor* (CBS, 2000–), involve hard physical trials and competitions in a range of survival skills, and even the more alluring *Temptation Island* (Fox, 2001–2003) dealt with stressful trials of fidelity and tested the degree of attachment between couples. Perhaps the closest comparison to *Paradise Hotel* is the immensely successful *Big Brother* show, and even though the contestants in that series also didn't do much apart from hanging around, a key difference was that *Big Brother* was mainly a popularity contest where the viewers ultimately decided who had to leave the house each week. In *Paradise Hotel* there is a weekly selection ceremony, resulting in one of the contestants being sent away, but this ceremony is not like the island counsel in *Expedition Robinson*, for example, where the entire group votes and a democratic verdict is reached. Decisions of who are allowed to stay and who must leave are usually down to one single contestant in *Paradise Hotel*.

In *Paradise Hotel* the criteria for success are therefore much more unclear, perhaps because the contestants live in an Eden, which is prior to right and wrong, and even in its production set-up, the rules and the ultimate goal is, apart from the very last week, in the background. Any viewer who has followed the show for some time will have noticed this; the finale is an anticlimax, almost as if the creators of the show haven't given it much thought beforehand. During the innumerable weeks when the show is aired, the guests and the viewers rarely get any hints from the programme hosts etc. about how long it will last. In narrative terms, *Paradise Hotel* is therefore much more about a staged happening than a narrative with a plot. One could even say that it is more about a specific state of mind than about a final end result based on an unfolding storyline. It is much less based on a linear master narrative than on numerous micro happenings that occur between the individuals involved. *Paradise Hotel* is less of a competition, and more of a late modern platform for the exposure of shamelessness.

There is no time and place

Concerning location, we are never told either by a visual map or a geographically spoken hint where the luxurious hotel is located. Like Eden itself, the televised paradise is outside time and space. This loss of feeling of place was clearly under-lined when one of the Norwegian contestants failed to successfully mark which part of the world she was in on a map. Unlike other reality shows, such as *The Bachelor* (ABC, 2002–), which occasionally is recorded in an exotic, foreign coun-try abroad, from where it originally is produced and aired, *Paradise Hotel* has no visible sponsored collaboration with the local authorities that makes the viewer see the local tourist attractions, integrated in the show, e.g. when couples are on a date. Although the pairs in *Paradise Hotel* also sometimes get awarded excur-sions – in line with the topological philosophy of the show – where they actually sojourn could be anywhere in the world, within a certain distance to the equator.

The dramaturgy of *Paradise Hotel* resembles tropical fictional shows like the classic *Fantasy Island* (ABC, 1978–1984) or the seemingly never-ending *Lost* (ABC, 2004–2010), where the viewer is left in the dark about geography. Both of these shows create an almost eerie feeling of bewilderment; both of them occurred on deserted islands and featured time travel. The much awaited ending and solution to the big mystery in *Lost* also underlines the idea that categories like time and place for the late modern subject are 'lost'. An early demonstration of this spatio-temporal confusion was perhaps provided in the American origi-nal of *Paradise Hotel* when Toni, in an impassioned plea directed at Dave, made the remark: 'This is temporary. Life is permanent.' Both the American, Danish and Norwegian versions of *Paradise Hotel* are shot in special strong colour filters, which produce a non-realistic and dream-like visual effect, resembling the three strip Technicolor technology used in movies like *The Wizard of Oz*, aesthetically emphasising the reality show's strong trait of unreality.

Paradise Hotel did not take place

From a strict commercial point of view, the creators' idea of creating a scene and narrative that simulates a postmodern theory about 'non-places' and the 'death of geography' is quite clever. It is well known that the contestants in *Paradise Hotel* are given a large amount of free alcohol and are encouraged by the production team to get inebriated since the odds for them to do stuff they otherwise would not do in front of the camera obviously increase. However, the whole set up, and the philosophy of no-place, helps to create a more fundamental, yet subtle, loss of attachment, bonds and, ideally, prohibitions, that is not as open to criticism of cynicism as giving a bunch of twenty-somethings unlimited amounts of alcohol and then recording their misconducts. Contemporary reality shows like *Paradise Hotel*'s mimicry of the apparent liquid, alcohol-like, postmodernity is ironic, in the sense that they fulfil Baudrillard's (in-)famous and often misinterpreted thesis about hyperreality. Fiction has not really become more real than the real – 'the real' still very much exists – but commercial media spectacles like *Paradise Hotel* persistently try to make us, the viewers, believe that all that is solid melts into air, and through this constant mimicry gradually creates a self-fulfilling prophecy. When the contestants return home, they often brutally become aware of 'the real', through death threats on Facebook, and sometimes even physical attacks, and, in a more long-term perspective, exclusions from future job opportunities due to a bad reputation etc. In accordance with present gender norms, female reality contestants are more vulnerable to this revenge of 'the real' than their male rivals.

Revenge of the nerds

The first season of the American version of *Paradise Hotel* consisted of a group of strong-minded and committed contestants with their eyes firmly fixed on the money prize throughout the weeks in the holiday resort. Thus, the importance of 'playing the game', forming alliances and manipulating other guests, quickly became a focus of action, perhaps helped by the selection criteria of the guests there, which fitted into the American college stereotypes pattern of the jocks, the nerds and the cheerleaders. In the finale, the typical nerd – the head smart Dave – had outlasted his more muscular rivals, but he was ultimately betrayed by his partner, the reserved beauty queen Charla, who broke their pact and took off with the whole prize money of $250,000 on her own.

Despite the constant conspicuous rivalry, both dictated by the rules of the game and the adversary conventions of the social world outside paradise in the American original show, a wholly different and much more casual attitude towards the goal of winning could be sensed in the Norwegian second series of

Paradise Hotel. The ultimately most successful couples, Carl and Tine and Even and Thea, shared a casual happy-go-lucky attitude towards their stay in *Paradise Hotel*. Their focus seemed to be on their own well-being here and now, without giving much thought and concern for winning and the strategic positioning necessary to secure this goal. Several of the other contestants, however, openly told the viewers at home, and other guests, that they would do anything in their power to win, and like their American predecessors stressed the importance of 'playing the game'. The most outspoken representative of this philosophy was perhaps Victoria, who rapidly became a hate figure among many viewers, which again underlies the conservative gender roles where women are allowed much less room for displaying strategic behaviours than their male rivals.

The differing attitudes towards what *Paradise Hotel* 'really was about' occasionally created tensions between the groups, and several members of the show felt that the male victor Carl was an unworthy winner since he refused to argue his case why he should win, and took an indifferent attitude towards duels, owing to his casual and careless philosophy. Hence, unlike many other reality shows, the object of winning, playing it tactically and getting allies, was not an apparent intent for the most successful group of the guests at *Paradise Hotel*. Paradoxically, the 'true winners' of *Paradise Hotel* were the contestants who were the most indifferent to the overall goals and plans (like winning) and most comfortable just 'being themselves' in a relaxing, charming and sometimes nude manner, without much thought for consequences – what the outcome would be *in* the show, and eventually what would happen on the outside when filming was over.

A showcase of shamelessness

With that being said, there still exist certain norms for what types of behaviour are wanted in the show. The visitors in *Paradise Hotel* all seem to be highly self-conscious that the show is about breaking taboos and revealing oneself either by physical or mental exposure. On the very first night of the Danish sixth season, a competition spontaneously broke out between the girls, after only hours of knowing each other, when several of them stripped off their tops and compared their breasts. Unlimited access to alcohol is of course also a major factor here, but the consistent revelations throughout the series, either by stripping clothes or confiding secrets, are so frequent in *Paradise Hotel* that alcohol alone does not fully explain this recurring sharing behaviour.

Likewise, new contenders who are permitted a stay in the hotel after one of the original guests has been forced to leave, are particularly vulnerable to social exclusion, and therefore are under extra strong pressure to swiftly demonstrate that they belong and are down with the show's contradictory, yet powerful, norms of shamelessness. The new female guest, the law school student Jeanette, in the second

Norwegian series, almost instantly asked other guests (men *and* women), extremely intimate questions about masturbation habits and sexual preferences. Most definitely inappropriate in any other social setting, yet, in *Paradise Hotel*, Jeanette only followed the norm and just did what was expected of her to demonstrate that she concurred to the unspoken rules of the show. To borrow a biblical phrase, we can say that to the pure, everything is pure, and such questions can be seen as innocent and childlike in the paradisiacal state beyond (or before) good and evil, but on another interpretation they are clearly meant as transgressing common morality.

Truth or dare

Regularly the guests of *Paradise Hotel* are engaged in different social games ('Twists!'), scripted by the producers in order to maintain the attention of the viewers. For instance, the contestants are instructed to play a version of the children's game 'Truth or dare'. In the Norwegian second series, the male and female guests were separated and asked to prepare questions to ask the other group. Not surprisingly, the content almost instantly took an intimate turn and was sometimes stretched to absurd levels of filth. The male members were asked the size of their private parts, a question that was pretty innocent in comparison to the boy's ultimate question to the girls (apologies to the reader for the transgressive question): 'If you had to suffer a double penetration in the same body opening, would you prefer it vaginal or anal?'

Later on, the contestants spontaneously played similar games of 'Truth or dare'. One version consisted of telling everybody, including the quarter of a million viewers, something that they had never revealed before. For instance, Stian recounted an embarrassing episode from his puberty when his mother accidentally caught him while he was masturbating. The show resembles the Freudian ethical ideal of bringing everything out in the open, and it is part of what Denzin (1995) has called a postmodern 'pornography of the visible' that assists in making everything visible, serving to realise 'the dream of a transparent society', criticised by Foucault (p. 190). In general, *Paradise Hotel* is a useful reminder of Foucault's critique of the limited potential of liberation that is left in the sexual revolution. The show could be said to represent a reality genre and medialised equivalent to hardcore pornography, which, after decades of close-ups, is running out of ideas on how 'to bring it to the next level'.

Full frontal

Body shame, an apprehensive sense of segregation at being revealed as unbearably naked in the face of an apparently omniscient community, is depicted in the original Fall (Katz, 1996). A frequent complaint among the male guests in the second season of the Norwegian *Paradise Hotel* was that of sexual frustration. They were constantly exposed to lightly dressed, attractive women, and given no option (yet) to sexually engage them. One of the male contestants, again Stian, sexually aroused by physically flirting in the pool, therefore 'relieved himself' one day. Accidentally, he was caught masturbating in the bathroom by two of the other male participants who came looking for him. Nevertheless, Stian didn't stop from embarrassment or cover his genitals like Adam and Eve (after having eaten the fruit), but carried on with the self-stimulation laughing in front of his comrades, testifying to the shamelessness prior to eating the fruit of wisdom. This episode became a much talked-about event among the guests at *Paradise Hotel*. Nevertheless Stian's popularity appeared only to increase amid the others for his misbehaviour. Hence, Stian both verbally and behaviourally in *Paradise Hotel*, acted out his inner demons: his super-ego (maybe his mother) which told him that masturbation was something private and shameful. Of course, as Foucault, and later authors like Michel Houellebecq have objected (see Chapter 8), sexual deliverances like these episodes have turned the idea of emancipation into a joke that is not funny anymore.

Fame monster

In the biblical story of Adam and Eve we learn that they are banished from the Garden of Eden before they get to eat of The Tree of Life which gives immortality. The equivalent mechanism in the postmodern story of Paradise is that the contestants are thrown out of Paradise's media stage before they reach modern immortality, namely, lasting fame. In fact, only a few people succeed in becoming 'true winners' and achieve the late modern celebrity status. The celebrity scene is limited, allowing only a certain amount of people on it at a time, which means that most *Paradise Hotel* contestants are not permitted a permanent stay there. We can speculate that it is here, in the failure to make fame enduring in the weeks, months and years after the TV cameras have been turned off, that we can rediscover the allegedly disappearing feeling of shame. The shame of being an unsuccessful reality-star, which even the winners of *Paradise Hotel* are not protected against. Finalist Thea, now impregnated from her stay in paradise, is asked whether she stills receives offers related to *Paradise Hotel*: 'No, it's not as if you demonstrate a talent in there which you can build upon. That is unless you want to join a drinking contest' [Our translation] (Danielsen, 2010). This shame, however, begins only after the banishment from *Paradise* (*Hotel*).

Adam and Eve gained self-reflexivity when they ate from the forbidden fruit – and man was from this point forever transformed from a creature to a creator. The shameless currents in Western consumer culture that *Paradise Hotel* attempts to emulate try to make us believe that the human being is undergoing a second transgression: we are on our way to becoming creators, without the price of living with shame. If some of the generations of young and beautiful guests at *Paradise Hotel* convincingly demonstrate that they really are *shameless* – with no fear of standing naked in front of the gaze of the modern God (the television camera) – does this mean that they must have lost freedom and their selves on the way, in a literal Kierkegaardian sense? We have argued that their freedom as reality celebrities is rather limited and consists of playing along with the show's commercial interests in nudity, drama and confessions, and afterwards, if they are lucky and permitted a permanent stay in the medial version of immortality, they must continue to play this role as the casual, shameless self. In the postmodern consumer culture, no one is allowed to say what freedom should consist of, but it seems uncontroversial to state that the room to re-create oneself, after the creation of oneself as a successful *Paradise Hotel* reality, is limited.

Conclusions: The shameful reality of everybody else

In this analysis, we have primarily focused on what takes place on TV for the inhabitants of Paradise. Yet, there is of course a real life for most young people (and ourselves) who comprise the interested audience that would like to become famous through shows like *Paradise Hotel*, but who fail to live up to its inclusion criteria of having a physical package of youth and beauty and an entertaining personality. Around the island of shamelessness that is *Paradise Hotel*, one probably finds shame on all fronts – the shame of not being twenty-something, the shame of not being beautiful, the shame of not being fit, the shame of not being sexually attractive and, ultimately, the shame of not being famous. A reality show like *Paradise Hotel* is first and foremost a mirror of current desires in the market society. Like most façades it is not always a beautiful sight when one starts to look behind the glamorous and shining surface.

In Eden, God was the omniscient observer, but in our world, the public, we, the viewers, are omniscient, witnessing every detail of the lives of the late modern Adams and Eves. In the previous chapter, Bjarne Riis confessed not to God, but to the public, and in *Paradise Hotel*, the eye of the camera has replaced the eye of God that sees everything. Like the original biblical myth of Eden, immortality is never reached – fame will not last: the shameless Self usually only lasts a short period of time. Shamelessness is temporary, but shame is permanent. This seems to be the lasting moral lesson of *Paradise Hotel* after all.

Reflections on the reading of *Paradise Hotel*

I have here provided an abridged version of our reading of *Paradise Hotel*. We have tried to read the show as a whole, in light of (an inverse version of) the biblical storyline. The show is part of the everyday life of the researchers; it is something we sometimes watch, and something that is talked about among friends and colleagues, and definitely something that fills the magazines on display in the Scandinavian supermarkets. Although many of us would be embarrassed to admit that we enjoy watching such a show, it seems fair to conclude that the show displays certain themes that are central to life in a postmodern world, such as visual exposure to others, sex, shame and shamelessness.

What have we done in order to read the show? The analytic process can be reconstructed in light of the six steps that I use in this book:

1 The *topic* was chosen by my co-writer and myself simply because the show interested and disturbed us. There was in this sense a clear breakdown in our understanding: Why does such a display of bad taste (according to conventional morality) become so popular? Does the show say anything about specific postmodern themes and/or about more persistent questions about selfhood?
2 We *collected materials* by watching the show and reading about it. There was no specific method of selecting individual episodes for analysis. We went along with whatever caught our attention, but still tried to provide a valid overview of episodes and happenings that was faithful to the spirit of the show.
3 The *literature* that we consulted was somewhat unusual. It consisted of the Bible, existential philosophy (Kierkegaard), and sociological theory of shame and selfhood (Katz). In this way, we strove for the kind of 'conceptual audacity' that Maffesoli (1989) emphasises as central to everyday life studies. The reading of *Paradise Hotel* as an inverse biblical story of the Fall was quite straightforward when we first noticed all the implicit biblical connotations in the show, and this storyline structured our analyses.
4 We *continued collecting materials* by going back and forth between theoretical readings and analyses of the show.
5 *Analytic writing* was not a separate stage, but something we used as a method of inquiry to develop our ideas and work towards a coherent perspective on the show that would enable us to mend the breakdown in understanding. I believe that the breakdown and the ensuing 'mystery' (Alvesson & Kärreman, 2011) have been solved, not least because of the mythological frame that we invoked to read the show.
6 The final step is publication, and this was an interesting case because I was only second author of the analysis, working together with a colleague who knew the show much better than I did. My main contribution was to provide the theoretical frame, while Ole Jacob Madsen did most of the actual writing and chose the empirical examples from the show. As I write these words, we are in the process of having the full paper published.

As was the case with the readings of the photograph earlier in this chapter, all three analytic strategies have been used in some way, however implicitly: we made the obvious obvious by describing evident (but often unnoticed) features of the show; we made the hidden obvious by reading the episodes in light of a storyline (from the Bible) that was not directly visible as such, but which simultaneously seems to work as an organising principle for the events; and we tried to make the obvious dubious by questioning whether the alleged transgression of moral norms, which are central to the show, are in fact socially transgressive or rather just reinforce prevailing norms in a postmodern consumer society (this aspect appears more clearly in the original article, though).

EXERCISE

A simple exercise for the reader who is interested in visual materials is just to browse through a magazine and look at the images. Whenever a picture seems particularly interesting, you should stop and do the following.

- Describe the image – make the obvious obvious. What is there to be seen in the image? You should continue writing down descriptions of the image for at least 15 minutes. Just write – don't stop or censor yourself. Keep going even if you feel you are just noting the obvious (this is exactly the point!).
- Then consider what is absent in the image – and try to make the hidden obvious. What could we have expected to find? Why is it not there? What do we know about how the image was constructed?
- After this you may try to destabilise your own understanding of the image – make the obvious dubious. What would we say had the image had different elements or had it been arranged differently?
- Finally, write down some reflections about why you noticed this specific image as particularly salient. Is there something about your own life that made it stand out? What are the obviousnesses in your life that this image broke down, or, less dramatically, meddled with?

The exercise can be done with images, but you can go through more or less the same procedure using films or television.

EIGHT

Books of fiction

For many of us, books of fiction have been formative. Some books are significant and have played a key role in making us who we are. This is obvious on personal as well as on cultural levels. Personally, I would not have been the same person had I not read (a children's version of) Herman Melville's *Moby Dick* as a child, Jean-Paul Sartre's *La Nausée* when I was in high school, Michel Houellebecq's *Atomised* when I was struggling with my doctoral dissertation, and Haruki Murakami's *The Wind-Up Bird Chronicle* as I had become an adult, a father, and was looking for more poetic, serene, but still fundamentally melancholic resources from which to experience the world. As I recently read Cormac McCarthy's *The Road*, I was moved like never before by prose, and was reminded of the fascinating evocative powers of written words. As in all hermeneutic processes, there is no one-way street here: I have surely been formed by the books that I've read, but it is just as certain that I picked up specific books because of the person that I had become. As in all our dealings with the world, there is a dynamic and transactional process at work, rather than a linear one.

This also applies to the cultural level. On this level, it goes without saying that books of fiction are shaping our social worlds and have done so historically. But it is also true that cultural factors have determined which forms of fiction have been produced. In any case, it is difficult to imagine what the world would have looked like without the invention of the modern novel. Benedict Anderson has even argued that without this particular literary genre, there would not have been nation states as we know them. The novel represented the technical means for re-presenting the kind of imagined community that is the nation (Anderson, 1991, p. 25). In this and many other ways, literature functions as a symbolic resource that at once gives us interpretative means with which to understand our social lives, but simultaneously assists in creating forms of individual and collective human living. Literature opens up new forms of experience and action and gives us new choices. Not always for the good. Sarbin recounts the story of the

'Werther epidemic', which followed the publication of Goethe's famous novel *The Sorrows of Young Werther*, published in 1774. This sentimental book (partly autobiographical) about unrequited love depicted Werther's suicide, which became a model for living and dying, leading to scores of people, in particular adolescents, committing suicide in the final quarter of the eighteenth century (Sarbin, 2004). Werther as a figure expressed the romantic sensibility, and we can today understand much about the late eighteenth century by reading the book.

In this chapter, I approach books of fiction as a resource for understanding human life. Such books represent everyday life materials in the sense that most of us own books, read books and use books when we think about our lives and our relationships. I thus approach books, in particular novels, as 'symbolic resources', which is a term used in particular by cultural psychologists (Zittoun, 2006). Not just literature, of course, but also films, music and religious discourses, for example, function as symbolic resources in our lives to regulate emotions (e.g. when we sing lullabies to our children) or make choices (e.g. when the devout Christian considers what Jesus would have done in a difficult situation). But I am not just interested in studying the symbolic contents and uses of literature. I am interested in the role of literature in qualitative inquiry in a more radical sense, namely as a form of qualitative inquiry in itself (Brinkmann, 2009). I shall argue that books of fiction can not only enter qualitative analyses as data – although this is one important function indeed – but also more radically as pieces of qualitative analyses in their own right.

Research, literature and the crisis of representation

All research that has been written down has a literary dimension. All texts make use of tropes and rhetorical effects, and this goes not just for innovative forms of writing in qualitative inquiry, but also for the most positivist article that reports on a scientific experiment. In the latter case, the rhetorical devices employed usually function to hide the author's person behind a standardised language of science, according to which one is not allowed to write 'I'. Rather than 'I did this and that...', such articles state that 'An experiment was conducted...', as if it had conducted itself. One has to write 'It can be concluded that...' rather than 'I believe that...', as if an experiment can draw its own conclusions without the interference of acting and judging human beings. A traditional scientific journal article is not built upon an absence of rhetorical elements, although these are generally not discussed in scientific debates (many people mistakenly think that they only concern 'form' rather than 'content'), but represents a literary genre of its own, with a specific set of rules that did not suddenly fall from the sky, but has a history and could have been very different.

Since the mid-1980s, qualitative researchers have increasingly turned their attention towards the literary dimensions of human and social science. A number of reorientations took place, following from what Denzin and Lincoln call the crisis of representation (Denzin & Lincoln, 2005a). This crisis was a complex event, when researchers of many stripes began to question whether it is possible to capture human experience accurately in scientific texts. In line with the post-modern ideas that emerged at that time, a certain scepticism arose concerning the possibility of devising valid descriptions of human lives. For if reality can only be understood perspectively, how can one know whether a description is valid? When we cannot leap out of language and compare our linguistic descriptions with the world as it is independently of our descriptions, how can we talk about descriptions being more or less true? Why bother representing anything, when it is clear that our descriptions do not mirror what we describe? Obviously, a description of the sunset does not 'look like' the sunset that is described. If so, how can it be that only one kind of representation of human experience – the so-called realistic one that leaves out the experiencing researcher as a person – counts as legitimate when it becomes increasingly clear that this kind of representation is a social construction, nothing more than a contingent product of historical circumstances (Rosenblatt, 2002)? Such questions became central during the crisis of representation and led to a literary turn in sociology and ethnography.

The literary turn implied qualitative researchers creatively turning their attention to different and alternative forms of literary representation. It has led to a general blurring of the traditional boundaries between scientific and literary forms of writing. The impetus to this blurring has much of its background in postmodernism, but more specifically, perhaps, in an emergence of a certain kind of philosophy of language. As Habermas said in a chapter on philosophy and science as literature:

> The levelling of the distinction between the genres of philosophy and science on the one hand and that of literature on the other hand is the expression of an understanding of literature that is derived from philosophical discussions. The context of these discussions is the turn from the philosophy of consciousness to the philosophy of language, specifically that variation of the linguistic turn that does away with the legacy of the philosophy of consciousness in a particularly relentless way. (Habermas, 1995, p. 207)

When Habermas refers to those who have tried to do away with the philosophy of consciousness in 'a particularly relentless way', he thinks more specifically of Heidegger and post-structuralists such as Derrida and Foucault, for whom all validity claims 'become immanent in particular discourses' (Habermas, 1995, p. 209). If taken seriously, this leaves scientific writing as just another genre without any of its modernist truth privileges. The late Richard Rorty (1980) can be said to have radicalised the view that philosophy (and science) is 'just' another form of literature or human conversation – and nothing else ('just' in quotation marks because for Rorty there is nothing more important than literature and conversation). Rorty's pragmatism led him to the view that all human productions, including literary ones, should be judged in terms of their edifying qualities, in terms of how well they enable us to cope with, rather than copy, the world. Famously, Rorty's institutional move from philosophy to the department of comparative literature at Stanford reflected his view that philosophy and literature are part of the same human conversation.

Before proceeding, I shall first introduce a distinction between three ways of using literature – fiction – in qualitative inquiry, and I will then discuss some objections to my idea that literature should count as qualitative research.

Writers as informants, inspirations or researchers?

If we frame the question in terms of how literary writers and their works can be received by qualitative researchers, I believe that there are three main roles in which we may cast writers of fiction: we can view them as *informants*, as *sources of inspiration*, or as *researchers in their own right* (see Table 8.1). I shall deal with each role in turn.

Writers as informants

In spite of being fictitious, there is no doubt that literature can provide us with one significant window into human experience in a given historical and cultural context. If we consider the first modern novel as an example, Cervantes' *Don Quixote* from 1605 (which I return to below), we can relate its contents and narrative structure to the historical transformation that was occurring at the time: from a premodern culture of chivalry and medieval folklore to a modern disenchanted culture that came to include a split between objectivity and subjectivity. The very genre – the novel – to which it belongs (and which it assisted in creating) testifies to this transformation, since the novel as a literary medium is quite different from premodern narrative forms in fairytales and folktales, where more

Table 8.1 Roles of works and writers of fiction in qualitative inquiry

Possible roles of writers of fiction in qualitative inquiry	Possible roles of works of fiction in qualitative inquiry
Informants	Data for research
Inspirations	Exemplary forms of representation
Researchers	Research reports

canonical situations – the same for everyone – were in focus, and where it did not matter much who the individual protagonist was, or how he or she individually experienced the world. In this quite straightforward sense, writers can be informants about a historical epoch, a culture, by supplying materials that researchers can analyse in order to say something interesting about the given time and place. Alternatively, but in a similar vein, writers can be informants about themselves, as when we analyse the personality dynamics of Kafka or Dostoevsky by using their works as externalised signs of who they were (what I called Self 2 in Chapter 4). Novels and other forms of writing here become *data* for researchers.

Writers as inspirations

Another role of works of fiction in qualitative understandings of human and social phenomena is as inspiration for researchers. This is perhaps the most widespread role today, at least judging from a reading of exemplary and contemporary postmodern analyses. Rosenblatt, for example, who is at once a social scientist and a novelist, argues that writing fiction (in addition to research papers), 'opens to possibility' for him and develops a 'better ear' in qualitative researchers (Rosenblatt, 2002, p. 907). Reading literature and experimenting with different forms of literary representation of human experience can develop more readable research with more aesthetic merit (Richardson & St. Pierre, 2005). According to proponents of investigative poetry, for example, this approach can also, by merging art and science, help us understand the social structures that are embodied as lived experience in individuals (Hartnett & Engels, 2005, p. 1044).

Richard Harvey Brown developed a poetics for sociology as early as the 1970s and analysed sociological texts as if they were novels, poetic or dramatic texts (Brown, 1977). An argument from the most radical of today's qualitative researchers is that sociology is nothing more than a particular literary-aesthetic practice. Consequently, aesthetic, but also ethical and political, criteria become decisive, when the quality of research is assessed. Some researchers will give up completely the traditional scientific criteria of validity, reliability and generalisability, and replace them with criteria that are grounded in a 'methodology of the heart', based on love, care, hope and forgiveness (Denzin, Lincoln, & Giardina, 2006, p. 770). This is a highly contested move (see Hammersley, 2008, for a critical discussion), but there is probably no doubt that the advocates of the 'methodology of the heart' articulate a significant tendency that forms the background to some of the discussions in the present chapter.

As Habermas (1995) reminds us in his essay on philosophy and science as literature, however, the merging of art and science is not a radically new dimension of social research. Famous human and social scientists, such as Freud and Adorno, were not just important as researchers, but also as *writers*. Thus, in 1930,

Freud received the Goethe prize for the literary qualities of his work, but as a scientist Freud would no doubt object to someone like Denzin or Rorty, if they were to advance the argument that the *only* relevant judgement to pass on Freud's work is one that concerns its literary qualities (in a broad sense).

From this perspective, where researchers look to fiction in order to learn how to write, novels and other forms of literature can be *inspirational*, both regarding the process of 'gathering data', where one must learn to see and observe perhaps the tiniest details of everyday life that escapes us in our more unreflective routines, but also regarding the production of the outcome of research, at least if we want to communicate our research in ways that are effective, touching, and moving. Richardson thus tells us that for her a qualitative research report should inspire to something beyond itself. She is 'inspired to do things because of aesthetics – aesthetic crafting creates the kinetic response in me' (Richardson & Lockridge, 1998, p. 330). If we take the pragmatist stance that was outlined in Chapter 2 and approach research as *kinesis*, as something that is meant to move us (in all senses of the word), as individuals and groups, rather than something that maintains status quo (*stasis*), then literature can be deeply inspiring and kinetic. Novels and other forms of writing here become *exemplary forms of representation* for researchers.

Writers as researchers

The role of fiction that I just addressed concerns the literary qualities of social and human science productions. I will now go in the reverse direction, so to speak, namely by addressing the scientific qualities of literary productions. Here, a good writer appears not simply as a source of data for researchers, nor as someone who (simply) inspires researchers, but as a researcher as such. This is admittedly a radical move, but it seems relevant to go in this direction since literary writers are often adept at depicting the qualities of everyday life. The argument can even be made that if we conceive 'life as literature' (Nehamas, 1985), then it seems that literary versions of life are in fact the truest ones – and definitely truer than any versions of life that empty it of its experiential and aesthetic qualities. Seen in this light, novels and other forms of writing can become *research reports* in themselves, as I hope to argue and illustrate more fully below.

One advantage of novels as 'research reports' is that unlike much 'proper scientific writing' that often works by synthesising, by presenting coherent narratives, and by crafting an order out of what is seemingly disordered (this is what most 'methods of analysis' recommend, directly or indirectly), literary writers normally have much more leeway in staying with the incoherent and disordered that often characterise our lives. Stephen Frosh (2007) has called for 'disintegrating qualitative research'. He specifically warns against the tendency in narrative qualitative research to have all aspects of human experience fit neatly into more or less coherent narratives. He argues that human subjects are not just integrated through narratives, but also fragmented, and he defends the idea that the human subject is '*never* a whole, is always riven with partial drives, social discourses that frame available modes of experience, ways of being that are contradictory and reflect the shifting allegiances of power as they play across the body and the mind' (p. 638). Frosh does not want us to abandon narrative or other order-seeking forms of analysis, but rather wants qualitative researchers to hold on to the dialectic of deconstructionist fragmentation and narrative integration when describing human experience. Qualitative research exists, as he says, in a tension between 'on the one hand, a deconstructionist framework in which the human subject is understood as positioned in and through competing discourses and, on the other, a humanistic framework in which the integrity of the subject is taken to be both a starting- and end-point of analysis' (p. 639). It seems to me that literary writers have some advantages here in being allowed to move more freely between the deconstructionist and the humanistic viewpoints. Someone who does exactly this is the French novelist Michel Houellebecq (born in 1958), whom I shall address below.

Not just fiction but also journalism has been discussed as a form of qualitative research in the past decades. Norman Denzin, for example, has defended a form of interpretive ethnography, according to which detective writing and journalism have become a very significant knowledge-producing genre in a postmodern world of ambiguities and violence (Denzin, 1997). Denzin is radical in his insistence that journalism and also crime fiction are legitimate, and perhaps even superior, sources of knowledge about contemporary society, compared to traditional qualitative methods such as interviewing or fieldwork. Must we say, then, that we can learn more about society and human lives from Elmore Leonard's novels than from Pierre Bourdieu's sociology, for example? No, this is too simplistic, and what I will defend instead is that we can learn different things, and that both are interesting, but also that it is futile to draw a sharp line between what we will count as literature and art (fiction) and what we call sociology and science (facts). The relationship between qualitative inquiry and journalism is thematised in Box 8.1.

BOX 8.1

Journalism as qualitative inquiry?

Journalists can be some of the most acute observers of everyday life, and much that goes by the name of journalism can perhaps also pass as qualitative research as such. Journalists do research, interviewing, observations, and they keep track of what they do – just as qualitative researchers. They rarely have explicit methods of

---

analysis, but they do have books on how to practise their craft, such as the volume edited by Walt Harrington: *Intimate Journalism: The Art and Craft of Reporting Everyday Life*. In the opening essay, Harrington describes the basic techniques of intimate journalism, or, as we might put it, the journalism of everyday life: think, report, and write in scenes; capture a narrator's voice; gather telling details from subjects' lives; gather real-life dialogue; gather 'interior' monologue; establish a time line that makes possible a narrative (beginning, middle, end); immerse yourself in the lives of the subjects; gather physical details; make the story resonate in readers; and: Don't make things up! (Harrington, 1997, pp. xx–xxi).

The best way to appreciate the qualities of good pieces of journalism as qualitative inquiry is to read some examples. One recommendation could be David Finkel's 'TV without guilt' (Finkel, 1997). It is a story about a family living a life with constant exposure to television. But, contrary to what one might think, it is not negativistic or critical, but takes a descriptive stance that it shares with much good ethnography. The piece begins by situating us in the family: 'The first TV to come on is the one in the master bedroom, a 13-inch Hitachi' (p. 77). And then it goes on to report on the day of the family, by including dialogues among family members and also some social science statistics. There are funny stories, like Bonnie (the mother) telling Finkel that 'Steven [her son] was born during the halftime of a Redskins game' (p. 79). About her daughter Ashley's birth, Bonnie remembers that she cut out the TV guide the day she was born (p. 80). TV completely structures Bonnie's life, but she has absolutely no guilt about it. Finkel writes descriptively, but perhaps with a gentle irony, which gives the reader a sense of ambivalence. By simply describing some of the TV shows that are on during the day (especially talk shows), Finkel shows us the absurdities of modern life without having to say it. The writing is evocative rather than argumentative. Not until the end of the piece, when Bonnie reveals that TV may be keeping her from thinking about more serious things, is there a more explicit criticism of the role of television in American life.

In Finkel's afterword to the article, written many years later, he writes that his story made people think, and he also reflects on the ethics of reporting the story. He received 70 letters from readers who were angry with Bonnie, and people also called Bonnie on the phone and told her that she should not be allowed to have children.

I have merely provided a glimpse of the concrete, descriptive richness of Finkel's journalistic ethnography of television viewing (a richness shared by many other pieces in the edited volume by Harrington), and I recommend this and similar stories to readers, who are interested in learning from good journalists who can capture and report particular details in precise and insightful ways.

Distinguishing qualitative inquiry from books of fiction?

Before moving on to an analysis of Houellebecq as an everyday life researcher, working with books of fiction as his medium, I will discuss four criteria of demarcation that have been invoked in an attempt to distinguish qualitative inquiry from fiction, but which – I shall argue – all ultimately fail. Reflecting upon these criteria may help in making clearer why and how books of fiction can be (and can be used in) qualitative inquiry. I refer to the four criteria as the phenomena, truth, methods and metaphors, respectively.

1 *The phenomena*: Can we find a difference between art (fiction) and research (facts) in those phenomena that the two activities address? Trivially, research can be said to address real phenomena (events, processes) while literature expresses the writer's free imagination. Is this a basic difference that allows demarcating the two genres from one another?

At first sight, this may sound very obvious. But if we look more closely, it turns out that it is far too simplistic. On the one hand, it ignores the fact that much research involves and produces fictions, and on the other, it forgets that much literature is concerned with 'real' phenomena. The former aspect was touched upon, when I referred to the crisis of representation: writing about the world is a poetic process in the original sense of the term. Poetic comes from the Greek *poiesis*, which refers to the act of creating something. And not just radical qualitative researchers, but also traditional quantitative people, are poetic in this sense, when they produce statistical averages that do not exist 'in reality' or tell us about real individuals. Averages do not refer to real, existing particulars. Still, this form of research can be very useful, and the same goes for other fictive objects that researchers produce (what matters, as the pragmatists would say, is what we can *do* with these objects). Another example from classical sociology could be Max Weber's ideal types that do not refer to real people, but may still inform us of significant features of society and thus increase our knowledge of the world.

On the other hand, art is not (at least rarely) a process of pure invention without connection to reality. Often, artists describe their practice as a practice of inquiry. They frequently refer to themselves as people who are *studying* the world. Artists study human experience and the great novels are almost always about the immortal themes in human life, such as love, finitude, guilt, deceit, etc. It is difficult to claim that such novels do *not* study these phenomena in ways that can give us insights that are at least as valid as those that come from sociology or psychology. David Foster Wallace put it in a very straightforward way: 'Fiction's about what it is to be a fucking human being'.

That fiction can produce knowledge about the phenomena of human life has been expressed very clearly by the Danish poet and filmmaker, Jørgen Leth. He refers to himself as an anthropologist, and his personal hero is the classical ethnographer Bronislaw Malinowski. Leth says that 'My basic idea is: I don't know anything, but I would like to know something' (Leth, 2006, p. 4). From this very basic idea, Leth conducts his studies through films, poems and essays. The classic avant-garde film, *The Perfect Human Being* from 1968, is referred to, by Leth, as a pseudo-anthropological film: 'The movements and behaviours of the persons are studied, as under a microscope. [...] It is not a story with a conclusion. It is a (fictive) investigation' (p. 3). It is hard not to acknowledge that Leth's films, although they are *directed*, nonetheless provide us with knowledge about human phenomena in line with traditional anthropological films (in *The Perfect Human Being* the topic is the phenomenology of human movements). Experiments and interviews are also, in a sense, directed processes. In short, I will argue that we cannot distinguish between art and research, using the phenomena as criteria, because both are practices that study human experience.

2 *Truth*: Can truth be a criterion? Can we say that the goal of research is to state truths while the goal of art is much more contested – some say that art should entertain, while others argue that it should be edifying or perhaps spiritual – but it cannot involve truth, can it?

Again, this is simplistic in a double sense, and it all depends on one's notion of truth. On the one hand, not everyone agrees that the goal of research is truth. From a pragmatic perspective, the goal of social science is to solve the problems that humans meet in history. So in order for this criterion to make sense, the concept of truth must at least be clarified, which is notoriously difficult. On the other hand, it is also problematic to keep art and fiction outside the domain of truth. For a pragmatist like Rorty, the true is the useful, and since art can be useful (edifying, insightful, emancipatory), it can be true in the same way as a scientific result. And Rorty himself read and analysed novels in the same way he read philosophical texts (Rorty, 1989).

Furthermore, in his essay on the origin of the work of art, Heidegger argued that for a work of art to be great, it has to be *true*. As he says: 'In the artwork, the truth of beings has set itself to work. Art is truth setting itself to work' (Heidegger, 1993, p. 165). For Heidegger, truth is not confined to science or logic, for a great work of art can convey an experience of the truth of Being. Truth, in Heidegger's sense, means that beings are brought into unconcealedness (*aletheia* in Greek). This is not truth as correct representation of the world, but truth as an *occurrence*, as something that happens (e.g. *as* a work of art). A work of art 'is not the reproduction of some particular entity that happens to be at hand at any given time; it is, on the contrary, the reproduction of things' general essence' (p. 162). Heidegger illustrates this point with a detailed analysis of van Gogh's famous painting of a pair of peasant shoes that point to the truth that 'this equipment belongs to the *earth*' (p. 159) in Heidegger's special terminology. Incidentally, the idea that truth is something that *happens*, something *set to work* (rather than an ethereal correspondence relation), unites Heidegger with the pragmatists and their *kinetic* notion of truth (cf. Richardson's view mentioned above). A painting – as well as well-crafted qualitative analyses – can *show* or *present* truths, but does not represent them (cf. the discussion of representation in Chapter 2).

In my opinion, we do not have to look to Heidegger's enigmatic words to appreciate the fact that the concept of truth is a much more problematic candidate for a criterion to distinguish art from science than one should think. All great art has the potential to increase human understanding and thus aspire to a form of truth, while much science likewise turns out to be aesthetically appealing. A recent analysis has been crafted by Lorraine Daston and Peter Galison in a thorough historical analysis of the concept of objectivity (Daston & Galison, 2007). The authors tell the story of changing notions of objectivity by analysing scientific atlases, not just geographical but also zoological, anatomical, botanical and astronomical atlases. They conclude that objectivity and the depiction of 'how things look' is a deeply historical and changing affair, and it becomes obvious that aesthetic aspects are inseparable from the cognitive aspects of science. And, to play along on the theme of objectivity, one could even argue that when the subject matter of research is human experience, then an aesthetically inspired form of research may turn out to be the *most* objective one – and thus the truest – since it comes as close as possible to the nature of the subject matter, which is one definition of objectivity (Kvale & Brinkmann, 2008).

3 *Methods*: What about methodology then? Supposedly, research becomes distinct from art by using standardised and well-controlled methods to produce knowledge? Art, on its side, is conversely governed by nothing but the individual idiosyncrasies of the artist and her wild, creative processes?

Again, this is too simplistic, and a look at methods cannot provide us with an adequate criterion. First, we can question the idea that research necessarily follows specific methodological steps. Philosopher of science Paul Feyerabend even concluded, in a book aptly entitled *Against Method*, that if scientists had in fact followed the methodological prescriptions of philosophers of science, then the great discoveries could not have been made (Feyerabend, 1975). Scientific progress is made, at least on a grand scale of paradigmatic shifts, when the rules are broken, and not when they are followed. And what counts as 'methodological rules' will vary from one paradigm to the next. In Chapter 2, we also saw in the quote from the anthropologist Jean Lave that it is misguided to say that there is 'a method' in anthropology. The person is the instrument – in art as in research.

Furthermore, on a looser definition of method, artists frequently refer to ways of working that are well tested and systematic and that usually lead to desired results – completely in line with scientific methods. We may once more refer to the poetics of Jørgen Leth, who does not talk much about methods, but about what he calls 'rules of the game'. His most general rules are: 'Find an area, delimit it, examine it, write it down' (Leth, 2006, p. 7). Together they form a quite specific way of working that has been developed to make use of what Leth calls 'the gifts of coincidence', where the world is allowed to show itself to the investigative researcher/artist. For Leth, studying an area demands what Jean Lave also describes: a personal involvement in the area, where one does not just observe the subject matter from the outside, but one must immerse oneself in it, and *live* it (see Barone & Eisner, 2012, for an account of arts-based research that is close to the poetics of Leth).

All in all, we may conclude in this case as well that it is difficult to draw a line between art and research. On a narrow interpretation of the concept of method, neither research nor art are sufficiently methodical (cf. Jean Lave on craftsmanship in Chapter 2). And, on a broader interpretation, both activities are methodical. Art can be methodical, and research can be based on craftsmanship rather than method rules (Kvale & Brinkmann, 2008, Chapter 5).

4 *Metaphors*: The final criterion of demarcation concerns metaphors. While scientific research speaks literally and aims to 'say it as it is', artistic inquiry is imaginative and employs metaphors.

This attempt to demarcate one from the other recognises that both research and art can provide us with knowledge or understanding, but the claim is that artistic understanding is radically different from the scientific one. Once more, I will argue that this rests on an illusion: that we can exorcise metaphors from our scientific descriptions and analyses. A metaphorical understanding is one where one phenomenon is understood in light of another phenomenon. For example, the sentence 'When he discovered the sodium-potassium pump, he took the first step toward the Nobel prize' rests on the metaphor 'A gain in understanding is moving through space' or 'Research is travelling'. Doing research is not (necessarily) literally travelling, but when we think about this activity in light of the embodied experience of moving through space, there are certain aspects of the activity that we understand better.

Recent theorising on metaphors has demonstrated that all abstract concepts are defined metaphorically (Johnson, 2007). This means that all concepts that are not tied to immediate sensory experience are meaningful only on the background of metaphors. And it is unthinkable that research in the human and social sciences can be cleansed of such metaphors. Theoretical concepts like social change, democracy and power are abstract in the sense that their meanings are not tied to immediate embodied experience, and they acquire their meaning from metaphorical processes instead. We simply cannot imagine research without metaphors; at least not if we wish to go beyond the logical positivists' reduction of scientific knowledge to immediate elementary sentences (like 'I see something red'). Rather than eliminating metaphors from our descriptions and analyses, we should instead pay closer attention to how our metaphorical ways of understanding and expressing ourselves determine the ways we see the world.

Literature as qualitative inquiry

After these general discussions, I will look more closely at one particular writer of fiction and try to see what happens if we read him as a qualitative researcher of everyday life. In Box 8.2, I have recycled the lyrical words of Michel Houellebecq to compose a simulacrum in the form of a fragment that condenses his 'lyrical sociology' as it could be called.

BOX 8.2

Using Michel's words – a simulacrum

At the dawn of the twenty-first century, tourism had become the world's largest industry. Members of the so-called Western societies travelled to more or less exotic places of the planet to experience the local varieties of food, drugs, and sex. Being a tourist could seemingly, for brief moments, cover up the intense loneliness and bitterness that had pervaded the civilisation. A more expensive alternative was psychotherapy. Most people would live according to the rules of work and consumption. Sometimes it would be tight, extremely tight, but on the whole, they would manage. Tax papers being up to date, bills paid on time. People would not leave their homes without their identity cards (and the special little wallet for the Visa). Yet they had no friends.

Some people had been capable of love, but this was no longer possible. A rare and overdue phenomenon, love can only flower under certain historical conditions, absolutely opposed to the freedom of morals, which characterised the era of modern materialism. Love as a kind of innocence and capacity for illusion, as a skill for epitomising the whole of the other sex in a single loved one, would seldom resist a year of sexual freedom, and never two. With ageing, people would become less seductive. The affection and interest in the world, so characteristic of the young members of the species, would be replaced by resentment and disgust, sickness and the anticipation of death. The historical passage from constraint and routine to autonomy and self-mastery was hailed by some as the final victory of the free, self-asserting individual. A few nostalgics would lament the passage into consumerism. The situation would not change until the advancement of scientific biology and organised New Age religion paved the way for the creation of posthuman individuals. A third metaphysical mutation would take place, succeeding those of Christianity and modern science.

A dream: He walks, reaches the border. Birds circle around something – probably a corpse. He is surrounded by hills of dry grass. The sunlight is unbearable, but he is no longer afraid.

He wakes, fully dressed, lying across his bed. He hears the truck unloading at the delivery entrance of the mall. The TV is on. It is a little after seven o'clock.

Crafting such fragments can be used as an evocative way of reporting the experience of living in a postmodern world (Baudrillard, 2007). Following from postmodern ideas, qualitative researchers have for more than twenty years addressed their research practice as one that essentially involves *writing*. It has become clear that there 'is no "natural" way of writing about social and cultural life. Even though we may be used to some ways of writing that we treat uncritically, this should not blind us to the fact that they are conventional resources' (Atkinson, Coffey, & Delamont, 2003, p. 173). Furthermore, writing is increasingly seen not just as an eventual reporting of results, a discrete final phase in the process of doing research, but as a method of inquiry in itself. As examples, we have sociologist Laurel Richardson addressing writing as a method of inquiry (Richardson & St. Pierre, 2005), and we have the ethnographic reflections on 'writing culture' in the ground-breaking collection by James Clifford and George Marcus *Writing Culture: The Poetics and Politics of Ethnography* (Clifford & Marcus, 1986). Sociologist Norman Denzin concludes about contemporary social science:

> The narrative turn in the social sciences has been taken. We have told our tales from the field. Today we understand that we write culture, and that writing is not an innocent practice. We know the world only through our representations of it. (Denzin, 2001b, p. 23)

If we only know the world through our representations, and if we literally write culture, can we then conclude that if want to live in a literary, poetic and aesthetic culture, for example, we should strive to write this culture into being? And who does this better than literary writers? 'No one' would be one obvious answer to this question. This means that we could think of such writers as qualitative researchers, and this is what I will attempt to do in what follows. Instead of simply seeing philosophy and social science as a form of literature (which was Rorty's move), I will approach the issue from the opposite direction by conceiving literature as a form of qualitative social and human inquiry, relevant to our everyday lives. And I will exemplify this approach to literature as qualitative inquiry by looking at the contemporary French novelist, Michel Houellebecq, whose style of writing represents a form of literary and even lyrical sociology. I will argue that we, as qualitative researchers, can learn as much from Houellebecq about contemporary human lives, experiences and sufferings, as we can from more traditional forms of empirical qualitative research.

Houellebecq does more than inform us about human experience in the contemporary Western world. He also disturbs our sense of narrative. Other contemporary writers, also within more conventional social science, have argued for the necessity of other, non-narrative forms of understanding. Recently, Abbott (2007) has advocated what he calls 'lyrical sociology' and positioned himself 'against narrative'. He argues that mainstream 'analytic social science and the new narratives of the 1990s and later are simply different versions of the same thing: stories in the one case of variables and in the other of actors' (p. 70). Obviously, given my emphasis on narratives and storylines for understanding everyday life, I will not join a call to be 'against narrative' as such, but I am interested in the constructive side of the project of lyrical sociology, and lyrical social science more broadly: What can it *add* to our ways of working in qualitative inquiry? According to Abbott, a lyrical approach is in a profound sense *not* narrative. For unlike a narrative that reports a *happening*, lyrical writings express a *state of affairs* (p. 69), and Abbott opens his piece with Harvey Zorbaugh's (1929) sociological paean to the city of Chicago, a lyrical description of how the city struck this classical sociologist. This passage is worth quoting at length:

> The Chicago River, its waters stained by industry, flows back upon itself, branching to divide the city into the South Side, the North Side, and 'the great West Side.' In the river's southward bend lies the Loop, its skyline looming towards Lake Michigan. The Loop is the heart of Chicago, the knot in the steel arteries of elevated structure which pump in a ceaseless stream the three millions of population of the city into and out of its central business district. The canyon-like streets of the Loop rumble with the traffic of commerce. On its sidewalks throng people of every nation, pushing unseeingly past one another, into and out of office buildings, shops, theaters, hotels, and ultimately back to the north, south, and west 'sides' from which they came. For miles over what once was prairie now sprawls in endless blocks the city. (Zorbaugh, 1929, p. 1)

There are no stories in lyric, no 'recounting, explaining, comprehending – but rather the use of a single image to communicate a mood, an emotional sense of social reality' (Abbott, 2007, p. 73). Unlike a narrative writer, who tries to tell us and explain what happened, a lyrical writer 'aims to tell us of his or her intense reaction to some portion of the social process' (p. 76).

To be fair, the narratives that Abbott claims to be against are rather modernistic, and postmodern writers have had other approaches to narratives. Denzin (1997, p. 158) mentions non-fiction writers such as Capote, Mailer and Wolfe, who challenge the modernistic narrative structure of plot, setting, characters, locale and temporality. Still, most social science writers on narrative, such as Czarnizawska (2004), are interested in narratives as meaningful wholes, ordered structures etc., often with reference to Labov's structural approach to narratives. In her fine book on *Narratives in Social Science Research*, for example, Czarniawska argues that plot is the means by which events 'are brought into one meaningful whole' (p. 7) and that explanations of human conduct are possible 'because there is a certain teleology – sense of purpose – in all lived narratives' (p. 13). Unlike this integrationist and explanatory use of narratives, lyrical writers are able to create experiences of events without plot, of that which defies explanation – which seem to characterise much of the postmodern world. Abbott observes that very few social science books are explicitly lyrical, possibly because scientists want to *explain*, and explanation is almost inevitably narrative in character. Consequently, he urges us 'to look for whatever pieces of lyrical sociology we can find' (Abbott, 2007, p. 73).

I wish to present one main contender in the field of lyrical social science by addressing the work of the contemporary French novelist, Michel Houellebecq. Both Houellebecq's style of writing and the themes that he writes about warrant a characterisation of him as a lyrical sociologist. Houellebecq is a writer of fiction who, in my view, enables his reader to gain a deep yet non-narrative understanding of contemporary social life. I have chosen to look at Houellebecq because he is a writer who has taken a postmodern turn that is congruent with the postmodern turn in qualitative inquiry, but who, in my opinion, represents better the postmodern position than many writers *on* postmodernism (my analysis of Houellebecq was published in Brinkmann, 2009, and the following will represent an example of using literature as material in everyday life inquiry).

Houellebecq between fact and fiction

A first thing to note about Houellebecq's novels is the way they problematise the boundary of fact and fiction. It is difficult to determine whether they are autobiographical with more than a grain of factual truth or novels of pure fiction. They constantly play with the boundaries between biographical facts and fiction, and also with those between art and science. Often, the main character in Houellebecq's books is very much like the public appearance of 'the real Houellebecq', and also often bears the first name Michel. In *Atomised* (which has also been published in the USA as *The Elementary Particles*), we even learn that one of the main characters grew up with his grandmother, after having been left there by his parents who were too busy with self-realisation practices: The parents 'quickly realised that the burden of caring for a small child was incompatible with their personal freedom' (Houellebecq, 2001, p. 26). Houellebecq's personal story is similar, and he very much conceives himself as a victim of a culture where a shared moral order has broken down. In Schjørring's (2005) reading of Houellebecq, she argues that his first three books, *Whatever* (1998), *Atomised* (2001) and *Platform* (2002), can simply be read as autobiographical confessions.

In addition to playing with the boundaries between autobiography and fiction, Houellebecq also plays with those between literary and scientific writing. His books are full of references to the social sciences, especially sociology, with a favourite thinker being Auguste Comte (see Brinkmann, 2008a). In line with the classical positivist approach, Houellebecq's style of writing is objectivist, sociological, behaviourist, and starkly anti-psychological. At the same time, however, it is strangely moving. Like social scientists, Houellebecq even conducts (fictitious) sociological experiments through his writings. Consider the following one, cited directly from *Whatever*, which concerns the display of sexual behaviours in young humans:

> Example number 1. Let us consider a group of young people who are together of an evening, or indeed on holiday in Bulgaria. Among these young people there exists a previously formed couple; let us call the boy François and the girl Françoise. We will have before us a concrete, banal and easily observable example.
>
> Let us abandon these young people to their amusing activities, but before that let us clip from their actual experience a number of aleatory temporal segments which we will film with the aid of a high-speed camera concealed in the environs. It is apparent from a series of measurements that Françoise and François will spend around 37% of their time in kissing and canoodling, in short in bestowing marks of the greatest reciprocal tenderness.
>
> Let us now repeat the experiment in annulling the aforesaid social environment, which is to say that Françoise and François will be alone. The percentage drops straightaway to 17%. (Houellebecq, 1998, p. 86)

The example is followed by a similar one, and together they are meant to present an image of the animalistic side of human beings that can be found through objectifying and simplifying experiments. The experiment has probably never been conducted, so there is no validity to the statistics that Houellebecq mentions, but it adds to what is at first sight a strange and troubling objectivist, even positivist, stance that Houellebecq wants to convey to his readers.

Like Comte (1830), who limited the study of human beings to physiology and sociology with no need for a psychology (which he considered as belonging to the 'theological stage' of human thought due to its reliance upon ethereal mental entities), Houllebecq explains human behaviour with exclusive references to bodily factors on the one hand, notably hedonist sexuality, and sociological factors in consumer capitalism, on the other. He sometimes makes explicit references to current social science discussions, for example in *Platform* (Houellebecq, 2002), a book about love and (sex) tourism as commodities, where he repeatedly quotes a number of theories about tourism and economic behaviour, and there is even a footnote with a reference to a fictitious article in the otherwise real *Annals of Tourism Research*.

Here I will approach Houellebecq as a sociologist, who expresses himself in literary tropes. Houellebecq not only uses social science in his novels, but also natural science, especially physics and biology. In some of the books (*Atomised, The Possibility of an Island* (2005)), he presents a technological 'solution' to the problems of the painful human existence in the hedonistic, postmodern world. In a near future, human beings are replaced by posthuman individuals (through cloning and other forms of biotechnology) that are unable to desire, suffer and love, but instead live eternal lives in a condition of indifference, which evokes images of Nirvana in Buddhism (Houellebecq, 2005). The depiction of this 'scientific religion' – with all the ambivalences that are attached to it – has obvious connections with Comte's prospects for a cultic and religious positivism.

Houellebecq's lyrical sociology

Houellebecq's works revolve around the sociological background question, which is posed explicitly in *Atomised*: 'How could society function without religion? It is difficult enough for an individual human being' (Houellebecq, 2001, p. 193). There is an echo of Durkheim in the assumption that without religion, there is little to hold society together. When nothing is sacred, human relations become an exchange of goods, where good relationships are those that maximise individuals' capacities to have pleasant and intense experiences, particularly concerning sex. A main theme for Houellebecq thus becomes the total marketisation of human life in consumer society. Tellingly, the chronicler in *Whatever* presents the sociological analysis that 'in societies like ours sex truly represents a second system of differentiation, completely independent of money; and as a system of differentiation it functions quite as mercilessly' (Houellebecq, 1998, p. 99). The losers in the novels are the unattractive people who have little to offer on the sexual marketplace, and prostitution plays a significant role, especially in *Platform*, and is described in positive terms on an individual level as a possibility for uninviting people to buy access to the market for sexual experience. And on a geopolitical level, sex tourism is depicted as a free market 'solution' to third world poverty. The novels unfold in a culture where love and family commitments have become reduced to pure sexual relationships; notice again the analytic sociological voice in the following quote: 'the couple and the family were to be the last bastion of primitive communism in liberal society. The sexual revolution was to destroy the last unit separating the individual from the market' (Houellebecq, 2001, p. 136). Although Houellebecq's protagonists long for love, the marketised society in which they live makes this an impossible dream.

In *Atomised*, we follow half-brothers Michel and Bruno, who act as lay sociologists throughout the book and analyse the contemporary consumer society – or 'the sex-and-shopping society', as Michel calls it (Houellebecq, 2001, p. 192) – 'where desire is marshalled and organised and blown up out of all proportion. For society to function, for competition to continue, people have to want more and more until it fills their lives and finally devours them' (p. 192). Bruno tells us of his life and his relationship with his son:

> I work for someone else, I rent my apartment from someone else, there's nothing for my son to inherit. I have no craft to teach him, I haven't a clue what he

might do when he's older. By the time he grows up, the rules I lived by will be meaningless – the world will be completely different. If a man accepts the fact that everything must change, then his life is reduced to nothing more than the sum of his own experience – past and future generations mean nothing to him. That's how we live now. (Houellebecq, 2001, p. 201)

As Bruno is aware, consumer society is an experience society (Schulze, 1992), where a person's life is reduced to the sum of his or her experiences. A life under postmodern conditions is thus not depicted as a narrative, but consists of different situations that follow one another, which in consequence cannot truthfully be represented in a narrative form. This explains why Houellebecq writes like a lyrical sociologist, who seeks to invoke emotions, rather than a narrative writer, who provides explanatory links between events.

The New Age and hippie movements of the 1960s are described as leading ideologies in this society of flexible, experience-seeking consumers. Houellebecq's moral verdict against these emancipatory movements is harsh and very provocative; they are seen as 'libertines forever in search of new and more violent sensations' (Houellebecq, 2001, p. 252):

> Having exhausted the possibilities of sexual pleasure, it was reasonable that individuals, liberated from the constraints of ordinary morality, should turn their attentions to the wider pleasures of cruelty. Two hundred years earlier, de Sade had done precisely the same thing. In a sense, the serial killers of the 1990s were the spiritual children of the hippies of the Sixties. (Houellebecq, 2001, p. 252)

People in the sex-and-shopping society consider life as worth living only if it provides them, continuously, with chances to have intense sensations and exciting experiences, and, as their bodies inevitably grow older and gradually decay, these chances are diminished:

> More than at any time or in any other civilisation, human beings are obsessed with ageing. Each individual has a simple view of the future: a time will come when the sum of pleasures that life has to offer is outweighed by the sum of pain [...]. This weighing up of pleasure and pain which, sooner or later, everyone is forced to make, leads logically, at a certain age, to suicide. (Houellebecq, 2001, p. 297)

The body plays a special role in the lives of Houellebecqian characters. Their identities are defined not only in social and commercial terms, but also in bodily (rather than psychological) terms: it is how their bodies look, move, dress, and suffer that define them as persons and constitute their identities. Reading Houellebecq is also an intense bodily experience for the reader. His extremely violent descriptions of sadistic and other pornographic practices literally move the reader. This marks a lyrical aspect of Houellebecq's writings: he tries to make us feel reality through concrete emotions (Abbott, 2007, p. 76). His works thus create a kinetic response, which Richardson has singled out as a sign of quality in writing (Richardson & Lockridge, 1998). The shocking and nauseous descriptions are quickly displaced by very beautiful descriptions of landscapes or brief moments of human tenderness in an otherwise brutal world. As it is said in *Atomised*, and illustrated concretely in the books: 'In the midst of nature's savagery, human beings sometimes (rarely) succeed in creating small oases warmed by love' (Houellebecq, 2001, p. 103). And further about tenderness, consider this glimpse of optimism nested in Houellebecq's otherwise pessimistic biologization of human life: 'Tenderness is a deeper instinct than seduction which is why it is so difficult to give up hope' (p. 61). A whole cloud of social science condensed into a drop of poetry.

Abbott points to the production of 'humane sympathy' as a goal of lyrical sociology, and in spite of (or because of?) Houellebecq's forceful portraits of shifting violent and beautiful situations, this exact emotion of sympathy is what is produced in some readers such as myself. Like other lyrical writers, Houellebecq 'aims to tell us of his [...] intense reaction to some portion of the social process seen in a moment' (Abbott, 2007, p. 76). He gives us full immersion into states rather than explanatory narratives about happenings. Tellingly, when Houellebecq made his debut as film director in August 2008, transforming *The Possibility of an Island* into a movie, he was attacked by critics who argued that his film was lacking in basic narrative structure!

Houellebecq presents us with a view of the body as that which identifies individuals as individuals – the rest is suprapersonal history and sociology, as we see in the following passage, where Michel considers the life of his half-brother:

> Was it possible to think of Bruno as an individual? The decay of his organs was particular to him, and he would suffer his decline and death as an individual. On the other hand, his hedonistic world view and the forces that shaped his consciousness and his desires were common to an entire generation. (Houellebecq, 2001, p. 212)

The 'forces' alluded to here are Comtean laws of 'social physics', governing human lives under conditions of advanced consumer capitalism (Varsava, 2005). So although Houellebecq is lyrical, he is willing to appeal to social science constructs such as social forces. These, rather than inner psychological properties, explain human behaviour: 'Like Zola, Houllebecq places his characters in certain social contexts and then portrays their reactions to various stimuli' (p. 153). Again, social contexts shift, often without connecting narratives, and are described lyrically. A lyrical sociologist 'looks at a social situation, feels its overpowering excitement and its deeply affecting human complexity, and then writes a book trying to awaken those feelings in the minds – and even more the hearts – of his readers' (Abbott, 2007, p. 70). One is moved by the emotional qualities of Houellebecq's descriptions of social situations – and not by narrative.

Houllebecq's perspective, with its positivist and behaviourist edges, is not just his own, as a writer, but is also conferred unto his characters in their interpersonal understandings that make them resemble the calculating, role-playing actors described, for example, in Goffman's sociology. A concrete example can illustrate this, again from *Atomised*, where Michel, who is a successful biologist, has decided to retire at a very young age from his laboratory and after a brief farewell reception says goodbye to the new female laboratory leader:

> When they reached his Toyota he offered his hand, smiling (he had been preparing himself mentally for this for several seconds, remembering to smile). Their palms brushed and they shook hands gently. Later, he decided a handshake lacked warmth; under the circumstances, they could have kissed each other on both cheeks like visiting dignitaries or people in show business. (Houellebecq, 2001, p. 12)

We hear little about the 'inner life' of the characters, and 'the social situation' is used to explain their conduct. They live and act in the here and now, are preoccupied with a Goffmansque presentation of self, and react to situational stimuli, driven almost entirely by an urge for (sexual) stimulation (thus in the example above, Michel has a sexual fantasy about the new laboratory leader immediately after having said goodbye to her).

Through his writings, Houellebecq tries to demonstrate the (no doubt hyperbole) sociologising point that we can explain human conduct entirely by looking at how historical forces (capitalism, consumerism) along with sexual desire in individuals together shape social situations, which in turn determine human behaviour. He makes us feel the despair that this disenchanted world affords. His fundamental naturalist, positivist and Darwinian perspective on human existence is coupled with a strong cultural-historical sensibility. For even though human desire is connected to the body, which as a biological entity is subject to the laws of natural science and thus doomed to decay, desire is not outside history. Here is Houellebecq the social scientist again: 'Pleasure and desire, which as cultural, anthropological and secondary phenomena explain little about sexuality itself; far from being a determining factor, they are in fact themselves sociologically determined' (Houellebecq, 2001, p. 292). In consumer society more specifically, desire and enjoyment 'become part of the process of *seduction*, and favour originality, passion and individual creativity (all qualities also required of employees in their professional capacities)' (p. 293). As Houellebecq himself has said, in an interview about the current commercialisation of desire: 'Today, we can no longer experience desire independently from advertising' (quoted in Grass, 2006, p. 2).

Irony and the scandalous

I believe that Houellebecq's writings contain precise sociological descriptions of central aspects of human life in postmodern consumer society. In this sense, we can read his works as literary and indeed lyrical sociology. This also seems to be the way he wants to be read, judged from his frequent references to Comte and other sociologists. In consumer society, identities have (at least partly) become aesthetic, touristic matters due to a general breakdown of a shared moral order. Tourism in Houellebecq's novels represents a kind of metaphysical homelessness (Grass, 2006). Needless to say, Houellebecq radicalises and caricatures some contemporary tendencies in order to develop certain ideal types, almost in the Weberian tradition. But although Houellebecq's descriptions are sometimes funny, they are not as such ironic. According to Abbott, this is another mark of lyrical writings: 'the lyrical writer does not place himself or herself outside the situation but in it. If there is an irony to the lyricism, it is an irony shared with the object and the reader, not an irony that positions the writer outside the experience of investigation and report' (Abbott, 2007, p. 74). In *Atomised*, there is a passage that explicitly deals with irony:

> Irony won't save you from anything; humour doesn't do anything at all. You can look at life ironically for years, maybe decades; there are people who seem to go through most of their lives seeing the funny side, but in the end, life always breaks your heart. Doesn't matter how brave you are, or how reserved, or how much you've developed a sense of humour, you still end up with your heart broken. That's when you stop laughing. After that, there's just the cold, the silence and the loneliness. You might say, after that, there's only death. (Houellebecq, 2001, p. 349)

Houellebecq is clearly part of the mess that he writes about, namely the mess we call consumer society. He is on an equal footing with his reader, and this creates a spark of hope in the otherwise gloomy world he describes: A message to the reader becomes 'you are not alone in feeling lost', and feeling lost and alone is a major theme for Houellebecq. *The Possibility of an Island* begins with a fable, allegedly conveyed to Houellebecq by a German journalist, who told him that, for her, it encapsulated his position as a writer:

> I am in a telephone box, after the end of the world. I can make as many telephone calls as I like, there is no limit. I have no idea if anyone else has survived, or if my calls are just the monologues of a lunatic. Sometimes the call is brief, as if someone has hung up on me; sometimes it goes on for a while, as if someone is listening with guilty curiosity. There is neither day nor night; the situation is without end. (Houellebecq, 2005, p. 1)

This is an intense lyrical presentation of human experience; sober, yet emotional; precise, yet mystifying.

It may be the non-ironical lyricism in Houellebecq that makes his work so scandalous in the eyes of many people. Indeed, his personal life has been publicly scandalous with several lawsuits in France, and, in some circles, Houellebecq has earned himself a reputation as indecent, especially with female journalists, while others reproach him as a right-wing, racist pornographer. Irony creates a distance and enables a speaker to hide, but with Houellebecq there is little distance. Although I am moved by Houellebecq's aesthetic lyricism, I also believe we should be critical of his sociology. First and foremost, his descriptions and conservative judgements of the postmodern as consumerist are hyperbolic and one-sided. The existential figure of the tourist, for example, could be re-described, contra Houellebecq, to include some positive sides that he does not touch upon, such as openness, curiosity, tolerance, and a willingness to learn from otherness. The same could be said of the hippie. But then again, it may exactly be because of Houellebecq's style, at once frank, one-sided and hyperbolic, that he is able to make his acute observations of human life. Or of *aspects* of human life, we should say.

More importantly, perhaps, Houellebecq's positive 'solutions' to the problem of human suffering in the form of a 'scientific religion' or a third 'metaphysical mutation' (especially in *Atomised* and *The Possibility of an Island*) must be criticised as scandalously unattractive dystopias. However, it is unclear if the posthuman world is one that is normatively advocated by Houellebecq (like B.F. Skinner's 1948 *Walden Two*), or if he describes the likely endpoint of humanity's current historical journey. In the first case, he should be met with political arguments, and in the second, he should be chided for the deeply questionable attempt to foresee the future on the basis of a stage-theory of history that he has inherited from Comte.

Fact and fiction in qualitative inquiry

After this reading of Houellebecq, we can return to more general discussions about fact and fiction in qualitative inquiry. Readers may object to my characterisation of Houellebecq as a lyrical sociologist and say that there is no social science in his books because they are fiction. How should that objection be dealt with? First, we can observe with Rosenblatt (2002) that the boundary between fact and fiction has blurred in the postmodern epoch, and that this boundary itself is a social construction. In a straightforward way, what we write is fiction in the sense of having been fashioned by us. It was not until the seventeenth century that the world of writing was divided into two separate kinds: literary and scientific (Richardson & St. Pierre, 2005, p. 960). In older European literature, there was no distinction between fiction and reality (Jauss, 1989). Cervantes' *Don*

Quixote can be singled out as one founding text of the modern epoch, sealing the end of the Middle Ages by taking the recent divorce between fiction and reality as its very theme (p. 9). In the book, Don Quixote, the last knight, opposes his own era and seeks to reinstall the enchanted but lost medieval world of heroes and lovers. This, however, makes him collide with the prosaic realities of the actual world, where things and events are no longer signs of a higher order. Things have become worldly, factual even, and Don Quixote consequently becomes a laughable figure. Cervantes' text can be described as the first modern novel, organising its storyline around particular subjective perspectives, which became central to modern forms of literary representation. A fact–fiction dichotomy was born, along with one of objectivity and subjectivity. Thus, the fact–fiction dichotomy is a historical construction.

Furthermore, we can say with Richardson and St. Pierre (2005) that literary/ fiction and scientific/factual writings differ only concerning the authors' claims for the text. Thus, it is rhetorical devices that make us classify a text as belonging to one genre rather than another. From this point of view, there are no inherent differences between science and art, social science and fiction. Umberto Eco, a noted writer of both 'science' and 'fiction', tells us the following about his own contributions to these fields:

> I understand that, according to a current opinion, I have written some texts that can be labelled as scientific (or academic or theoretical), and some others which can be defined as creative. But I do not believe in such a straightforward distinction. [...] There is not some mysterious ontological difference between these two ways of writing, in spite of many and illustrious 'Defences of Poetry'. The differences stand, first of all, in the prepositional attitude of the writers – even though their prepositional is usually made evident by textual devices, thus becoming the prepositional attitude of the texts themselves. (Eco, 1992, p. 140)

Whenever he writes, Eco tells us, he starts 'from the same lump of experiences' (Eco, 1992, p. 140), and then must choose either to propose a coherent conclusion to readers (which results in a 'scientific' text) or stage a play of contradiction (resulting in a 'creative work'), thereby allowing readers to choose a conclusion or even decide that there is no possible choice. But, significantly, both forms of writing are, for him, ways of conveying a 'lump of experiences'.

With the literary turn in contemporary social science, even the rhetorical devices that Eco consciously uses to mark the chosen genre are progressively getting more and more opaque. We thus have autoethnography (Ellis, 2004), investigative poetry (Hartnett & Engels, 2005), creative analytical practices (CAP) ethnographies (Richardson & St. Pierre, 2005) and many other 'experimental' forms of qualitative writings that eschew modernist, objectivist and scientific rhetoric, and instead insert the researcher as an observing, experiencing and reflecting I, who reports on lived experience in the first-person singular, using literary and aesthetic forms of (re)presentation. Often, the result is similar to Eco's description of creative work: a play of contradictions without clear conclusions. As in modern novels, the world is experienced, enjoyed and suffered through the first person – or, in more postmodern variants, through multiple perspectives and polyphonic voices that are sometimes reported side by side as in Lather and Smithies' *Troubling the Angels* (Lather & Smithies, 1997).

The anthropologist Margery Wolf once asked how 'one is to differentiate ethnography from fiction, other than in preface, footnotes, and other authorial devices' (Wolf, 1992, p. 56). And according to narrative researcher Barbara Czarniawska (2010), this is a standing concern, but one that should not worry qualitative researchers. Rather than being worried about the fictive element in qualitative inquiry, researchers should ask and answer this question again and again in a productive communal reflection over the genres. Czarniawska advocates what she calls 'creative borrowing' between the genres of fact-producing science and fiction-producing literature and she reminds us that etymologically 'facts' comes from the Latin 'facere' and are literally fabrications. Seen in this way, 'science' is no longer a priori distinct from 'literature'. Rosenblatt (2002) argues further along these lines that fiction may be a legitimate outcome of qualitative research, and we can add that most kinds of research in fact involve fictions, also outside the postmodern and qualitative fields of research. There have been continuities between ethnography and fiction at least since the early years of ethnographic sociology at the University of Chicago, where the 'urban sociologists and novelists of 1920s Chicago had common subject matter and adopted similar approaches to the production of texts' (Atkinson, Coffey, & Delamont, 2003, p. 174). And, as I pointed out above, also the calculated averages of quantitative surveys and experiments are fictions that do not represent concretely existing persons or entities, but may still be useful for a range of societal purposes.

I believe that the most fruitful way of navigating the issue of fact and fiction is to say with the pragmatists that human knowledge is a matter of testing different kinds of fictions (Banks & Banks, 1998, p. 15). From this point of view, the opposite of fact is not fiction, but rather something like error (p. 13). If I utter something that is not true, what I say is not thereby rendered fiction. And, conversely, what we call fiction can be *right*, e.g. if it allows us to understand something better or lead better lives. On reflection, then, the supposed clarity of the distinction between fiction and fact quickly breaks down. Qualitative research and art should not be bifurcated, and when I speak here of social science and fiction, I speak mainly of different prepositional attitudes (as Eco said) or different forms of rhetoric, and *not* of different forms of knowing. Knowledge can be conveyed with both forms of rhetoric, and both can result in error.

Concluding comments

In this chapter, I have given an example of how to read novels as qualitative inquiry into our everyday lives in the postmodern epoch. The market-ruled consumer society analysed by Houellebecq has been presented as saturated with demands for new, unique, and passionate experiences related to individual creativity. We have seen a focus on the surface, not least the surface of the body, and, for a psychologist like me, Houellebecq is particularly challenging because of his sociological anti-psychologism. Sometimes, his characters are even openly hostile to the psychologised world in which they live: at the end of *Whatever*, for example, when Michel has been admitted to a psychiatric hospital, he talks to the female psychologist there: 'I've always hated female psychology students: vile creatures, that's how I perceive them' (Houellebecq, 1998, p. 145). At first, Michel recounts:

> ... our relations were not easy. She took me to task for speaking in general, overly sociological terms. This, according to her, was not interesting: instead I ought to involve myself, try and 'get myself centred'.
> – But I've had a bellyful of myself, I objected.
> – As a psychologist I can't accept such a statement, nor encourage it in any way. In speaking of society all the time you create a barrier behind which you can hide; it's up to me to break down this barrier so that we can work on your personal problems. (Houellebecq, 1998, p. 145)

The barrier is never broken down, or perhaps it is, but there is nothing behind it. Michel (the character *and* the author, I would add) sees the world clearly and realistically from his sociological stance, whereas the psychologist's vision is clouded in mythical psychological entities with a focus on an (illusory) self. The final chapter in the book begins with a quote from the Buddhist Sattipathana-sutta that there is a road to travel, and yet no traveller and: 'Acts are accomplished, yet there is no actor' (Houellebecq, 1998, p. 151). The very last words in the book are moving – and at the same time fundamentally mundane: 'the goal of life is missed. It is two in the afternoon' (p. 155). Everything is finally brought down to earth in every sense of the term, situating everyone, fictional characters and readers, in the here and now.

Following from the Houellebecqian blurring of the boundary between literature and social science, I would like to end by asking the following questions: In spite of being 'fictitious' (if indeed they are just that?), do we not learn as much from Houellebecq's lyrical descriptions of life in a postmodern consumer culture as we do from reading, say, Zygmunt Bauman, Richard Sennett, or Jean Baudrillard on the same issue? Are Houellebecq's literary writings not every inch as *true* as those of Bauman, Sennett and Baudrillard? Has he not, to use the words of Heidegger, reproduced an artful 'general essence' (Heidegger, 1993, p. 162) of human experience in consumer society, thereby making himself a candidate for saying something indisputably true? And are we not *moved* by Houellebecq to an even greater degree than by the otherwise fine prose of these sociologists (whom I all admire)? Cannot poetry and the aesthetic in a broad sense be as *valid* as what we traditionally call the scientific?

My goal in this chapter has been to investigate the possibility of giving affirmative answers to these questions, and I believe a case can be made for including at least some literary works in the great social and human science conversation that is currently going on, for example about everyday life in postmodern consumer cultures. I have argued that literature can be considered as qualitative research in itself. Like traditional forms of research, literature can be done well or poorly, but when done well, it enables readers to understand the world and themselves better than they did before, and may even animate them to act differently, both of which are legitimate aims of research.

Using books of fiction in qualitative inquiry

The research that is reported in this chapter – the analysis of Houellebecq as a qualitative researcher – has been published as a journal article (Brinkmann, 2009), and I originally chose to engage in this form of analysis for the straightforward reason that I felt I had learned much from reading these books. But I wanted to find out exactly what it was that I had learned. And I wanted to discuss whether it could be legitimate to use books of fiction not just as data or as an inspirational form of writing, but as qualitative research in its own right. My reading of Houellebecq as a qualitative researcher is probably closest to the strategy of 'making the obvious obvious'. His books do not deconstruct or criticise, but aim for clear descriptions of human life under specific historical circumstances. The very argument that literature can be qualitative research, however, is probably closer to 'making the obvious dubious', since it destabilises or even 'breaks down' conventional understandings of the dichotomy of art (fiction) and research (fact). To me, at least, it became something of a mystery (Alvesson & Kärreman, 2011) what the difference between these sides of the conventional dichotomy could be, and I used this mystery productively in writing about fiction and Houellebecq's novels.

My engagement with Houellebecq can be depicted in terms of the six steps that I have outlined in this book: (1) My *topic* was literary analyses of consumer society, (2) my *collection of materials* was easy, because I had in many ways come to this topic through reading Houellebecq's books, so they became my empirical corpus, (3) I then *consulted the literature*, which, in this case, mainly consisted of discussions about the relationship between fact and fiction, research and literature. I would then (4) *continue collecting materials* by going back to Houellebecq and reading more of and about him, before (5) doing *analytic writing*, the result of which became (6) *a published article* (Brinkmann, 2009), some of which is reproduced above. Unlike the empirical example in Chapter 5, for example, which involved much of my own life in the meeting with Thomas, the analysis in this chapter is in a sense more impersonal, in line with Houellebecq's rather objectivist stance. I could perhaps have included a more autobiographical part, but I believed that it would not add much to the discussion in this case, although I personally expanded my horizon greatly during the process of working with fiction as qualitative inquiry. I will encourage others to use novels and other texts of fiction in this way.

EXERCISE

How to do it? Here are some suggestions inspired by Laurel Richardson:

- Find your favourite book or books. It can be those books that you enjoy reading the most, those that have challenged your views, those that make you laugh or cry or those that have inspired you to do something. Write down your immediate explanations as to why these books have had the influence on you that they have had. Just write. Do not stop and do not censor yourself. This is the personal or biographical side of the process of studying everyday life through books.
- Then ask what these books tell you about the social world. What images of culture do these books convey? How do they portray gender, class and race issues? Are the characters' experiences human universals (like the experiences of death and suffering), or are they historically specific (like the experience of participating in the Second World War)? Again, you should write without stopping and censoring yourself. One page or two will do. This is the social side of the process.
- You now have some words about your personal relationship to the book(s) and about the social life portrayed in them. You should now compare the two sets of words in order to write from the point of intersection between the biographical and the social, as Mills advocated (Mills, 1959). This is where the sociological imagination is put to work. You should formulate some analytic questions to the materials (the books and your own descriptions). These can arise from specific research questions that you are interested in. (What is the existential role of resentment in a human life? How do we make sense of suffering? How has the idea of good work changed? etc.)
- Next go to the library (your supervisor, colleagues, etc.) – if you haven't already done so – and find what you can about the topic to be analysed in the books. This is where you make use of theoretical concepts to develop theoretical audacity that can enable you to say something potentially interesting about the materials. In the case of Houellebecq, I was surprisingly led to the classical positivism of Comte as a way of understanding Houellebecq's novels, but also to the religious-scientific

culture that is at work in curious ways in the contemporary postmodern world. I had not thought before I began working on this that I was going to read Comte's theoretical pieces on positivism from the early nineteenth century.

- In the process, remember that there is no mechanical way of producing knowledge. You have to use writing as a method of inquiry (Richardson & St. Pierre, 2005). This is perhaps not very methodical, but it is an interpretative affair that has its own rigour. By going through the steps described here, there is some systematicity that I expect will work for many. But, as Mills said: 'Let every man be his own methodologist; let every man be his own theorist; let theory and method again become part of the practice of a craft' (Mills, 1959, p. 224). We should not let what we can insightfully say about the social world be determined by a set of rigid methods. Our ways of working with everyday life materials should rather be 'determined instead by the nature of the phenomenon, what's interesting about it, and what's worth saying' (Freeman, 2004, p. 71). Freeman recognises that it is difficult to differentiate his work in narrative analysis from literary criticism, but this is a true virtue if life is literature (Nehamas, 1985). If so, it may be that only a literary approach to life can aspire to a true 'fidelity to the phenomena' that ought to be part of all research (Freeman, 2004, p. 64).

NINE

Conclusions: On quality

This book has advocated a way of working in social and psychological research that uses objects and episodes from the researcher's everyday life as a key to open up an understanding of the larger social and cultural life. Qualitative inquiry in everyday life takes place in the intersection of the researcher's life, on the one hand, and the larger social and cultural history, on the other. The argument is that it is valuable to use the breakdowns, which frequently occur in our understanding as we go about living our lives, as an occasion for research. The goal is to gain a deeper and better understanding of the social world, but a side-effect is that it is often enjoyable to use the objects, situations and people that one cares about in a research process. A philosophical premise for this kind of research is that there is no qualitative difference between living a life (which is an ongoing interpretative process of inquiry) and doing research.

The structure of a research project

Ideally, the structure of a research project based on the ideas of this book would look something like this:

First, the researcher is surprised, encounters a problem or *experiences a breakdown* in her understanding of some phenomenon (some x) in her everyday life. This corresponds to what I have called the 'Choose a topic' phase of qualitative inquiry. Sometimes a topic almost 'chooses itself', by being so pressing that one simply finds a need to study it, but more often we are as living, inquiring beings engaged in trying to understand something anyway (e.g. because we are taking a course in 'research methods'), and can thus work to become open to surprises, astonishment and breakdowns.

Secondly, the researcher *gathers materials* that appear to be relevant in relation to the issue in question. This is conventionally called 'data collection' in the methodological literature. However, as I have argued, we should not think of data as 'givens', but as 'takens', something we pick up for the purpose of understanding something better. These materials can come from the media, from fiction, from informal conversations, from formal interviews, from observations or from documents. At the outset, there are few limits as to what to include, but there should be a continual back and forth process between gathering materials, choosing exemplars to analyse more thoroughly and deciding what to exclude. In principle, by using the strategies of this book, *anything can be singled out as 'data'*. Everything from the room you are in to the clothes you wear can be taken as interesting material for everyday life analyses (what do your clothes say about who you are? How were they constructed? How did you acquire them? How do people react to them – if at all? Why do you wear clothes at all?).

Thirdly, from the materials, and from readings of extant literature, the researcher makes an analysis or interpretation, typically by engaging in *abductive* reasoning: 'If y is the case, then x makes sense – so, for the time being, we work from the idea that y is the case.' Theories are particularly relevant as aids in the process of using one's imagination abductively in the interpretative moment.

Fourthly, the researcher's interpretations must be written down, i.e., materialised on paper, in order for anyone (including the researcher) to judge their validity. This is what I have called *analytic writing*, which means using analytic concepts to order, unpack and understand problematic situations. The researcher will often go back and forth between reading, writing and collecting empirical materials. Not only is *writing* a method of inquiry – this also goes for *reading*, although few scholars have analysed systematically what it means to read as part of a research process. As a starting point, we can point to Pelias, who has given the following piece of advice to the qualitative researcher: 'Accept that you cannot read without holding a pencil in your hand. Develop your own system of marking the important points you want to remember. Think of your system as aesthetic' (Pelias, 2004, p. 143). In addition, one's system should be *ethical*, and the ethical issues (Will your study be beneficial to anyone? How will you handle informed consent and confidentiality? What is your own role in the process?) should continually be addressed.

Fifthly, I have advocated different *analytic strategies* that can be tried out: making the obvious obvious (a phenomenological stance), making the hidden obvious (a critical stance) and making the obvious dubious (a deconstructive stance). These need not be mutually exclusive, but can inspire researchers to different readings of the same materials. The researcher can also ask which kind of *self* is at stake in the situation that one investigates, i.e., the persons that participate in the social process can be understood in terms of their experiential point of view (Self 1), interpreted properties (Self 2) or social discourses and norms (Self 3). Likewise, what I have called *the ontological triangle* may inspire us to viewing our complex social life from the side of experience, discourse or objects. It is not possible to decide in advance which angles are most helpful, but researchers must experiment with different approaches and readings.

All in all, and given the many-sided view of the social process, this book has advocated a pragmatic approach to qualitative inquiry, according to which theories and analytic frameworks are *tools* that are employed by researchers, who can favourably think of themselves as *craftspersons*. Like other craftspersons, the quality of the work of the researcher is inherent in the products rather than in specific methodological procedures. I have also referred to this way of working as *empirical philosophy*, since careful philosophical and theoretical reflection will go hand in hand with empirical description and analysis. Theoretical concepts without empirical materials are empty, but empirical analyses without theory are blind.

In contrast to the ideal structure depicted here, however, one is often obliged to do a specific kind of research, or answer a specific question, possibly because one is a student that has been given an assignment. In such a case, I believe that it is still possible to work according to the research logic of this book. Most themes and methodologies can be accommodated to the interpretative-pragmatic approach of this book, and even if one is not allowed (e.g. by one's teacher) to concentrate fully on everyday life situations and objects, it is often possible to include examples from one's everyday life to illustrate a point or perhaps even as a main empirical case.

When one does not proceed from a genuine breakdown in understanding, however, one should be particularly careful to defamiliarise oneself with the field that is studied, or employ other heuristics that generate at least a pseudo-breakdown that can facilitate exciting and audacious analyses of the mundane. Topics such as emotions (e.g. shame, guilt, happiness, jealousy, loneliness), personal troubles, experienced marginalisation, processes of social positioning, interpersonal relationships and other micro sociological and psychological phenomena are particularly well suited to qualitative everyday life analyses. In such cases, it is possible to use one's own life and experiences to unpack and understand larger social issues. Using one's own perspective as a researcher should not be understood as contrary to a search for more general features of social life. Rather, we should bear in mind that when we talk about the social and psychological reality, the general is found in the particular (Valsiner, 2007, p. 388). And, as I have argued, we approach the general by using the tools of theoretical concepts and ideas that can, to some extent, travel between situations and episodes.

Quality in everyday life analyses

How, then, does one judge the quality of the everyday life analyses that one makes or reads about? One answer, which is almost too general to be helpful, says that one's analysis has quality when it enables one to understand and act. That is, when what used to be unclear or unsettling becomes clearer and perhaps when some life equilibrium and potential to act is regained. There are many ways to accomplish this, however, and I shall here point to three overarching sets of criteria in relation to which we can raise the question of quality. These are epistemic, aesthetic and moral criteria.

Truth – epistemic criteria

In spite of postmodern critiques, we should not shun a word like truth. At least not if we remember to spell it with a lower-case t. In our everyday lives, we quite simply need a distinction between true and false accounts, and, in so far as qualitative inquiry is just one reflexive form that everyday life can take, there is reason to keep the notion of truth in research as well. That something is true in this sense does not mean that it is true from a view from nowhere (Nagel, 1986). Rather, it means that we have uncovered something from somewhere, and doing so is not a province of the sciences alone, for, as we saw in the previous chapter that cited Heidegger on art and truth, works of art can also be true if they succeed in uncovering aspects of reality. Qualitative analyses can be true when they are honest, when the researcher specifies her theoretical perspective, when she situates the persons, episodes and objects that she addresses, when she gives examples that back up her conclusions, when she offers a coherent account of that which can be represented coherently – and offers fragments of that which is fragmented – and when she creates a story that resonates in the reader (Elliott, Fischer, & Rennie, 1999). These are all epistemic criteria that are signs of quality in everyday life analyses.

Beauty – aesthetic criteria

Invoking resonance as an epistemic criterion of quality already takes us to the aesthetic dimension. Qualitative researchers such as Richardson (Richardson & Lockridge, 1998; Richardson & St. Pierre, 2005) and Bochner (2002) have stressed this dimension as perhaps the most important one in qualitative inquiry, for if the reader is not *moved* – in some way – by what she reads, the text will not make a difference. Bochner finds that aesthetic qualities are improved when the researcher reports many concrete details, including their own feelings and doubts, communicates structurally complex narratives with honesty, credibility and vulnerability, relates to some process of human development and is based on ethical self-consciousness. This list is not definitive or exhaustive, and the important point here is simply that researchers should think more about the aesthetics of their reports. Writing is a craft, and arguably the single most important practice of qualitative researchers, and given its centrality in the research process, it is surprising how little attention writing is given in most departments, programmes and courses in qualitative research. Writing is often thought of as a mere 'postscript' to the research process, and the result is often boring and unappealing research reports that are unlikely to have an impact (Richardson & St. Pierre, 2005).

Goodness – moral criteria

With the third set of criteria we are delving into difficult waters, but given this book's emphasis on the pragmatic dimension of research – the capacity to act and make a change in fruitful ways – it becomes very important to discuss what is meant by 'fruitful'. Even though pragmatism stands as the most important approach that evaluates research in terms of its (moral) effects, the emphasis on morality goes back as far as Aristotle. As he stated in his *Ethics*, the political sciences (or what we would call the social sciences today), are species of *phronesis* (Aristotle, 1976, p. 213) (practical wisdom) because they are dealing with human conduct as a highly particularistic, versatile and changing phenomenon, and practical knowledge about such things consequently 'involves knowledge of particular facts, which become known from experience' (p. 215). We *know* about the social world (which is the goal of the social sciences) when we are able to *act well* as participants in our communities.

In recent years there has been a resurgence of interest in the Aristotelian view of the social sciences. For example, Robert Bellah and colleagues have developed what they call 'social science as public philosophy' (Bellah, Madsen, Sullivan, Swidler, & Tipton, 1985). This perspective accentuates the fact that the social researcher is within the society she is studying, and also within one or more of its moral traditions (p. 303). As we saw in Chapter 1, we should think of the everyday life researcher as a *participant* in social life, and as someone who addresses human *experience* through *audacious* analyses. Social science as public philosophy is public in the sense that it is part of the ongoing discussion of the meaning and value of our common life, and, as such, it ideally engages the public. Bent Flyvbjerg has argued quite specifically that the social sciences are – or must become, if they want to matter – *phronetic* (Flyvbjerg, 2001). *Phronetic* researchers place themselves within the context being studied and focus on the values of the practices of communities by asking three 'value-rational' questions: Where are we going? Is this desirable? What should be done? (p. 60). The *raison d'être* for the social sciences is, Flyvbjerg thinks, developing the value-rationality of society, i.e., enabling the public to reason better about values.

One of my arguments in this book has been that qualitative inquiry in everyday life is *one* form that *phronetic* social science may take. This involves opening up the social process 'from within', so to speak, i.e., using one's own life and experience to understand how society works in order to understand it better, act adequately in it and possibly improve it. When researchers succeed in this regard, they can be said to contribute to making qualitative research into 'a democratic project committed to social justice in an age of uncertainty' (Denzin & Lincoln, 2005b, p. x). This, obviously, is not a simple thing to do, and whenever we talk about quality criteria – whether they are epistemic, aesthetic or moral – we should bear in mind the pragmatic point that criteria are 'temporary resting places constructed for specific utilitarian ends'; a criterion is what it is 'because some social practice needs to block the road of inquiry, halt the regress of interpretations, in order to get something done' (Rorty, 1982, p. xli).

Criteria are always temporary and practical, created for instrumental purposes to be able to move things further, just like qualitative inquiry itself is an open-ended life process that never stops as long as human beings are alive. A sign that one has succeeded in one's pursuits as a qualitative everyday life researcher is, from the *phronetic* and pragmatic perspectives, that one's everyday life has been enriched. Either because one has solved a problem, achieved a deeper understanding of something or acquired a capacity to act in more fruitful ways, or simply because one has become able to enjoy life more fully by using one's powers of observation, conversation and reflection to become astonished by the richness of the mundane.

The greatest challenge to the kind of research logic that has been advocated in this book is not just to learn how to do it well (this is already difficult enough), but relates to having this form of research accepted as legitimate in the many corners of the social sciences. Some disciplines and research milieus may not accept it, but it is comforting to bear in mind that a worldwide qualitative community, which includes congresses, centres, handbooks and journals that are totally open to what I have called qualitative everyday life analyses, now exists. A committed and vibrant group of scholars from many different disciplines have for years articulated critiques of the emerging global audit culture and evidence-based model of science 'that privileges an instrumental, engineering model of social science that feeds on metrics to establish "what works"' (St. Pierre, 2011, p. 611). Many of these discussions can be found in *The SAGE Handbook of Qualitative Research*, edited by Denzin and Lincoln, currently in its fourth edition (as of 2011). Readers who are looking for places to present and publish qualitative everyday life analyses are also welcome to contact me, and I will then do my best to guide them in relevant directions. As with life itself, the best piece of advice on how to get started is simply to begin. Or, rather, to discover that one has been doing *it* – qualitative inquiry in everyday life – all along.

References

Abbott, A. (2004). *Methods of Discovery: Heuristics for the Social Sciences*. New York: W.W. Norton & Co.

Abbott, A. (2007). Against narrative: A preface to lyrical sociology. *Sociological Theory, 25*: 67–99.

Adorno, T.W., Frenkel-Brunswik, E., Levinson, D.J., & Sanford, R.N. (1950). *The Authoritarian Personality*. New York: W.W. Norton & Co.

Agar, M. (1986). *Speaking of Ethnography*. Thousand Oaks, CA: Sage.

Altheide, D. (1996). *Qualitative Media Analysis*. Thousand Oaks, CA: Sage.

Altheide, D. (2003). The mass media. In L.T. Reynolds & N.J. Herman-Kinney (Eds), *Handbook of Symbolic Interactionism*. Walnut Creek, CA: AltaMira Press.

Alvesson, M. & Kärreman, D. (2011). *Qualitative Research and Theory Development: Mystery as Method*. London: Sage.

Anderson, B. (1991). *Imagined Communities* (Revised and extended edition). London: Verso.

Aristotle (1976). *Nichomachean Ethics*. London: Penguin.

Atkinson, P., Coffey, A., & Delamont, S. (2003). *Key Themes in Qualitative Research: Continuities and Change*. Walnut Creek, CA: AltaMira Press.

Averill, J.R. (1982). *Anger and Aggression: An Essay on Emotion*. New York: Springer.

Bacchi, C.L. (2009). *Analysing Policy: What's the Problem Represented to Be?* Frenchs Forest, Australia: Pearson Education.

Banks, A. & Banks, S.P. (1998). The struggle over facts and fictions. In A. Banks & S.P. Banks (Eds), *Fiction and Social Research: By Ice or Fire*. Walnut Creek, CA: AltaMira Press.

Banks, M. (2007). *Using Visual Data in Qualitative Research*. London: Sage.

Barone, T. & Eisner, E.W. (2012). *Arts Based Research*. Thousand Oaks, CA: Sage.

Baudrillard, J. (2007). *Fragments: Cool Memories III, 1990–1995*. London: Verso.

Bauman, Z. (2007). *Consuming Life*. Cambridge: Polity Press.

Baumeister, R.F., Stillwell, A.M., & Heatherton, T.F. (1994). Guilt: An interpersonal approach. *Psychological Review, 115*: 243–267.

Bellah, R.N., Madsen, R., Sullivan, W.M., Swidler, A., & Tipton, S.M. (1985). *Habits of the Heart: Individualism and Commitment in American Life*. Berkeley, CA: University of California Press.

Benedict, R. (1946). *The Chrysanthemum and the Sword*. Boston, MA: Houghton Mifflin.

Bernstein, R.J. (2010). *The Pragmatic Turn*. Cambridge: Polity Press.

Birch, M., Miller, T., Mauther, M., & Jessop, J. (2002). Introduction. In M. Mauther, M. Birch, J. Jessop, & T. Miller (Eds), *Ethics in Qualitative Research*. London: Sage.

Blumer, H. (1969). *Symbolic Interactionism: Perspective and Method*. Englewood Cliffs, NJ: Prentice-Hall.

Bochner, A.P. (2002). Criteria against ourselves. In N.K. Denzin & Y.S. Lincoln (Eds), *The Qualitative Inquiry Reader*. Thousand Oaks, CA: Sage.

Briggs, C. (2003). Interviewing, power/knowledge, and social inequality. In J.A. Holstein & J.F. Gubrium (Eds), *Inside Interviewing: New Lenses, New Concerns*. Thousand Oaks, CA: Sage.

Brinkmann, S. (2004). Psychology as a moral science: Aspects of John Dewey's psychology. *History of the Human Sciences*, 17: 1–28.

Brinkmann, S. (2005). Human kinds and looping effects in psychology: Foucauldian and hermeneutic perspectives. *Theory & Psychology*, 15: 769–791.

Brinkmann, S. (2007a). Could interviews be epistemic? An alternative to qualitative opinion-polling. *Qualitative Inquiry*, 13: 1116–1138.

Brinkmann, S. (2007b). Practical reason and positioning. *Journal of Moral Education*, 36: 415–432.

Brinkmann, S. (2007c). The good qualitative researcher. *Qualitative Research in Psychology*, 4: 127–144.

Brinkmann, S. (2008a). Comte and Houellebecq: Towards a radical phenomenology of behavior. In K. Nielsen, S. Brinkmann, C. Elmholdt, L. Tanggaard, P. Museaus, & G. Kraft (Eds), *A Qualitative Stance: Essays in Honor of Steinar Kvale*. Aarhus: Aarhus University Press.

Brinkmann, S. (2008b). Identity as self-interpretation. *Theory & Psychology*, 18: 404–422.

Brinkmann, S. (2009). Literature as qualitative inquiry: The novelist as researcher. *Qualitative Inquiry*, 15: 1376–1394.

Brinkmann, S. (2010). Guilt in a fluid culture: A view from positioning theory. *Culture & Psychology*, 16: 253–266.

Brinkmann, S. (2011a). *Psychology as a Moral Science: Perspectives on Normativity*. New York: Springer.

Brinkmann, S. (2011b). Towards an expansive hybrid psychology: Integrating theories of the mediated mind. *Integrative Psychological and Behavioral Science*, 45: 1–20.

Brinkmann, S. & Kvale, S. (2005). Confronting the Ethics of Qualitative Research. *Journal of Constructivist Psychology*, 18: 157–181.

Brinkmann, S. & Kvale, S. (2008). Ethics in qualitative psychological research. In C. Willig & W. Stainton-Rogers (Eds), *The SAGE Handbook of Qualitative Research in Psychology*. London: Sage.

Brinkmann, S. & Tanggaard, L. (2010). Toward an epistemology of the hand. *Studies in Philosophy and Education*, 29: 243–257.

Brown, R.H. (1977). *A Poetics for Sociology: Toward a Logic of Discovery for the Human Sciences*. Chicago, IL: University of Chicago Press.

Burman, E. (1997). Minding the gap: Positivism, psychology, and the politics of qualitative methods. *Journal of Social Issues*, 53: 785–801.

Cavell, S. (2004). *Cities of Words: Pedagogical Letters on a Register of the Moral Life*. Cambridge, MA: Harvard University Press.

Clarke, A. (2003). Situational analyses: Grounded theory after the postmodern turn. *Symbolic Interaction*, 26: 553–576.

Clarke, A. (2005). *Situational Analysis: Grounded Theory after the Postmodern Turn*. Thousand Oaks, CA: Sage.

Clifford, J. & Marcus, G. (1986). *Writing Culture: The Poetics and Politics of Ethnography*. Berkeley, CA: The University of California Press.

Comte, A. (1830). *Introduction to Positive Philosophy* (this edition 1988). Indianapolis, IN: Hackett Publishing Company.

Corner, J. (2002). Performing the real: Documentary diversions. *Television & New Media*, 3: 255–270.

Costall, A. (2007). The windowless room: Mediationism and how to get over it. In J. Valsiner & A. Rosa (Eds), *Cambridge Handbook of Sociocultural Psychology*. Cambridge: Cambridge University Press.

Coupland, D. (2009). *Generation A*. New York: Scribner.

Curt, B. (1994). *Textuality and Tectonics: Troubling Social and Psychological Science*. Buckingham: Open University Press.

Czarniawska, B. (2004). *Narratives in Social Science Research*. London: Sage.

Czarniawska, B. (2010). Narratologi og feltstudier [Narratology and field studies]. In S. Brinkmann & L. Tanggaard (Eds), *Kvalitative metoder: En grundbog [Qualitative Methods: A Textbook]*. Copenhagen: Hans Reitzels Forlag.

Danielsen, H. (2010). Han ble sjuk av all alkoholen [Alcohol made him sick]. *Dagbladet*, 25 September.

Daston, L. & Galison, P. (2007). *Objectivity*. New York: Zone Books.

Davies, B. & Harré, R. (1999). Positioning and personhood. In R. Harré & L. van Langenhove (Eds), *Positioning Theory: Moral Contexts of Intentional Action*. Oxford: Blackwell.

de Certeau, M. (1984). *The Practice of Everyday Life*. Berkeley, CA: University of California Press.

Denzin, N.K. (1995). *The Cinematic Society: The Voyeur's Gaze*. Thousand Oaks, CA: Sage.

Denzin, N.K. (1997). *Interpretive Ethnography: Ethnographic Practices for the 21st Century*. Thousand Oaks, CA: Sage.

Denzin, N.K. (2001a). *Interpretive Interactionism* (2nd edition). Thousand Oaks, CA: Sage.

Denzin, N.K. (2001b). The reflexive interview and a performative social science. *Qualitative Research*, 1: 23–46.

Denzin, N.K. (2003). Cultural studies. In L.T. Reynolds & N.J. Herman-Kinney (Eds), *Handbook of Symbolic Interactionism*. Walnut Creek, CA: AltaMira Press.

Denzin, N.K. (2004). The art and politics of interpretation. In S.N. Hesse-Biber & P. Leavy (Eds), *Approaches to Qualitative Research: A Reader on Theory and Practice*. Oxford: Oxford University Press.

Denzin, N.K. & Lincoln, Y.S. (2005a). Introduction: The discipline and practice of qualitative research. In N.K. Denzin & Y.S. Lincoln (Eds), *The SAGE Handbook of Qualitative Research*. Thousand Oaks, CA: Sage.

Denzin, N.K. & Lincoln, Y.S. (2005b). Preface. In N.K. Denzin & Y.S. Lincoln (Eds), *The SAGE Handbook of Qualitative Research* (3rd edition).Thousand Oaks, CA: Sage.

Denzin, N.K. & Lincoln, Y.S. (2011). Introduction. In N.K. Denzin & Y.S. Lincoln (Eds), *The SAGE Handbook of Qualitative Research* (4th edition). Thousand Oaks, CA: Sage.

Denzin, N.K., Lincoln, Y.S., & Giardina, M. (2006). Disciplining qualitative research. *International Journal of Qualitative Studies in Education*, 19: 769–782.

Dewey, J. (1891). Moral theory and practice. *International Journal of Ethics*, 1: 186–203.

Dewey, J. (1896). The reflex arc concept in psychology. *The Psychological Review*, 3: 357–370.

Dewey, J. (1910). *How We Think* (this edition 1991). Amherst, NY: Prometheus Books.

Dewey, J. (1925). *Experience and Nature*. Chicago, IL: Open Court.

Dewey, J. (1929). *The Quest for Certainty* (this edition 1960). New York: Capricorn Books.

Dewey, J. (1938). *Logic: The Theory of Inquiry*. New York: Henry Holt & Co.

Dewey, J. & Bentley, A. (1949). *Knowing and the Known* (this edition 1960). Boston, MA: Beacon Press.

Dreier, O. (2008). *Psychotherapy in Everyday Life*. Cambridge: Cambridge University Press.

Dreyfus, H. (1991). *Being-in-the-World: A Commentary on Heidegger's Being and Time, Division I*. Cambridge, MA: The MIT Press.

Duncombe, J. & Jessop, J. (2002). 'Doing rapport' and the ethics of 'faking friendship'. In M. Mauther, M. Birch, J. Jessop, & T. Miller (Eds), *Ethics in Qualitative Research*. London: Sage.

Eco, U. (1992). Reply. In S. Collini (Ed.), *Interpretation and Overinterpretation*. Cambridge: Cambridge University Press.

Ekelund, C.Z. (2007). Kommunikationsekspert: Danske medier er ukritiske over for Riis. [Communications expert: The Danish media are too uncritical of Riis]. *Politiken*, 1 June. Retrieved 24 April 2008, from http://politiken.dk/cykling/article316096.ece.

Elias, N. (1998). On the concept of everyday life. In J. Goudsblom & S. Mennell (Eds), *The Norbert Elias Reader*. Oxford: Blackwell.

Elliott, K., Fischer, C.T., & Rennie, D.L. (1999). Evolving guidelines for publication of qualitative research studies in psychology and related fields. *British Journal of Clinical Psychology*, 38: 215–229.

Ellis, C. (1991). Sociological introspection and emotional experience. *Symbolic Interaction*, 14: 23–50.

Ellis, C. (2004). *The Ethnographic I: A Methodological Novel about Autoethnography*. Walnut Creek, CA: AltaMira Press.

Ellis, C., Adams, T.E., & Bochner, A.P. (2011). Autoethography: An overview. *Forum: Qualitative Social Research*, 12, Article 10. Retrieved 19 March 2012, from www.qualitative-research.net/index.php/fqs/article/viewArticle/1589/3095.

Evans, A., Elford, J., & Wiggins, D. (2008). Using the internet for qualitative research. In C. Willig & W. Stainton-Rogers (Eds), *The SAGE Handbook of Qualitative Research in Psychology*. London: Sage.

Ferguson, H. (2009). *Self-Identity and Everyday Life*. Abingdon: Routledge.

Feyerabend, P. (1975). *Against Method*. London: Verso.

Finkel, D. (1997). TV without guilt. In W. Harrington (Ed.), *Intimate Journalism: The Art and Craft of Reporting Everyday Life*. Thousand Oaks, CA: Sage.

Flyvbjerg, B. (2001). *Making Social Science Matter: Why Social Inquiry Fails and How It Can Succeed Again*. Cambridge: Cambridge University Press.

Flyvbjerg, B. (2006). Five misunderstandings about case-study research. *Qualitative Inquiry*, 12: 219–245.

Fog, J. (2004). *Med samtalen som udgangspunkt* [*With the Conversation as Starting Point*] (2nd edition). Copenhagen: Akademisk Forlag.

Fontana, A. & Frey, J.H. (2005). The interview: From neutral stance to political involvement. In N.K. Denzin & Y.S. Lincoln (Eds), *The SAGE Handbook of Qualitative Research* (3rd edition). Thousand Oaks, CA: Sage.

Freeman, M. (2004). Data are everywhere: Narrative criticism in the literature of experience. In C. Daiute & C. Lightfoot (Eds), *Narrative Analysis: Studying the Development of Individuals in Society*. Thousand Oaks, CA: Sage.

Frosh, S. (2007). Disintegrating qualitative research. *Theory & Psychology*, 17: 635–653.

Gadamer, H.G. (1960). *Truth and Method* (2nd revised edition 2000). New York: Continuum.

Garfinkel, H. (1967). *Studies in Ethnomethodology* (this edition 1984). Cambridge: Polity Press.

Gerrod Parrott, W. (2003). Positioning and the emotions. In R. Harré & F.M. Moghaddam (Eds), *The Self and Others: Positioning Individuals and Groups in Personal, Political, and Cultural Contexts*. London: Praeger.

Gerrod Parrott, W. & Harré, R. (2001). Princess Diana and the emotionology of contemporary Britain. *International Journal of Group Tensions*, 30: 29–38.

Giorgi, A. (1975). An application of phenomenological method in psychology. In A. Giorgi, C. Fischer, & E. Murray (Eds), *Duquesne Studies in Phenomenological Psychology II*. Pittsburgh, PA: Duquesne University Press.

Giorgi, A. & Giorgi, B. (2003). The descriptive phenomenological psychological method. In P.M. Camic, J.E. Rhodes, & L. Yardley (Eds), *Qualitative Research in Psychology: Expanding Perspectives in Methodology and Design*. Washington, DC: American Psychological Association.

Glassner, B. & Hertz, R. (Eds) (1999). *Qualitative Sociology as Everyday Life*. Thousand Oaks, CA: Sage.

Goffman, E. (1959). *The Presentation of Self in Everyday Life*. New York: The Overlook Press.

Grass, D. (2006). Houellebecq and the novel as site of epistemic rebellion. *Opticon 1826*, 1: 1–10.

Habermas, J. (1995). Philosophy and science as literature? In J. Habermas (Ed.), *Postmetaphysical Thinking*. Cambridge: Polity Press.

Hall, T., Lashua, B., & Coffey, A. (2008). Sound and the everyday in qualitative research. *Qualitative Inquiry*, 14: 1019–1040.

Hammersley, M. (2008). *Questioning Qualitative Inquiry: Critical Essays*. London: Sage.

Harper, D. (2005). What's new visually? In N.K. Denzin & Y.S. Lincoln (Eds), *The SAGE Handbook of Qualitative Research* (3rd edition). Thousand Oaks, CA: Sage.

Harré, R. (1983). *Personal Being*. Oxford: Basil Blackwell.

Harré, R. (1998). *The Singular Self: An Introduction to the Psychology of Personhood*. London: Sage.

Harré, R. (2004). Staking our claim for qualitative psychology as science. *Qualitative Research in Psychology*, 1: 3–14.

Harré, R. & Moghaddam, F.M. (2003). Introduction: The self and others in traditional psychology and in positioning theory. In R. Harré & F.M. Moghaddam (Eds), *The Self and Others: Positioning Individuals and Groups in Personal, Political, and Cultural Contexts*. London: Praeger.

Harré, R. & van Langenhove, L. (1999). The dynamics of social episodes. In R. Harré & L. van Langenhove (Eds), *Positioning Theory*. Oxford: Blackwell.

Harrington, W. (1997). A writer's essay: Seeking the extraordinary in the ordinary. In W. Harrington (Ed.), *Intimate Journalism: The Art and Craft of Reporting Everyday Life*. Thousand Oaks, CA: Sage.

Hartnett, S.J. & Engels, J.D. (2005). 'Aria in time of war': Investigative poetry and the politics of witnessing. In N.K. Denzin & Y.S. Lincoln (Eds), *The SAGE Handbook of Qualitative Research*. Thousand Oaks, CA: Sage.

Heidegger, M. (1927). *Being and Time* (this edition 1962). New York: HarperCollins.

Heidegger, M. (1993). The origin of the work of art. In D.F. Krell (Ed.), *Martin Heidegger: Basic Writings*. London: Routledge.

Hektner, J.M., Schmidt, J., & Csikszentmihalyi, M. (2007). *Experience Sampling Method: Measuring the Quality of Everyday Life*. Thousand Oaks, CA: Sage.

Holquist, M. (2002). *Dialogism: Bakhtin and His World* (2nd edition). London: Routledge.

Holstein, J.A. & Gubrium, J.F. (1995). *The Active Interview*. London: Sage.

Holstein, J.A. & Gubrium, J.F. (2003). Inside interviewing: New lenses, new concerns. In J.A. Holstein & J.F. Gubrium (Eds), *Inside Interviewing: New Lenses, New Concerns*. Thousand Oaks, CA: Sage.

Horgan, B. (2010). The presentation of self in the age of social media: Distinguishing performances and exhibitions online. *Bulletin of Science, Technology & Society*, 30: 377–386.

Houellebecq, M. (1998). *Whatever*. London: Serpent's Tail.

Houellebecq, M. (2001). *Atomised*. London: Vintage.

Houellebecq, M. (2002). *Platform*. London: Willam Heinemann.

Houellebecq, M. (2005). *The Possibility of an Island*. London: Weidenfeld & Nicolson.

Husserl, E. (1954). *Die Krisis der europäischen Wissenschaften und die tranzendentale Phänomenologie* [*The Crisis in the European Sciences and the Transcendental Phenomenology*]. The Hauge: Martinus Nijhoff.

Illouz, E. (2007). *Cold Intimacies: The Making of Emotional Capitalism*. Cambridge: Polity Press.

Ingold, T. (2011). *Being Alive: Essays on Movement, Knowledge and Description*. London: Routledge.

Jacobsen, M.H. (2009). The everyday: An introduction to an introduction. In M.H. Jacobsen (Ed.), *Encountering the Everyday: An Introduction to the Sociologies of the Unnoticed*. Basingstoke: Palgrave Macmillan.

James, W. (1890). *The Principles of Psychology* (this edition 1983). Cambridge, MA: Harvard University Press.

Janesick, V. (1999). A journal about journal writing as a qualitative research technique: History, issues, and reflections. *Qualitative Inquiry*, 5: 505–524.

Janesick, V. (2004). *'Stretching Exercises' for Qualitative Researchers* (2nd edition). Thousand Oaks, CA: Sage.

Jarzombek, M. (2000). *The Psychologizing of Modernity: Art, Architecture, and History*. Cambridge: Cambridge University Press.

Jauss, H.R. (1989). *Question and Answer: Forms of Dialogic Understanding*. Minneapolis, MN: University of Minnesota Press.

Johnson, M. (2007). *The Meaning of the Body: Aesthetics of Human Understanding*. Chicago, IL: University of Chicago Press.

Kahneman, D., Krueger, A.B., Schkade, D.A., Schwartz, N., & Stone, A.A. (2004). A survey method for characterizing daily life experience: The day reconstruction method. *Science*, 306: 1776–1780.

Katz, J. (1996). The social psychology of Adam and Eve. *Theory & Society*, 25: 545–582.

Kierkegaard, S.A. (1844). *The Concept of Anxiety* (this edition 1981). Princeton, NJ: Princeton University Press.

Kvale, S. & Brinkmann, S. (2008). *InterViews: Learning the Craft of Qualitative Research Interviewing* (2nd edition). Thousand Oaks, CA: Sage.

Lather, P. & Smithies, C. (1997). *Troubling the Angels*. Boulder, CO: Westview Press.

Latour, B. (1996). On Interobjectivity. *Mind, Culture, and Activity*, 3: 228–245.

Latour, B. (2000). When things strike back: A possible contribution of 'science studies' to the social sciences. *British Journal of Sociology*, 50: 107–123.

Latour, B. (2005). *Reassembling the Social*. Oxford: Oxford University Press.

Lave, J. & Kvale, S. (1995). What is anthropological research? An interview with Jean Lave by Steinar Kvale. *Qualitative Studies in Education*, 8: 219–228.

Lefebvre, H. (1968). *Everyday Life in the Modern World* (this edition 1971). London: Penguin.

Leth, J. (2006). Tilfældets gaver: En filmisk poetik [The gifts of the present: A poetics of film]. *Kritik*, 2–10.

Løgstrup, K.E. (1956). *The Ethical Demand*. (this edition 1997). Notre Dame, IN: University of Notre Dame Press.

Loizos, P. (2000). Video, film and photographs as research documents. In M.W. Bauer & G. Gaskell (Eds), *Qualitative Researching with Text, Image and Sound*. London: Sage.

Lyotard, J.-F. (1984). *The Postmodern Condition: A Report on Knowledge*. Manchester: Manchester University Press.

MacIntyre, A. (1985). *After Virtue* (2nd edition with postscript). London: Duckworth.

Madsen, M.V. (2007). Second Life – Second Identities? Unpublished Master's thesis. University of Aarhus: Department of Psychology.

Maffesoli, M. (1989). The Everyday Perspective: Editorial Preface. *Current Sociology*, 37: v–vi.

Mannheim, B. & Tedlock, B. (1995). Introduction. In B. Tedlock & B. Mannheim (Eds), *The Dialogic Emergence of Culture*. Urbana, IL: University of Illinois Press.

Markham, A. (2005). The methods, politics, and ethics of representation in online ethnography. In N.K. Denzin & Y.S. Lincoln (Eds), *The SAGE Handbook of Qualitative Research* (3rd edition). Thousand Oaks, CA: Sage.

McAdams, D.P. (1997). *The Stories We Live By*. New York: Guilford Press.

McDermott, R.P. (1993). Acquisition of a child by a learning disability. In S. Chaiklin & J. Lave (Eds), *Understanding Practice*. Cambridge: Cambridge University Press.

McDermott, R.P. & Tylbor, H. (1995). On the necessity of collusion in conversation. In B. Tedlock & B. Mannheim (Eds), *The Dialogic Emergence of Culture*. Urbana, IL: University of Illinois Press.

McLennan, G. (2010). The postsecular turn. *Theory, Culture & Society*, 27: 3–20.

Mead, G. H. (1962). *Mind, Self, and Society: From the Standpoint of a Social Behaviorist* (First published 1934). Chicago, IL: University of Chicago Press.

Menand, L. (2002). *The Metaphysical Club*. London: Flamingo.

Merleau-Ponty, M. (1945). *Phenomenology of Perception* (this edition 2002). London: Routledge.

Milgram, S. (1992). *The Individual in a Social World: Essays and Experiments*. New York: McGraw-Hill.

Mills, C.W. (1959). *The Sociological Imagination* (this edition 2000). Oxford: Oxford University Press.

Mills, C.W. (1963). The man in the middle. In I.L. Horowitz (Ed.), *Power, Politics, and People: The Collected Essays of C. Wright Mills*. New York: Ballantine.

Mol, A. (2008). I eat an apple: On theorizing subjectivity. *Subjectivity*, 22: 28–37.

Mulhall, S. (2002). *On Film*. London: Routledge.

Mulhall, S. (2007). *The Conversation of Humanity*. Charlottesville, VA: University of Virginia Press.

Nagel, T. (1986). *The View from Nowhere*. Oxford: Oxford University Press.

Nehamas, A. (1985). *Nietzsche: Life as Literature*. Cambridge, MA: Harvard University Press.

Noblit, G.W. & Hare, R.D. (1988). *Meta-Ethnography: Synthesizing Qualitative Studies*. Newbury Park, CA: Sage.

Norris, C. (1987). *Derrida*. London: Fontana.

Nussbaum, M.C. (1986). *The Fragility of Goodness: Luck and Ethics in Greek Tragedy and Philosophy*. Cambridge: Cambridge University Press.

Packer, M. (2011). *The Science of Qualitative Research*. Cambridge: Cambridge University Press.

Parker, I. (1996). Discursive complexes in material culture. In J. Haworth (Ed.), *Psychological Research: Innovative Methods and Strategies*. London: Routledge.

Parker, I. (2005). *Qualitative Psychology: Introducing Radical Research*. Buckingham: Open University Press.

Pelias, R. (2004). *A Methodology of the Heart: Evoking Academic and Daily Life*. Walnut Creek, CA: AltaMira Press.

Plato (1987). *The Republic*. London: Penguin.

Polkinghorne, D. (2000). Psychological inquiry and the pragmatic and hermeneutic traditions. *Theory & Psychology*, 10: 453–479.

Polkinghorne, D. (2004). *Practice and the Human Sciences*. Albany, NY: SUNY Press.

Potter, J. & Wetherell, M. (1987). *Discourse and Social Psychology*. London: Sage.

Richardson, F.C., Fowers, B.J., & Guignon, C.B. (1999). *Re-envisioning Psychology: Moral Dimensions of Theory and Practice*. San Fransisco, CA: Jossey-Bass.

Richardson, L. & Lockridge, E. (1998). Fiction and ethnography: A conversation. *Qualitative Inquiry*, 4: 328–336.

Richardson, L. & St. Pierre, E.A. (2005). Writing: A method of inquiry. In N.K. Denzin & Y.S. Lincoln (Eds), *The SAGE Handbook of Qualitative Research* (3rd edition). Thousand Oaks, CA: Sage.

Ricœur, P. (1991). Life in Quest of Narrative. In D. Wood (Ed.), *On Paul Ricœur: Narrative and Interpretation*. London: Routledge.

Rodriguez, N. & Ryave, A. (2002). *Systematic Self-Observation*. Thousand Oaks, CA: Sage.

Rogers, C. (1945). The non-directive method as a technique for social research. *The American Journal of Sociology*, 50: 279–283.

Rorty, R. (1980). *Philosophy and the Mirror of Nature*. Princeton, NJ: Princeton University Press.

Rorty, R. (1982). *Consequences of Pragmatism*. Brighton: Harvester.

Rorty, R. (1989). *Contingency, Irony, and Solidarity*. Cambridge: Cambridge University Press.

Rorty, R. (1991). Habermas and Lyotard on postmodernity. In R. Rorty (Ed.), *Essays on Heidegger and Others. Philosophical Papers Volume 2*. Cambridge: Cambridge University Press.

Rose, D. (2000). Analysis of moving images. In M.W. Bauer & G. Gaskell (Eds), *Qualitative Researching with Text, Image and Sound*. London: Sage.

Rosenblatt, P.C. (2002). Interviewing at the border of fact and fiction. In J.F. Gubrium & J.A. Holstein (Eds), *Handbook of Interview Research*. Thousand Oaks, CA: Sage.

Salvatore, S. & Valsiner, J. (2010). Between the general and the unique: Overcoming the nomothetic versus idiographic opposition. *Theory & Psychology*, 20: 817–833.

Sanders, C.R. (1999). Earn as you learn: Connections between doing qualitative work and living daily life. In B. Glassner & R. Hertz (Eds), *Qualitative Sociology as Everyday Life*. Thousand Oaks, CA: Sage.

Sarbin, T.R. (2004). The role of imagination in narrative construction. In C. Daiute & C. Lightfoot (Eds), *Narrative Analysis: Studying the Development of Individuals in Society*. Thousand Oaks, CA: Sage.

Schjørring, M.A. (2005). *Michels krop – læsninger i Michel Houellebecqs forfatterskab* [*Michel's body: Readings in the works of Michel Houellebecq*]. Odense: Syddansk Universitetsforlag.

Schulze, G. (1992). *Die Erlebnisgesellschaft: Kultursoziologie der Gegenwart* [*The Experience Society: A Cultural Sociology of the Present*]. Frankfurt: Campus.

Schwandt, T. (2000). Three epistemological stances for qualitative inquiry: Interpretivism, hermeneutics, and social constructionism. In N.K. Denzin & Y.S. Lincoln (Eds), *The SAGE Handbook of Qualitative Research* (2nd edition). London: Sage.

Scott, S. (2009). *Making Sense of Everyday Life*. Cambridge: Polity Press.

Sellars, W. (1997). *Empiricism and the Philosophy of Mind* (first published 1956). Cambridge, MA: Harvard University Press.

Shotter, J. (1993). *Conversational Realities: Constructing Life through Language*. London: Sage.

Skinner, B.F. (1948). *Walden Two*. Indianapolis, IN: Hackett Publishing Company.

Slocum-Bradley, N. (2009). The positioning diamond: A trans-disciplinary framework for discourse analysis. *Journal for the Theory of Social Behaviour*, 40: 79–107.

St. Pierre, E.A. (2011). Post qualitative inquiry. In N.K. Denzin & Y.S. Lincoln (Eds), *The SAGE Handbook of Qualitative Research* (4th edition). Thousand Oaks, CA: Sage.

Taylor, C. (1985a). Atomism. In *Philosophy and the Human Sciences: Philosophical Papers 2*. Cambridge: Cambridge University Press.

Taylor, C. (1985b). Self-interpreting animals. In *Human Agency and Language: Philosophical Papers 1*. Cambridge: Cambridge University Press.

Taylor, C. (1989). *Sources of the Self*. Cambridge: Cambridge University Press.

Taylor, C. (1995). Overcoming epistemology. In *Philosophical Arguments*. Cambridge, MA: Harvard University Press.

Taylor, C. (2004). *Modern Social Imaginaries*. Durham, NC: Duke University Press.

Toulmin, S. (1981). The tyranny of principles. *Hastings Center Report*, 11: 31–39.

Trevarthen, C. (1993). The self born in intersubjectivity: The psychology of an infant communicating. In U. Neisser (Ed.), *The Perceived Self*. Cambridge: Cambridge University Press.

Turkle, S. (1997). *Life on the Screen: Identity in the Age of the Internet.* New York: Touchstone.

Valsiner, J. (2006). Dangerous curves in knowledge construction within psychology. *Theory & Psychology*, 16: 597–612.

Valsiner, J. (2007). *Culture in Minds and Societies: Foundations of Cultural Psychology.* New Delhi: Sage.

Varsava, J.A. (2005). Utopian yearnings, dystopian thoughts: Houellebecq's *The Elementary Particles* and the problem of scientific communitarianism. *College Literature*, 32: 145–167.

Winch, P. (1963). *The Idea of a Social Science and Its Relation to Philosophy* (first published 1958). London: Routledge & Kegan Paul.

Wittel, A. (2001). Toward a network sociality. *Theory, Culture & Society*, 18: 51–76.

Wittgenstein, L. (1981). *Zettel* (2nd edition). Oxford: Blackwell.

Wolf, M. (1992). *A Thrice-Told Tale.* Stanford, CA: Stanford University Press.

Young, I.M. (1980). Throwing like a girl: A phenomenology of feminine body comportment, motility and spatiality. *Human Studies*, 3: 137–156.

Zagzebski, L. (1996). *Virtues of the Mind: An Inquiry into the Nature of Virtue and the Ethical Foundations of Knowledge.* Cambridge: Cambridge University Press.

Zittoun, T. (2006). *Transitions: Development through Symbolic Resources.* Greenwich: Information Age Publishing.

Zittoun, T. & Gillespie, A. (2010). Using diaries and self-writings as data in psychological research. In E. Abbey & S. Surgan (Eds), *Developing Methods in Psychology.* New Brunswick, NJ: Transaction Publishers.

Zorbaugh, H. (1929). *The Gold Coast and the Slum.* Chicago, IL: University of Chicago Press.

Zuckerman, P. (2008). *Society without God.* New York: New York University Press.

Index

heuristics, 46–7
Hobbes, Thomas, 137
Holmes, Oliver Wendell, 38
Holstein, J.A., 90–1
Horgan, B., 109
Houllebecq, Michel, 5, 145, 155, 161–4, 167–76
human life seen as a process of inquiry, 6–7, 15, 57
Husserl, Edmund, 66–7, 75–7

Illouz, Eva, 109
images, 131–4; polyvocality of, 128
induction, 45–6
informed consent, 53–6, 60, 113
Ingold, Tim, 4, 42
inquiry, process of, 39–42
'instances' (Denzin), 48
interactive media, 108
internet research, 115
internet resources, 108–9, 113–15
interpellation, 27–8
'interpretation' of life on an everyday basis, 42–3
interpretive interactionism, 40
intersubjectivity, 65
interval-contingent sampling, 75
interviewing for research purposes, 75, 84–94, 105–6; different conceptions of, 89–91; of groups, 85; *structured* or *semi-structured*, 85–6
investigative poetry, 153, 172
irritation, 120

Jacobsen, M.H., 16, 18
James, William, 38–9, 68–9
Janesick, V., 79
Jarzombek, M., 103
Jessop, J., 56
journal writing, 79
journalism, 155–6
Joyce, James, 102

Kafka, Franz, 153
Kahneman, D., 76
Kantianism, 61
Kärreman, D., 44, 93
Katz, Jack, 139–40
Kierkegaard, Søren, 138
knowing: as a causal process, 92; as a human activity for coping with life, 32–3, 40
knowledge: definition of, 91–2; production of, 88, 91, 105; theory of, 39
Kracauer, Siegfried, 134
Kvale, Steinar, 7, 49

Lascaux cave drawings, 129
Lashua, B., 21–2
Lather, P., 173
Latour, Bruno, 14, 35, 48
Lave, Jean, 49, 159
Leonard, Elmore, 155
Leth, Jørgen, 121, 157–60
'life world' concept, 17, 41, 67
Lincoln, Y.S., 19–20, 183
'literary turn' in social science, 151, 172
literary versions of life, 154
literature searches, 13
literature seen as qualitative inquiry, 161–4, 175–6
logical positivism, 160
Løgstrup, K.E., 57
Loizos, P., 131
lying, 77–8, 80
Lyotard, Jean-François, 5
'lyrical sociology' (Abbott), 162–4, 167–71

McCarthy, Cormac, 149
MacIntyre, Alasdair, 85, 103
Madsen, Jacob, 147
Madsen, Maria Virhøj, 113
Maffesoli, M., 18, 30, 147
Marcus, George, 162
Markham, Annette, 114
Marx, Karl (and Marxian theory), 23, 95
mass media, 109–13; goals of, 110
Mass-Observation Archive, 72
'material turn' in social science, 35
materialist social constructionism, 35
Mead, G.H., 68–9
'media', definition of, 110
media materials, 112–15
media research, procedure in, 112
mediation, problem of, 65
mediators, material, 36
Menand, Louis, 38
Merleau-Ponty, Maurice, 26, 66–7, 77
meta-ethnography, 22
metaphors, 160
'methodolatry', 1, 48
'methodology of the heart', 153
Milgram, Stanley, 68, 73–4
Mills, C. Wright, 4–5, 43, 49, 111
Moghaddam, F.M., 118
Mol, Annemarie, 6, 29–30
moral questions raised by research, 55, 58, 61, 117–19, 182; *see also* ethical issues
motivations for research, 53
Mulhall, Stephen, 84, 134–5
Murakami, Haruki, 149

Nanook of the North (film), 130
narrative reports on self observation, 77–8
'narrative turn' in social science, 162
naturalistic materials, 129, 131–6
Nazism, 134
Noblit, G.W., 22
non-directive method of research, 89
non-ergodic phenomena, 76
novels, 149–50, 173; of Michel Houellebecq, 164–5; seen as 'research reports', 154, 174
Nussbaum, M.C., 58

objectivity, 48, 159
online ethnography, 114–15
'ontological triangle', 34–6, 70–1, 111, 127, 179–80
ontology of the social world, 33–6
oral history projects, 130

Packer, Martin, 36
panopticon concept, 128
Paradise Hotel (television show), 131–3, 136–48
Parker, Ian, 27–8, 35, 48, 81, 87
Parrott, Gerrod, 119, 123
Peirce, Charles Sanders, 38–9, 46
Pelias, R., 23, 179
The Perfect Human Being (film), 157–8
phenomenological interviewing, 90
phenomenology, 18–19, 23–6, 33–6, 74–5; traditions of, 66–8
'philosophical anthropology', 33, 66, 83
philosophy, study of, 6; *see also* 'empirical philosophy'
phronesis and phronetic researchers, 59, 182
Plato and Platonic dialogue, 92, 104
Popper, Karl, 45
positioning theory, 87, 117–20, 125; and the emotions, 119–20
positivism, 32, 164–5l; *see also* logical positivism
possessive individualism, 110–11
The Possibility of an Island (film), 168–71
postmodernity and postmodernism, 15–16, 33, 96–7, 111, 116, 137, 151, 162, 164
post-structuralism, 151
Potter, J., 91
'pragmatic maxim', 46
pragmatic pluralism, 34
pragmatism in qualitative inquiry, 4, 33–40, 47, 158, 180, 182
psychoanalysis, 28
publication of research texts, 14, 106, 126

qualitative inquiry: *craft* approach to, 7, 49, 180; defining features of, 1–2, 12, 15–21; definition of, 19–20; *disintegrating*, 154–5; as distinct from fiction, 156–60; as distinct from quantitative research, 20; as empirical philosophy, 5–6; in the form of literature, 161–4; goals of, 4

rapport with research participants, 56
reality television, 137, 140–3, 148
receptive interviewing, 90
reconceptualisation, 47
reduction, technique of, 66
're-enchanting' the world, 30
relativism, 33
religion, 95–9, 103, 166
research reports: aesthetic aspects of, 181–2; structure of, 178–80
research topic, choice of, 13, 80, 106, 125, 178, 180
researchers, role of, 53–6, 59–61
rhetorical devices, 150, 172–3
Richardson, F.C., 41, 43
Richardson, L., 5, 14, 79–80, 154, 162, 168, 172, 181
Riis, Bjarne, 110, 112, 115, 120–5, 146
Rodriguez, N., 72, 77
Rogers, Carl, 89
Rorty, Richard, 39–40, 151–2, 158, 162, 183
Rose, Diana, 135–6
Rosenblatt, P.C., 153, 171, 173
rule-breaking, 45
Ryave, A., 72, 77

St Pierre, Elizabeth, 64, 172, 183
Sanders, Clinton, 2
Sarbin, T.R., 149–50
Sartre, Jean-Paul, 66
Schjørring, M.A., 164
Schleiermacher, Friedrich, 40
Schwandt, T., 42
scientific methodology and understanding, 6, 159
scientific writing, 150–1
Scott, S., 18, 44
Second Life, 109, 113–14
secularism, 96
segregation of boys and girls, 11–12, 56
self, concepts of, 68–71, 109, 179
self observation, 65–82; coding of data from, 76; diary method of, 76, 79; *direct* and *indirect*, 71–4; narrative reports on, 77–8; starting a project on, 80–2
Sellars, Wilfrid, 91–2
sexual relationships, 166

shame, 66–72, 77, 80, 139–40, 146–7
shamelessness, 136, 138, 141–7
Shotter, John, 84
signal-contingent sampling, 75
situational analysis, 36–7
small-scale inquiries, 3–4
Smithies, C., 173
'the social', concept of, 16–17, 20
social atomism, 34
social networking sites and other social
    media, 109, 127
social practices, 21, 40–1, 47
social science, 15–18, 22, 35, 43, 47, 49, 151,
    162, 172; as public philosophy, 182;
    raison d'être for, 182
socialisation, 110, 119
Socrates and Socratic dialogue, 91–3, 98,
    104–6
The Sorrows of Young Werther, 150
spirituality, 100, 104
'stepping back' from a text, 28
story-telling, 42
storylines in positioning theory, 118
Straus, Erwin, 24–5
subjectivity, 30
symbolic interactionism, 33, 40
symbolic resources, 103, 149–50
systematic self-observation (SSO), 74–80

taken-for-granted assumptions, 45
Taktsang Dzong monastery, 99
Taylor, C., 41, 84
television viewing, 127, 135–7; time taken by,
    135; *see also* reality television
theories and theoretical concepts, 4, 6, 19,
    31, 179; as tools for thinking, 58, 180

'thick' descriptions, 29, 79
thinking, definition of, 39
'throwing like a girl', 24–7, 34, 48
Tipton, Steven, 94
toothpaste, use of, 27–8, 35–6
Toulmin, Stephen, 58
Tour de France, 120–1
transactional media, 108
transcendence, 26
truth, concept of, 158–9, 181

validity of analysis, 47–8
Valsiner, J., 74
van Gogh, Vincent, 158
visual culture, 127–8, 133
visual materials, 128–33; reasons for use
    of, 128–9

Wallace, David Foster, 157
Weber, Max, 157
Wetherell, M., 91
Winch, Peter, 6
Wittgenstein, Ludwig, 68, 118
Wolf, Margery, 173
writers' role in qualitative inquiry: as
    informants, 152–3; as *inspirations*, 153–4;
    as *researchers*, 154–5
writing: as an intrinsic part of research, 80; as
    a method of inquiry in itself, 162; *see also*
    research reports

Young, Iris Marion, 24–7, 34, 48, 58

Zabel, Erik, 121
Zola, Émile, 168
Zorbaugh, Harvey, 163